Beyond
Sweatshops

Beyond Sweatshops

Foreign Direct Investment and Globalization in Developing Countries

THEODORE H. MORAN

BROOKINGS INSTITUTION PRESS
Washington, D.C.

Copyright © 2002
THE BROOKINGS INSTITUTION
1775 Massachusetts Avenue, N.W., Washington, D.C. 20036
www.brookings.edu

Library of Congress Cataloging-in-Publication data

Moran, Theodore H., 1943–
    Beyond sweatshops : foreign direct investment and globalization in developing countries / Theodore H. Moran.
        p.   cm.
    Includes bibliographical references and index.
    ISBN 0-8157-0616-2 (cloth : alk. paper) — ISBN 0-8157-0615-4 (pbk. : alk. paper)
    1. Investments, Foreign, and employment—Developing countries. 2. Foreign trade and employment—OECD countries. 3. Manufacturing industries—Developing countries—Employees. 4. Investments, Foreign—Moral and ethical aspects—Developing countries. 5. Investments, Foreign—Government policy—Developing countries. 6. Economic development. I. Title.
    HD5710.75.D44 M67   2002
    331.1′09172′4—dc21   2002003528

9 8 7 6 5 4 3 2 1

The paper used in this publication meets minimum requirements of the American National Standard for Information Sciences—Permanence of Paper for Printed Library Materials: ANSI Z39.48-1992.

Typeset in Sabon

Composition by
Betsy Kulamer, Washington, D.C.

Printed by
R. R. Donnelley and Sons
Harrisonburg, Virginia

Contents

Beyond
Sweatshops

1 *Introduction*

Following in the tradition of *Globaphobia: Confronting Fears about Open Trade,* by Gary Burtless, Robert Z. Lawrence, and Robert Litan, this volume was designed to address fundamental questions about foreign direct investment and development:

—What impact do foreign investors and their subcontractors, in sectors other than natural resources and infrastructure, have on the lives of workers and average citizens in the developing world?

—How can developing countries minimize or escape the dangers and abuses that often accompany foreign direct investment in low-skill, labor-intensive operations?

—What role might the international community play in improving the treatment of workers in foreign-owned and foreign-controlled plants? Should the World Trade Organization (WTO) be turned into the central multilateral actor in this endeavor?

—How might the globalization of industry, via foreign direct investment, affect the lives of workers and average citizens in developing countries, other than through the creation of low-skill jobs free from abusive treatment?

—Under what conditions might foreign direct investment in progressively higher-skill activities transform the development trajectory of a host economy? Under what conditions might foreign direct investment damage a host country's development prospects?

—Finally, what is the impact of the globalization of industry, via foreign direct investment, on the well-being of workers and average citizens in the home country of the investor?

Globaphobia, which focused on workers, firms, and consumers in the developed world rather than in developing countries, summarized age-old debates about trade liberalization, and reinterpreted them in light of resurgent arguments about the sources of wage inequality in modern economies. The intention in this volume was to use a similar approach to explore a different topic: the impact of foreign direct investment on jobs and workers, and on growth and welfare, in developing countries. It soon became apparent, however, that the task was more challenging and complex than it had at first appeared. The impact of the globalization of industry, via foreign direct investment, is more complicated and problematic than that of trade. Moreover, the effects of trade have been more comprehensively studied and the policy alternatives more fully explored. The current volume therefore had to fill in gaps in both evidence and analysis. The more far-reaching arguments and proposals presented in this volume will, it is hoped, offer a stronger foundation than has heretofore been possible for the continued investigation of the impact of foreign direct investment on both developed and developing countries.

Chapters 2 through 6 focus on less-skilled and least-skilled workers in foreign-owned or foreign-controlled plants—those who are most likely to labor in poor conditions and to be subject to mistreatment or abuse. Chapter 2 explores the perils and the benefits of foreign direct investment in export-oriented, labor-intensive operations—such as those producing garments, footwear, toys, and sports equipment—where sweatshop-type conditions frequently (but not always) occur. The inventory of potential opportunities and dangers turns out to be both more extensive and more complex than is commonly supposed. To launch an investigation of how developing countries might maximize the benefits and avoid the dangers of foreign investment, the chapter investigates the record of less developed countries that have tried to use export processing zones (EPZs) to accommodate foreign investors and their subcontractors. That record is in fact quite spotty; by tracing the experiences of Mauritius and Madagascar—relatively favorable examples of the EPZ approach to development—the chapter delineates the criteria for success or failure.

Chapter 3 expands the horizon, investigating how host countries might use foreign direct investment to provide a path up from the lowest-skill, lowest-paid jobs to slightly higher-skill, higher-paid, and more promising occupations. What happens to the treatment of workers in foreign-owned and subcontractor plants when host countries are successful in this endeavor? Drawing on the examples of EPZs in the Philippines, the Dominican Republic, and Costa Rica, the chapter offers evidence that as foreign investors engage in higher-skill operations—and therefore have to attend more closely to the quality and reliability of their products, and to attract and retain more desirable workers—the treatment of workers improves. This transformation occurs, moreover, not only in the newer and more sophisticated plants but in older plants and in those engaged in lower-skill operations as well.

However, even when the transition from lower-skill to higher-skill operations leads to improvements in the treatment of workers, the results will be far from perfect, and new controversies will inevitably arise. Chapters 4, 5, and 6 create a sequence that explores the ways in which multilateral mechanisms might be used to help settle the disputes that emerge and to investigate and punish the labor abuses that remain. Chapter 4 begins by inquiring what might be included in the list of core labor standards for treatment of workers around the world. It examines the challenge of gaining international consensus about the kinds of obligations imposed on members by the four most widely accepted core labor standards promulgated by the International Labor Organization (ILO). The chapter also considers the addition of a fifth standard—either a minimum wage or a "living wage"—and examines the distortion and discrimination that would likely result from efforts to implement a wage-related standard.

As chapter 4 points out, however, even without the added complexity of a wage standard, obtaining multilateral agreement on the definitions of the core labor standards—as well as on what would constitute a violation, and on how such violations would be investigated and punished—would be a difficult task requiring extraordinarily difficult international negotiations. Moreover, the very areas in which complaints associated with foreign direct investment are most likely to arise—interference in the representation of workers, antiunion discrimination, incomplete recognition of the right to strike, and threats to close down plants that vote to establish unions—are those in which agreement is likely to be most difficult to obtain.

Finally, chapter 4 considers a formula in which nations simply enforce their own laws and adhere to their own interpretation of ILO core standards, an approach that is embodied in the labor side-letter to the NAFTA and in the U.S.-Jordan Free Trade Agreement. The chapter investigates whether, within the context of a hypothetical WTO-based international dispute-settlement and appellate system, such a formula could provide a shortcut around painstaking international negotiations about the definition of an actionable violation.

The next two chapters turn to the debate about how the international community can most effectively monitor the treatment of workers and punish violators. One option, explored in chapter 5, is to employ the WTO as an authoritative structure to enforce core labor standards; another, explored in chapter 6, is to rely on corporate codes of conduct, certification organizations, and compliance labeling to improve the treatment of workers.

There is a vast literature on the "public goods" character of labor standards, and on the "collective action" problems associated with voluntary enforcement systems. But the logic that the international community should, or could, turn the WTO into a "benevolent dictator"—to combat the cheating and free riding of producers, retailers, and consumers around the world—and the recommendation that the ILO should move decisively in the same direction, require rather more careful scrutiny.

Chapter 5 examines the ways in which a hypothetical WTO-based system might function in practice. Drawing on evidence from chapter 3, chapter 5 demonstrates that the design of the enforcement mechanism would be crucial to whether a WTO-based system might prove harmful to the interests of workers in the developing world; crucial to whether the WTO-based system might be captured by protectionist interests in importing countries; and crucial to whether the WTO-based system could weaken the ability of international investors and retailers to maintain discipline over the treatment of workers in their own supply chains. The chapter also compares the possible use of fines, rather than trade sanctions, to punish violators. Chapter 5 concludes by considering the merits of a related, but analytically distinct, proposal to use the WTO to retaliate against possible "unfair advantages" gained by countries that tolerate substandard working conditions. The chapter investigates whether such unfair advantages actually exist, and if so, to what extent they can truly be said to injure firms and workers in importing countries.

Chapter 6 considers the use of voluntary measures—which depend on cooperation, persuasion, and public exposure, rather than on trade sanctions or fines—to improve the treatment of workers. Although the evidence presented in the chapter suggests that the common-sense standards and overlapping investigative procedures associated with a corporate codes of conduct, certification organizations, and compliance labeling might actually have more widespread and more rapid effects than a WTO-based alternative, there is still room to strengthen and improve the voluntary regime—in particular, to increase the autonomy of monitoring and remediation procedures. Chapter 6 concludes by examining recent changes in the work of the ILO, which has taken on increasing responsibility for monitoring labor practices, mediating labor disputes, and providing training in dispute resolution and modern human-resource management. Specifically, the chapter considers whether the ILO should, in addition to its current and highly successful work, take on a stronger role in the enforcement of labor standards.

Thus chapters 2 through 6 concentrate on the risks and opportunities involved in creating jobs, via foreign direct investment, for lower- and least-skilled workers. Chapter 7 shifts the focus of the volume in order to place this type of job creation into a broader context. The treatment of employees in, for example, the garment, footwear, and toy industries is an area of legitimate concern, but it is only a small part of any assessment of the overall impact of foreign direct investment on workers and economies in developing countries.

The flow of foreign direct investment to the more advanced industrial sectors in developing countries—including electrical equipment, electronics, semiconductors, auto parts, industrial machinery, chemicals, medical equipment, and pharmaceuticals—is roughly twenty-five times larger than the flow to low-skill, labor-intensive operations (see table 1-1). If accumulated stock is used as the basis for comparison, the ratio of foreign direct investment in the more advanced sectors to foreign direct investment in the lowest-skill sectors is more than ten to one. If chemicals are left out of the calculations (since many of the chemical investments are made in countries that are members of the Organization of Petroleum Exporting Countries), the flow of investment to industrial sectors in the developing world is approximately ten times larger per year than the flow to garments, textiles, and footwear, and the accumulated stock is four times larger.

Since foreign investment in garments, textiles, footwear, and other similar products relies extensively on subcontracting, some analysts have suggested that a more accurate estimate of the flow of investment

Table 1-1. *Foreign Direct Investment and Wages in Developing Countries*

Sector	Stock (in billions of $)[a]	Flow of investment (in billions of $)[a]	Country	Hourly rate ($)[b]
Chemicals	85	14	Vietnam	0.86–2.17
			China	0.95–3.37
			Philippines	0.96–5.97
			Malaysia	2.00–8.20
			Mexico	6.02–7.39
Electronics and electrical machinery	37	5	Vietnam	0.53–2.17
			China	0.69–3.37
			Mexico	0.78–10.38
			Philippines	0.83–5.97
			Thailand	1.36–8.04
			Malaysia	1.67–8.20
Transportation equipment, machinery, and industrial equipment	19	6	Vietnam	0.53–3.37
			China	0.75–3.37
			Thailand	0.80–8.04
			Mexico	1.60–10.38
			Philippines	1.02–5.97
			Malaysia	2.20–8.20
Textiles, clothing, leather, and footwear	14	1	China	0.18
			Bangladesh	0.20
			Vietnam	0.22
			Honduras	0.44
			Thailand	0.49–0.76
			El Salvador	0.84
			Philippines	0.88

Sources: Statistics for stocks and investment flow are from *World Investment Report 1999* (Geneva: United Nations Conference on Trade and Development, 1999). Statistics for textiles, clothing, and footwear are from Center for Economic and Social Applications, University of Ho Chi Minh-Vietnam (now Truong Doan), "Workers' Voices: A Study of the Assets and Needs of Factory Workers in Vietnam" (www.theglobalalliance.org [February 26, 2002]); Chulalongkorn University Social Research Unit, "Needs Assessment for Workers and Communities" (www.theglobalalliance.org [February 26, 2002]); individual factory reports posted by the National Labor Committee at its Web site (www.nlcnet.org [February 26, 2002]); and Mark Jacobson, "The Philippines: The Case of Economic Zones," in *Alleviating Poverty through Foreign Direct Investment: Country Case Studies* (World Bank, 1999). Statistics for other industrial sectors are from American Chamber of Commerce, *Survey of Salaries 2000* (Mexico City: October 1999), and *Survey of Salaries 2001* (Mexico City: October 2000); the wage survey conducted by the International Trade Research Office of the Ministry of International Trade and Industry of Japan, which covers Japanese firms in Mexico, Thailand, the People's Republic of China, Malaysia, and the Philippines; the Research and Development Committee of the Automotive Industry Board Foundation in the Philippines; Mark Jacobson, "The Philippines: The Case of Economic Zones," in *Alleviating Poverty through Foreign Direct Investment: Country Case Studies* (World Bank, 1999); the Economist Intelligence Unit, *Business Asia* (London: June 1997); the U.S. Foreign Commercial Service in Thailand and the Philippines; the Office of Automotive Affairs of the U.S. Department of Commerce; the Bureau of Labor Statistics, U.S. Department of Labor; Bonwick Associates, *Salary Survey of Foreign Investors in Vietnam* (July 1, 2000); and personal communications from Professor J. P. Tuman, Texas Tech University, September 2001.

Note: Because finding data that are both accurate and comparable is extraordinarily difficult, the figures shown here should be taken as indicative rather than precise. They are presented primarily to illustrate the order of magnitude that separates lowest-skill jobs in garments, textiles, and footwear from the higher-skill jobs in more advanced industrial sectors.

a. As of 1997, expressed as 2000 dollars.

b. The figures reflect combined wages and benefits for production workers and production supervisors from the period 1997–2000, translated into 2000 dollars; because the elements included in the calculation of wages and benefits vary, as does the definition of production supervisor, figures are indicative only.

to that sector would be twice as high as the figures ordinarily used. But this approach ignores the fact that foreign investment in more advanced manufacturing operations can also achieve impressive levels of subcontracting and other backward linkages to local suppliers, under conditions examined in chapter 7. Nevertheless, an arbitrary doubling of the flow figure for low-skill, labor-intensive goods still results in foreign direct investment in higher-skilled sectors that is five times higher than the level of investment in lower-skill operations.

In short, by far the largest flows of foreign direct investment go to sectors that pay production workers two to five times more than what is found in garment, textile, and footwear plants within the same country; and, across developing countries, the multiples may be several times higher. For indigenous production supervisors in host countries, the difference is even greater, and for the more sizable proportion of employees who are technicians, engineers, and quality-control specialists (as well as local managers) the difference is often larger still.

Although comparisons of compensation rates in different sectors, different regions, and different countries raise a number of statistical difficulties, the evidence presented in this volume indicates that the greatest flows of foreign direct investment are not directed toward the lowest-skill occupations, or toward workers who can be taken advantage of because they are inexperienced, or timid, or have no other options except abysmal jobs in agriculture or village households. Indeed, the data introduced here show, again and again, that perhaps the most consistent characteristic of foreign investors across varied industries—even including products such as textiles, garments, and footwear—is the search for energetic, reasonably well-educated workers who live close enough to industrial hubs and commercial centers to have other job possibilities.

Thus, a major theme that emerges in chapters 2 and 3, and reappears in chapter 7, is that developing countries are best served when they adopt a "build-up" rather than a "trickle-down" approach to capturing the benefits of foreign direct investment. A build-up approach requires a number of strategies on the part of host-country authorities: first, sound macroeconomic management, including realistic exchange rates and trade liberalization; second, the provision of reliable infrastructure and of dependable commercial and regulatory institutions; third, the creation of policies that allow indigenous firms, as well as foreign investors, equal access to benefits and incentives; fourth, the creation (and ongoing support) of a work force that is at least modestly skilled and trainable; and fifth, efforts to maximize backward linkages and spillovers to small and medium-sized, as well as to large indigenous firms. Various methods for strengthening backward linkages are described in detail in chapter 7.

In addition to exploring the creation of higher-skill and higher-paying jobs, chapter 7 illustrates how the globalization of industry, via foreign direct investment, can transform the overall development profile of an entire host country, and thereby redefine the economic prospects of hundreds of thousands—even millions—of workers who are not directly employed in foreign plants. Drawing on the experiences of the automotive and computer and electronics industries in Latin America and Southeast Asia, the chapter illustrates the fruitful connections that are forged when foreign subsidiaries are tightly integrated into the parent firm's regional and international sourcing networks. To protect their standing in international markets, parent firms position their subsidiaries on the cutting edge of industry practices and generate dynamic backward linkages to suppliers in the local economy. These steps, in turn, create spillovers and externalities that can reshape the development of the entire host economy.

Where trade and investment liberalization allows the globalization of industry to proceed unhindered in a developing country, how large might the benefits be? And where trade and investment restraints inhibit globalization, how large might the costs be? The methods of computation suggested in chapter 7 avoid faulty conventional measurements of the impact of foreign direct investment on a developing country economy, while pushing contemporary estimation techniques a step or two beyond their current limitations. But the chapter provides a cautionary look, as well, at the circumstances in which foreign direct investment might hold back and damage the host economy.

Reversing the perspective of the preceding chapters, chapter 8 considers the impact of the globalization of industry, via foreign direct investment, on workers in the home country. Concern about foreign direct investment in developing countries has focused on whether such investment would ultimately create, in Ross Perot's words, a "giant sucking sound"—as jobs, rather than products, leave home countries for host countries. Chapter 8 concludes, however, that outward investment supports "good" jobs and high-value-added activities in the home economy, and that developed countries would fare much worse if outward investment were hindered or prohibited altogether. Contrary to fears that the globalization of industry, via foreign direct investment, constitutes a zero-sum struggle between home and host economies, the evidence presented in chapter 8 reveals, somewhat counterintuitively, that globalization may be a win-win proposal for workers and communities in developed and developing countries alike.

The final chapter sums up the previous evidence and arguments, arranging them thematically in twelve overlapping sections.

2 Foreign Direct Investment in Low-Wage, Low-Skill Activities

The list of dangers and difficulties linked to foreign direct investor and associated subcontractor operations in low-skill, labor-intensive operations is quite long—but, perhaps somewhat surprisingly, so is the list of possible benefits and opportunities.

This chapter catalogues the various kinds of mistreatment and abuse to which some low-skilled workers are exposed, and contrasts this appalling picture with evidence that in some cases, plants in the same industries provide better treatment of workers and offer various kinds of scarce—and sometimes unique—advantages to both the workers and the host countries.

What factors generate better treatment for workers? Why are other workers vulnerable to mistreatment and abuse? How might host countries design development strategies to maximize the benefits and opportunities of foreign direct investment in labor-intensive operations, and minimize or eliminate the dangers and difficulties? The investigation of these questions begins here, and continues through the next four chapters.

To obtain even the chance of capturing the potential benefits, host countries need to attract a vigorous flow of foreign investment into low-skill activities in the first place. But many of the poorest developing countries experience difficulties with this initial step, even when they go to great lengths to set up special export processing zones or free trade zones (FTZs) to accommodate foreign firms and their subcontractors.

This chapter examines both the failures and successes of EPZs in host countries, drawing on Mauritius and Madagascar as examples of poorer countries in which the creation of export processing zones has yielded relatively positive outcomes. The experiences of these two countries provide a first look at some of the ingredients that help generate better working conditions in foreign-owned and foreign-controlled export plants.

But this chapter only sets the stage for what follows: chapter 3 examines a much more powerful force for improving the treatment of workers—namely, when developing countries begin to build a path up from foreign investment in the lowest-wage, lowest-skill operations to slightly more sophisticated, higher-skill, higher-wage operations. The transition to that phase of development is the subject of chapter 3.

A Bleak Picture

Working conditions and the treatment of workers in plants that produce garments, textiles, footwear, handbags, toys, soccer balls, and other labor-intensive products for export vary widely. On the one side, conditions in foreign-owned and subcontractor plants offer extensive evidence of harm, and of the exploitation and abuse of workers.[1] Workers may be paid no more than a few dollars a day and may be required to work six days a week; during peak periods, such as the pre-Christmas season, regular work hours plus mandatory overtime may total more than eighty hours a week. Firm managers may insist that employees work two successive shifts, sometimes without any break in between.[2] There may be disciplinary fines for coming in late, for talking, or for going to the restroom more frequently than some arbitrary standard permits. Sometimes disciplinary penalties take the form of corporal punishment: workers have been required to stand in the sun with their arms raised, to run laps around the factory, or to have their mouths taped shut.

Once workers have been attracted from distant regions to work in a factory, various coercive techniques—including deception and debt bondage—may be used to prevent them from leaving their jobs. In the extreme, recruiters and agents set up networks in which family members arrange to pay off loans by selling their children into contract labor.

Local enforcement of minimum wages and other labor standards may be weak or nonexistent. Workers may receive no health benefits, be denied social security benefits, and have penalties deducted from their earnings if they fail to meet quotas. New hires may be paid "training wages"—a fraction of the standard wage—for extended periods of time, and more experienced workers may be repeatedly fired and rehired (a practice known as churning) to prevent them from building up the seniority to qualify for various benefits.

Factories may be noisy, hot, and stuffy, with heavy fumes and little ventilation. Some factory operators require their employees to work with toxic and carcinogenic chemicals such as toluene, a shoe adhesive, and benzene, a spot remover.[3] Despite high injury rates, many factories have no first-aid facilities and offer only meager instruction in the proper use of machinery. Fires that have broken out when safety exits were blocked or sealed shut have led to tragic losses; examples include the disaster at the Kader toy factory, in Thailand, in which 188 workers died and 496 were injured, and the more recent fire at the Chowdhury Knitwear subcontractor, in Bangladesh, in which fifty-two workers were trampled in a single stairway exit.[4]

Workers may be housed near the factory, sleeping together on the floor of shacks that are poorly supplied with water or sanitation facilities. Or they may live far from the workplace, in areas with poor lighting, poor security, and little public transport at the hours when they begin and finish work.

Minimum age regulations may be poorly enforced. The work force in garment, footwear, and toy factories, for example, is filled with young women—some younger than eighteen—who have little prior experience in the formal economy and are vulnerable to physical and sexual abuse.

Wages for women are typically lower than for men. While the difference may sometimes reflect lower productivity and skill levels, survey evidence shows that plant managers believe that young women can be paid less simply because they are more passive and docile than male workers. In justifying lower wage rates for women, plant owners also express the opinion, erroneously or opportunistically, that women require no more than a supplement to the main family income. In fact, however, a large percentage of female workers are divorced, widowed, or otherwise the sole source of household income. In the well-known case of Wendy Diaz, the fifteen-year-old Honduran who worked in a plant that produced clothing endorsed by Kathie Lee Gifford and sold at Wal-Mart, the truth emerged that the young worker was an orphan who had supported herself and her three younger brothers since she was thirteen.

Managers report, in addition, that they prefer to hire men for administrative and managerial posts. In some plants women account for a lower proportion of supervisory positions even when they constitute a higher fraction of the skilled labor in the plant.

Some employers limit their training programs to the inculcation of obedience and the repetition of single tasks. This approach may be part of a deliberate strategy to limit the workers' mobility: according to testimony from managers, if women employees are taught to do only one step rather than to make an entire garment, they will be less likely to leave and set up their own shops.

A More Promising Portrait

Despite what is frequently a grim picture, there is evidence to support a much more positive appraisal of the effects of foreign direct investment, and foreign-controlled subcontracting, in low-skill, low-wage sectors of developing countries. Surveys by the International Labor Organization, for example, have regularly found that the pay for workers in EPZs, while extremely low by the standards of developed countries, is higher than what would be available in the villages from which the workers come.[5] Similarly, the U.S. Department of Labor reports that firms producing footwear and apparel generally pay more than the minimum wage and offer conditions substantially better than those that prevail in agriculture.[6] Other surveys have found that, on average, jobs in foreign-owned, export-oriented factories offer higher pay and better working conditions than comparable jobs in domestic companies.[7]

Do wages that are better than the next-best alternative represent a promising opportunity? Or are they part of what the ethicist Michael Walzer has called desperate exchanges, in which people in distress are coerced by circumstances into accepting terrible occupations?[8] There is extensive evidence on both sides.

Reports by the National Labor Committee and other nongovernmental organizations (NGOs) regularly include the testimony of export-plant workers struggling to make ends meet. "Made in China: Behind the Label"; "Bangladesh: Wal-Mart's Shirts of Misery"; and "Behind Closed Doors: Honduras," for example, provide interviews with workers who testify that they can hardly live or support their families—let alone save or cope with emergencies—on their earnings.[9] At the same time, survey evidence from three footwear and two apparel factories in Thailand shows that 72 percent of workers considered their overall income from factory work to be fair, with 60 percent reporting that their wages allowed them to accumulate savings.[10] Seventy-one percent characterized the relationship between workers and supervisors as good, and three-quarters said that they felt recognized by factory management. (The most popular form of recognition was a pay raise.) Of workers surveyed at seven apparel and footwear plants in Vietnam, more than 70 percent reported that their work gave them a feeling of personal satisfaction (71 percent), that they were treated with respect at work (71 percent), that they would recommend their factory as a good place to work (71 percent), and that they were provided with an opportunity to improve their skills (78 percent).[11] No comparable survey data are available from Bangladesh—which, along with China and India, provides the lowest pay for unskilled workers. But while garment workers in Bangladesh take home an average wage of only $35 to $40 a month, these meager earnings are nevertheless 25 percent higher than the country's average monthly per capita income.[12]

The examples of Mauritius, Madagascar, the Philippines, the Dominican Republic, and Costa Rica, considered later in this chapter and in the next, provide extensive evidence that wages and working conditions in foreign-owned or foreign-controlled factories compare favorably with those of alternative occupations. Around the world, when new export plants open, demand for the available jobs tends to be strong; and when first-time workers leave their villages after the holidays, the likelihood that they will return to the same plants is high.

In some garment and footwear plants, workers receive an employer contribution of 15 to 20 percent of wages for social security benefits, a one-month cash bonus for a full year of service, and paid annual leave of twelve working days thereafter. Many workers live in factory-provided dormitories, some with three free meals, others with one free meal (often breakfast, to encourage prompt arrival). Some employers provide free or subsidized transportation. Some firms set up in-house safety and health committees, disseminate safety-related information, and ensure workers an adequate supply of protective gear. Some firms provide medical services and day care, or locate plants where these services are nearby.

In contrast to what the ILO calls the "work harder" approach to human resources, which emphasizes discipline and the repetition of single tasks, the ILO has found evidence of the growing use of "work smarter" strategies. Even in the lowest-skill occupations, such as garment sewing, employers themselves provide testimony about the combined benefits of training workers in multiple skills and using teams to produce the final product—strategies that enable workers to replace one another in case of absences, reduce the amount of repetitive work (thereby cutting down on incidences of occupational disability), minimize the need for supervision, and help to foster a more positive working atmosphere.[13] Working with education officials from the host country, some employers have helped to arrange evening classes, certified by public school authorities, through which workers can obtain credits toward a degree. Other employers, working with NGOs, sponsor night classes in data processing, business administration, or English.

Working in foreign-owned or subcontractor export plants may make benefits available to host-country workers that extend beyond simple economics. In some countries foreign firms and their subcontractors may provide access to the formal economy for otherwise "repressed segments" of the work force. In Bangladesh, for example, Muslim traditions prohibited single women from working in factories, a practice that foreign investors and their local subcontractors lobbied at the highest national levels to change. Today, approximately 95 percent of the 1.4 million garment-sector employees in Bangladesh are women; and of all women employed in the formal sector of the economy, more than 70 percent work in the export garment industry.[14]

According to surveys of female workers in Asia and Latin America, factory work offers a measure of autonomy, status, and self-respect that is otherwise hard to obtain. Women in textile, garment, and shoe-assembly factories in Indonesia reported that their jobs strengthened their positions in relation to their nuclear families back in their village and helped them gain control over their lives; 82 percent indicated that working in a factory provided better status than being a housewife.[15]

In Mexico, work in foreign-owned or foreign-controlled export factories strengthened the self-respect of female workers and created a more equal power balance in their relations with their husbands.[16] In Malaysia, employment in foreign electronics plants afforded female workers "experience in independent living, greater personal autonomy and more personal choice in everything from consumer purchases and leisure activities to marriage partners and future family size."[17] Thus, in addition to improving the overall welfare of workers, employment in foreign-owned plants provides many female workers with what Nobel laureate Amartya Sen has called enhanced "agency."[18]

The social benefits of women's employment in low-skill export plants may extend beyond increased status and autonomy on the individual level.[19] As a result of higher female participation in the labor force, a higher proportion of household income is directed toward basic family needs such as health, nutrition, and education, which reduces the inter-generational transmission of poverty.[20] Working in factories also appears to militate against early marriage, and may raise awareness about family planning, thereby lowering fertility rates. The long-term positive social externalities from the globalization of labor-intensive industries merit much more extensive study.[21]

Foreign investment in labor-intensive operations is labor-intensive in itself. Later chapters will analyze the impact of foreign investment in higher-skill manufacturing sectors, such as automotive parts or comput-ers, on the development of host countries. But a full-scale auto-engine export plant, however desirable for many reasons, is likely to employ fewer than 1,000 relatively highly skilled workers—even if the plant operates with three shifts, around the clock. In the apparel and footwear industries, in contrast, a single plant can employ between 10,000 and 18,000 workers, thereby providing workers with minimal skills a tremendous opportunity for entry into the formal economy. The global-ization of more complicated, capital-intensive operations simply cannot create jobs on a comparable scale in a short period of time.

For host countries, the presence of foreign investors and foreign-controlled subcontractors thus represents a complicated mix of dangers and opportunities. Where are the dangers, rather than the opportunities, more likely to be found? The available statistics show that workers are more likely to be treated poorly—or even abused—at plants that are older or smaller, that require the lowest levels of skill, that are owned by countries that do not belong to the Organization for Economic Cooper-ation and Development (OECD), that produce nonbranded products, or that are located in publicly rather than privately administered EPZs or in isolated, poverty-stricken regions.[22]

But how can these statistics be translated into useful policy recom-mendations that will enable developing countries to maximize the bene-fits—and minimize or avoid the dangers—of foreign direct investment in labor-intensive activities? That question requires complex analysis that begins in this chapter and continues through the next. The central issues are how to attract larger numbers of investors, increase demand for workers, break down isolated labor markets, mix higher-skill operations with lower-skill activities, upgrade the administration of enterprise zones, and improve national supervision of the treatment of workers. These efforts, in turn, must be backed by build-up—rather than trickle-down—strategies that are designed to harness the potential of foreign direct investment; as will be discussed in more detail in chapter 3, build-up strategies combine vocational education and skill training with programs that strengthen the connections between foreign investors and local suppliers, and generate spillover benefits for indigenous firms and workers.

However, as noted earlier, many developing countries have had trouble even getting started.

Getting Started: Attracting Foreign Firms to Low-Skill Export Operations

The most common strategy used by developing countries to attract foreign investors to low-wage export industries is to establish special export processing zones or free trade zones.[23] But EPZs and FTZs have a very problematic record. What separates the successes from the failures?

The objective of establishing EPZs and FTZs is to provide foreign investors and their subcontractors with freedom from duties on the capital equipment and components used in assembly operation, to enable them to operate with modern infrastructure, and to offer them sanctuary from the adverse business conditions (red tape, corruption, delays) evident in other parts of the economy. Most developing countries offer, in addition, special tax treatment—and, sometimes, subsidized rates for buildings and services. Many governments also offer exemption from various labor regulations in the zones (including the right of workers to organize unions, a subject of special concern in later chapters).

There are variations on the EPZ model in which host-country authorities grant EPZ status to foreign investors and their subcontractors without limiting their activities to a spatially designated zone. The two most prominent variations are bonded warehouses and duty-drawback arrangements. Bonded warehouses are single-factory EPZs, with a customs agent at the site and a bond posted against any duty-free imports diverted to the domestic market. The duty-drawback approach also applies to specific export factories where duties on imported inputs are reimbursed upon export of the final product. Like plants in EPZs, bonded warehouses and duty-drawback plants may enjoy special tax breaks and special labor regulations.

What differentiates the more successful EPZs from the less successful ones?[24] A first ingredient for success in attracting foreign investors and launching successful operations is a favorable macroeconomic environment—in particular, a realistic exchange rate. The boom in exports from EPZs in Mauritius and Madagascar, examined later in this chapter, and from the Dominican Republic, analyzed in the next, occurred only after exchange rates had been brought down to realistic levels. In contrast, macroeconomic distortions in the Kenyan economy led some 60 of the 70 bonded warehouses operating in the early 1990s to close down in subsequent years. In Egypt, the provision of generous incentives and new facilities failed to compensate for an overvalued exchange rate. A second ingredient is the EPZ's ability to provide reliable and competitively priced utility services, transportation, and communications facilities. Without rapid and dependable delivery of inputs and outputs, export-oriented firms cannot function cost-effectively. Similarly, investment is likely to be deterred by telecommunication services that are slow or that cost two to three times the going international rate, and by the need to build backup generators for use during blackouts. A third ingredient is a transparent, efficient, and reasonably stable institutional structure of laws and court systems to protect private property (including intellectual property) and enforce contracts—with a minimum of red tape, corruption, or administrative uncertainty. Among alternative arrangements for attracting investment, duty-drawback systems that require foreign firms or their subcontractors to pay an import tax and then apply for a rebate have been particularly subject to delay, and sometimes to manipulation.

The need for a well-functioning infrastructure complicates efforts to use EPZs as a tool to directly reduce poverty. Countries that have tried to place EPZs or FTZs in poor, remote regions have encountered difficulty in attracting investors or generating a rapid expansion in exports. And those firms that do set up operations in such areas may become monopsonistic (that is, sole-source) providers of jobs—and, as such, may be subject to minimal external supervision. As the examples of the Philippines and the Dominican Republic in the next chapter will show, monopsonies are not a promising recipe for good treatment of workers or harmonious labor relations.

The objective of expanding the use of host-country products as inputs for exported products (that is, the creation of "backward linkages" to the local economy) also militates against isolating foreign investors in the most depressed areas. As chapter 7 explores in some depth, the generation of backward linkages requires that the exporting firms be surrounded by vibrant domestic companies that enjoy good infrastructure and business-friendly treatment—including exemption from duties—similar to those granted to the exporters themselves.

In this chapter and the next, it will become clear that the export processing strategy is likely to remain a very limited vehicle for capturing the benefits of foreign direct investment—unless the zone approach gives way to a model in which foreign plants are incorporated into integrated commercial and industrial hubs throughout the host country; are located in proximity to better educated (or at least modestly better educated) labor pools, rather than in the midst of the most desperate workers; and are nourished by nationwide liberalization of trade and investment. Nevertheless, EPZs and FTZs remain a starting point for many developing countries' efforts to attract foreign direct investment.

Mauritius: An Early Model

Mauritius provides a model that hosts and would-be hosts—even among the poorest developing countries—can find reason to emulate.[25] In the 1960s Mauritius depended on sugar production for 99 percent of its exports, and employment in domestic industry was limited to sectors that had been given trade protection so that local production could replace imports. Preparatory to independence, the British commissioned a study (entitled *Mauritius: A Case Study in Malthusian Economics*) that concluded that young workers with higher levels of education should be encouraged to emigrate.[26]

In the early 1970s the government of Mauritius turned from import substitution to an export-oriented development strategy: it liberalized trade, adopted a realistic exchange rate, and opened up the economy to foreign investors—many from Hong Kong—with expertise both in garment production and in maneuvering through the complexities of international textile quotas.

In 1971 nine firms with EPZ status provided 644 jobs. By 1978 EPZ employment had grown to 17,000. After a slowdown associated with the worldwide recession of the early 1980s, growth in EPZ employment resumed, and had reached 90,000 by 1990. Between 1970 and 1990, the increase in EPZ jobs accounted for two-thirds of the total expansion of employment, and by the end of this period EPZ jobs amounted to one-third of all jobs on the island. Agriculture grew more slowly than EPZ industrial employment. During the 1990s wage rates rose rapidly in the zones, and EPZ jobs fluctuated between 80,000 and 90,000 as investors weighed the cost of producing goods in Mauritius against the cost of producing them elsewhere.[27]

Between 1971 and 1986, export earnings from manufacturers in Mauritius climbed from 3 to 53 percent of total export earnings, overtaking sugar exports for the first time. By 2000 export earnings from EPZ firms, valued at more than $1.2 billion, amounted to approximately 70 percent of total export earnings.[28] Investors from France, Germany, the United Kingdom, China, and Taiwan joined those from Hong Kong. Steven Radelet shows that between 1970 and 1996, among low- and middle-income countries around the world, Mauritius—with an average annual growth rate of 2.9 percent a year—ranked seventh among the fifteen top-performing exporters of manufactured products, a ranking that placed it below Singapore, Taiwan, and Hong Kong but ahead of better-known examples of economic progress such as Israel, Portugal, and Thailand.[29]

Although the average number of years of schooling (4.5) was not extraordinarily high, foreign investors reported being attracted to the work force in Mauritius, which was relatively better educated than those of nearby countries. In the same region, Sri Lanka had higher literacy rates (75 percent, versus 60 percent for Mauritius), and the labor force had a higher average number of years of schooling (6.2 years). But, as Paul Romer points out, Sri Lanka refused to abandon its import-substitution strategy or to welcome foreign direct investment in the way Mauritius had.[30] Thus, despite Sri Lanka's superior human-resource base, the growth rate in per capita income in Mauritius was more than twice that of Sri Lanka—a pattern that continued for more than two decades.

The labor-relations system in Mauritius EPZ provided the firms with zone status greater flexibility in the treatment of workers than other firms in the economy.[31] Overtime was calculated on a weekly basis rather than daily (the norm elsewhere in the economy, once the weekly total had exceeded forty-five hours), and workers could be required to work up to ten hours a day and for seven consecutive days; for firms outside the zones, national labor law permitted only six consecutive days of work. Zone legislation limited women to a maximum of three maternity leaves; there was no such limit for nonzone companies. Finally, zone legislation made no provision for pension payments, which were required for firms without zone status.

Between 1985 and 1996, real wages in duty-free manufacturing rose by 57 percent.[32] During the same period, regulations governing severance pay were reformed, and new regulations called for workers to be notified in advance if overtime would be required.

Although union organizing had always been permitted among firms with zone status, no more than 9 percent of the work force in the EPZ sector ever belonged to trade unions.[33] Complaints to the ILO about the mistreatment or abuse of workers were more rare in Mauritius than in the Philippines, the Dominican Republic, or Costa Rica—a difference that may be due, in part, to the somewhat atypical practice in Mauritius of treating EPZ status as essentially an administrative designation for exporters wherever they chose to locate throughout the country: as long as firms exported their output, they could enjoy duty-free imports of machinery and materials, no restrictions on ownership or repatriation of profits, and a ten-year income-tax holiday. While one-third of EPZ enterprises did choose to locate in special industrial estates created as part of the export-promotion strategy, the remaining two-thirds of the firms applying for EPZ designation chose their own independent plant sites.[34] Because exporters were not limited to particular geographic enclaves in remote regions, the Mauritian system contained less potential for single employers or small groups of employers to dominate local labor markets—and, hence, less potential for mistreatment or abuse of workers.

Although information about on-the-job training and the development of skills among employees of foreign firms is less detailed for Mauritius than for some other countries, the aggregate data show that EPZ workers and managers gained expertise in foreign-owned plants and then used their know-how to set up their own companies.[35] The cumulative effect was substantial. When Mauritius began its outward-oriented development approach in the 1970s, foreign investors owned nearly all of the firms with EPZ status. By 1995 indigenous investors accounted for 50 percent of the total equity capital in firms with EPZ status.[36]

Madagascar as a Follow-on to Mauritius

Mauritius does not stand alone among smaller, poorer economies that have had some success in reshaping the host-country economy around foreign investment in lowest-skill exports. Following the example of Mauritius, Madagascar opted to liberalize its economy, adopt a realistic exchange rate, and establish an EPZ-led growth strategy in 1989.[37] Not only was the model the same (EPZ status for investors regardless of where they chose to locate), but so were many of the participants. Madagascar managed to entice both Hong Kong firms based in Mauritius, and Mauritian firms that had acquired EPZ expertise, to invest in Madagascar.

Whereas it had taken ten years for the first hundred EPZ firms to become established in Mauritius, Madagascar boasted 120 firms with EPZ status within its first five years.[38] By 1996 the country had 158 firms and EPZ employment of more than 36,000. Between 1994 and 1998 (the most recent year for which statistics are available), EPZ exports grew from $64 million (14 percent of all exports) to $195 million (37 percent of all exports).[39] The wages and benefits for workers in EPZs were not only higher than those in low-skill agricultural occupations but superior to those for comparable jobs throughout the country. After correcting for education level, extent of professional experience, and length of tenure in the enterprise, Mireille Razafindrakoto and Francois Roubaud found that Madagascar's EPZ workers earned between 15 and 20 percent more than workers across all sectors of the economy.[40]

Mauritius, meanwhile, had begun the slow process of trying to diversify beyond the lowest-skill EPZ operations into relatively more sophisticated, higher-skill operations. The next chapter, which investigates the impact on the treatment of workers when higher-skill operations are introduced alongside lower-skill operations, turns to countries where this diversification has proceeded further, and where more extensive data are available on the evolution of working conditions in EPZs.

3

*Improving the Treatment of
Workers at the Bottom by
Providing a Path Up from Below*

This chapter continues to examine, in more depth and detail, how developing countries might be able to maximize the benefits that foreign direct investment provides for low-skilled and least-skilled workers, while minimizing the dangers and difficulties. The examples of Mauritius and Madagascar in the previous chapter—which illustrated how the rising number of investors and the increasing demand for labor augmented the number of jobs and boosted wages for workers in garment, footwear, and other labor-intensive export industries—provided some important preliminary insights. This chapter considers the experiences of three countries—the Philippines, the Dominican Republic, and Costa Rica—that offer more extensive evidence about the circumstances that generate poor treatment of workers in EPZs, as well as about the elements that lead to broad-based improvements in the treatment of workers. In particular, the experiences of these three countries illustrate the improvements in working conditions that occur as the pattern of foreign investment shifts from lowest-skill operations that are limited to export processing enclaves to relatively higher-skill operations that are more thoroughly incorporated into the host economy.

The examples of the Philippines, the Dominican Republic, and Costa Rica offer an opportunity to scrutinize the hypothesis that when firms are required to pay greater attention to the quality and reliability of production, they are more likely to undertake measures that foster better labor-management relations. The evidence introduced here, however, goes beyond a consideration of the behavior of individual firms under shifting market conditions. The experiences of the three countries detailed in this chapter indicate that changes in the treatment of workers are not limited to plants engaged in higher-skill, more sophisticated operations, but spread to other plants in the same EPZs that engage in lower-skill, less sophisticated operations—and even spill back to plants that engage the least-skilled workers and are located in the oldest and least advanced EPZs. Further, the evidence indicates that the movement from lowest-skill to relatively higher-skill operations is accompanied by a more extensive institutional transformation in the treatment of workers. Facilitating this transition will prove to be the most powerful tool that developing countries possess for improving the treatment of workers in their economies. But this process is not a cure-all: individual abuses do not entirely disappear, and new controversies about the structure of worker-management relations inevitably emerge.

The task, therefore, is to determine whether international procedures to punish abuses and deal with controversies will weaken—perhaps even undermine—this broad, worker-friendly evolution in labor-management relations. Or, can such external initiatives be designed instead to complement the institutional transformation in the treatment of workers? The findings offered here will turn out to be indispensable in assessing proposals, in the chapters that follow, for international enforcement of core labor standards.

The Self-Interest of Firms and the Treatment of Workers

Sophisticated economic models show how the behavior of firms toward their workers might vary under different market conditions. According to these models, and perhaps contrary to expectations, the conditions under which firms can enhance their competitive position through a strategy of labor suppression—that is, by holding wages and benefits artificially low (below the value of what the workers produce), and by skimping on expenditures for ventilation, light, or health and safety—are quite limited.[1] If, for example, workers have few alternatives, are immobile, or lack information about employment in other regions, a monopolistic employer or a collusive set of employers in an isolated labor market might be able to derive additional profit from pushing wages, benefits, and other expenses related to workers below the marginal revenue product of the workers. But as these conditions disappear—as labor markets become more national, as workers learn of alternative sources of employment, and as demand for employees with experience in the formal sector increases—a firm's attempts to increase profits by keeping wages below the amount by which the employees' labor increases the firm's profit, and by imposing unappealing and intolerable working conditions, should damage its ability to attract the kinds of workers that the firm needs. To the extent that the firm persists in using labor suppression, it is likely to be less productive and less competitive, and to suffer declines in both output and profits.

Another factor that would be expected to limit the effectiveness of labor suppression is the requirement that manufactured goods meet international standards of quality and dependability. Thus, companies that export more complicated products—electronics, medical equipment, and automotive parts, for example, rather than toys, garden implements, and costume jewelry—have to attract and retain good workers. Again, the firm's self-interest should lead it away from a strategy of labor suppression, and toward the implementation of measures designed to retain desirable workers.

So far, however, these are only hypotheses. As competition among employers grows, as labor markets become less isolated, and as the operations in foreign-owned plants become increasingly sophisticated, what evidence is there of visible change in labor-management relations? Are shifts in the treatment of workers reflected only in the behavior of individual employers—or are there signs of cumulative improvement in the treatment of workers across EPZs and across industrial sectors?

Despite the difficulty of finding comparable data over long periods of time, the experiences of the Philippines, the Dominican Republic, and Costa Rica provide a remarkably clear and consistent picture of evolution in the treatment of workers as labor-market conditions change in EPZs.

The Philippine Experience: From Labor Unrest to Greater Labor-Management Cooperation

Two months after martial law was declared in 1972, President Ferdinand Marcos signed a decree establishing the Bataan Export Processing Zone.[2] Located in a mountainous area some 160 kilometers from Manila, the site of the new zone lacked adequate transportation, communications, water, and power facilities. However, the central government hoped that a combination of extensive, publicly funded infrastructure improvements and the prospect of cheap labor would lure foreign investors to the EPZ, transforming it into a showcase for manufactured exports.

Initial investment was almost exclusively in garment factories, where the value of exports reached more than $134 million by 1980. The first systematic collection of data on working conditions in the Bataan EPZ—three surveys undertaken between 1982 and 1986—reveals many of the characteristics of labor suppression: a large percentage of the work force earned wages that were less than or just equal to the statutory minimum wage; the average work week was fifty-four hours, with a "significant number" of workers spending considerably more hours on the job; 46 percent of the workers surveyed were often required to work two successive shifts; some reported that they were allowed a short break between shifts, and others that they were not.[3] Employers testified that they limited workers to the repetition of a single task in a deliberate effort to limit their mobility.[4] A 1984 study by the Ministry of Labor and Employment on health and safety conditions recorded complaints of fatigue, inadequate ventilation, dust, fumes, and unpleasant odors.

During the period covered by the surveys, recurrent strife characterized the relations between workers and management. The Bataan EPZ was "badly shaken" by strikes, many industries closed operations, and the value of exports declined by more than one-half between 1980 and 1986.[5] By 1986, with only twelve firms remaining, the EPZ had fallen far below the original projections for occupancy rates, exports, and foreign-exchange earnings.

Despite the expenditure of nearly $200 million in public funds to improve the physical infrastructure, the Bataan operation failed to pass even leniently constructed cost-benefit tests published in 1987 by Peter Warr. As a result of Warr's study and the attention it engendered, the notion of using EPZs to achieve economic growth gained a bad reputation among development strategists worldwide that lasted for more than a decade.[6]

But the next three major Philippine EPZ initiatives—originating at Mactan in 1979, at Baguio City in 1980, and at Cavite in 1982—began to offer, almost immediately, important contrasts to the Bataan experience. Situated near urban industrial centers, all three sites offered proximity to large numbers of better-educated workers, which helped persuade investors with higher-skill operations to settle alongside plants engaged in lower-skill activities.

The Mactan zone was set up not far from Cebu, the second-largest city after Manila. The earliest investors produced textiles and garments, housewares, and toys. Over the course of the 1980s, the number of plants devoted to these and similar goods continued to grow, but the proportion of such firms declined to less than half of all firms in the EPZ. The foreign managers reported that the number of technical and postsecondary educational institutions in the province, and the supply of skilled and professional workers, were important "pull factors" in encouraging their investments.[7]

The trend toward higher-skill foreign operations continued during the next decade. By the end of the 1990s only 29 of 105 firms exported garments, textiles, apparel, or footwear; the rest—72 percent—were engaged in metal fabrication or produced electronics, automotive parts, chemicals, machinery, optical equipment, medical equipment, or software. Rather than use the lowest-skilled and lowest-wage workers, the new investors took advantage of the area's educational resources: of the female employees, 55 percent had high school degrees, and an additional 37 percent had education beyond high school; of the male employees, 21 percent had high school degrees, and an additional 65 percent had education beyond high school.[8] Although the data do not break out educational level by industry sector, the fact that only 8 percent of all female employees and only 14 percent of all male employees had less than a high school education suggests that even the garment, footwear, and toy plants sought out better-educated workers.

Whereas Bataan employers had tried to limit the skills that workers acquired, foreign firms at Mactan devised on-the-job training programs to develop multiple skills among workers, with the goal of giving them the flexibility needed to adjust to new designs, processes, and products.[9] Survey data identify two separate approaches to the common objective: U.S. firms assigned workers to handle ten to eighteen interrelated tasks; enterprises from Japan, the United Kingdom, and Taiwan assigned workers to one or two fixed tasks, then rotated them from job to job every three or six months. In each case, managers reinforced the training by granting promotions to workers who participated successfully. Over the course of the 1990s, there was also a trend among U.S. and Japanese firms to assign women to supervisory positions.[10]

Providing an even more stark contrast with Bataan, the employers in the Mactan zone—according to interviews carried out by Elizabeth M. Remedio, a researcher from the economics department at the University of San Carlos—initiated their own efforts to head off the kind of labor unrest that had plagued other regions in the Philippines. In this endeavor, the Chamber of Exporters and Manufacturers, working through a human-resource association made up of personnel managers from all the companies in the zone, undertook a self-policing effort to ensure that firms complied with all national labor regulations. Companies that violated national labor laws received reprimands, and one firm that was unwilling to respect the standards set by the chamber (which led to a strike) appears to have been expelled from the zone.[11]

The chamber, which represented the firms in the zone, was "particularly vigilant" about wages, allowing individual firms to set their own rates but ensuring that compensation met or exceeded legal minimums. Benefits offered to workers included paid sick leave and holidays, social security, uniforms, canteen facilities, and transport to and from the zone. When labor problems or complaints arose, the chamber played a mediating role without waiting for intervention—or lack thereof—on the part of government officials or zone administrators.

The avowed aim of the chamber and its human-resource association was to preserve "industrial peace." Union organizing was allowed by law, and took place from time to time.[12] The employers clearly hoped, however, to preempt the appeal of unions, and to some extent succeeded: in the mid-1990s, when workers in one of the enterprises called for an election for trade-union recognition, fewer than 5 percent of the workers voted in favor.[13]

In the Baguio City EPZ, launched in 1980—one year after Mactan—the treatment of workers shows some of the same characteristics. Because of the role Texas Instruments had played in lobbying for its creation, the Baguio City industrial park was often referred to as the TI zone. Texas Instruments developed a reputation for setting a high standard for wages, benefits, working conditions, and human-resource practices[14]—and, according to one local study, it also served as a model for empowering women workers.[15] It is not clear whether the employers in the Baguio City EPZ played as active a role in preempting the formation of unions as they had in Mactan—but, while union organizing was allowed, no unions were formed.[16]

In Baguio City, the mountain atmosphere (which lacks the corrosiveness of saltwater air) and the educational resources that came with being the main urban center in the north combined to create a favorable locale for electronics investment. Across all sectors, the educational levels of employees in the Baguio City Zone were the highest of all Philippine EPZs: at the end of the 1990s, 63 percent of all male employees and 66 percent of all female employees had some postsecondary education, and 34 percent of all male employees and 38 percent of all female employees had a college degree.[17] Although the electronics firms that followed TI into the Baguio City Zone constituted the largest proportion of investors, one-quarter of the investors came from the garment industry and set up plants side by side with the electronics plants. Over the course of the 1990s, local Filipino firms came to constitute one-third of all the firms in the EPZ. Average monthly earnings in the zone—for textile and apparel, as well as for electronics firms—were two to three times higher than at the other Philippine EPZs ($2.26 an hour in 1995 dollars; $2.76 an hour in 2000 dollars).

The EPZ at Cavite, the zone that experienced the most rapid growth in the Philippines, had access to the diverse labor supply of metropolitan Manila and to the superior infrastructure of Aquino International Airport and Manila South Harbor. Perhaps because of its proximity to a large labor pool that was experiencing persistent unemployment, wages and working conditions at Cavite rivaled those of Bataan as the worst among the major Philippine EPZs.[18] During the late 1980s and early 1990s the International Textile, Garment and Leather Workers' Federation (ITGLWF) and the International Confederation of Free Trade Unions (ICFTU) registered complaints about firms at Cavite because of low wages, poor working conditions, insecure employment, and hostility toward unions.[19]

At Cavite, the shift from lowest-skill to higher-skill activities began in 1987. Within a decade, 72 percent of the investors represented the electronics, automotive parts, machining, metal fabrication, plastics, and rubber products industries. However, wages at the end of the 1990s averaged between $1.01 and $1.45 an hour for automotive parts and industrial machining, and $0.88 an hour for garments—less than half the average rate at Baguio City.[20]

At Cavite, employers also took the initiative to shape labor-management relations, setting up the Council of Industrial Peace and Productivity to help members head off worker unrest. Some firms hired professional human-relations specialists and consultants to help with labor strategy.[21] According to employers, the "industrial peace" in the zone during the 1990s was a major attraction for foreign firms, which numbered more than two hundred by the end of the decade, making Cavite the largest of all Philippine EPZs.

Union organizing was permitted, and the ILO reported that a "progressive business group" of zone employers collaborated with the Associated Labor Unions–Trade Union Congress of the Philippines to help advance "trade-union rights."[22] In 1995 workers in three of the 142 firms in the zone voted to form unions. The Trade Union Congress of the Philippines received backing from the U.S. Agency for International Development to establish a labor education and counseling center, and launched a drive to organize workers in the Cavite zone in 1997. The zone remained free of strikes throughout the decade.

In the Philippines, the growing proportion of foreign firms engaged in more sophisticated industrial operations came about largely through the natural "pull" of zones that were located near relatively well-educated labor populations and backed by reasonably good infrastructure. But the Philippine experience also reflects a profound change in host countries' efforts to upgrade the composition of foreign investment in their economies. This change will be much more pronounced in the examples of the Dominican Republic and Costa Rica, which will be considered next. Two factors stand out as central to such initiatives: first, satisfied investors can play a strong role in attracting other participants from the same industrial sectors. Texas Instruments, Toyota, and an array of other high-profile U.S., Japanese, Taiwanese, and European corporations became prime exhibits in helping Philippine authorities to sign up follow-on investors in the same industries. This parallels the part played by companies like Westinghouse and GTE (Verizon) in the Dominican Republic, and by Motorola, Baxter Healthcare, and ultimately Intel in Costa Rica. Second, private developers can be highly valuable in identifying and delivering new foreign investors. Although the use of private operators to create and manage EPZs was initially greeted with considerable skepticism by development strategists,[23] it soon became apparent that the self-interest of the developers—in recruiting investors (frequently from the developer's home country), and in ensuring levels of service that would keep the investors satisfied and growing—meshed closely with the objectives of the host country.

In the Philippines, the fastest-growing sectors in the privately administered zones have been electronics and electrical equipment, followed by automotive parts, watches and clocks, metallic minerals, plastics, wood products, and chemicals.[24] Among the services that they provide, many of the private zone developers include help in recruiting appropriately skilled labor. Working with public sector agencies, private administrators have also incorporated worker housing, transportation, and access to commercial infrastructure into the initial design of zones, sometimes using international builders—such as the Santa Monica Development Corporation or the Regent Crest Corporation—in project development. In the Philippines and elsewhere a large portion of the fees that private zone administrators charge investors come from providing transportation, security, medical care, day-care, and recreational facilities for the firms and their employees. Some private developers have been able to generate as much as 50 percent of their revenues from such support services, and foreign investors with higher-skill, more sophisticated operations have forgone much lower zone fees elsewhere to secure such services.[25]

The changes in the treatment of workers associated with foreign investors in higher-skill EPZ operations did not remain limited to those investors, or those zones, or those activities. By 2001 direct employment in the Philippine EPZs totaled approximately 225,000. Statistics from the 1990s show that wages in the Philippine zones were higher than the average for the region in which each zone was located, and were generally rising in both peso and dollar terms.[26] Across all zones, workers' self-assessments of their socioeconomic status before and after employment in an EPZ indicated that they were better off financially than they had been before getting a job in the EPZ.[27] Before employment in the zone, 9 percent of workers surveyed were able to accumulate savings; after employment, 47 percent were able to. Even in Bataan, 56 percent of the workers surveyed reported that they could accumulate savings from their EPZ earnings, versus 11 percent before employment in the zone.

Data from the 1980s offered clear evidence of division of labor by gender, with men predominating in supervisory roles. But by 1998, across all zones, the proportion of men holding the position of line leaders, foremen, inspectors, controllers, supervisors, and engineers was 24 percent, and the proportion of women holding these positions was 22 percent.[28] The proportion of women holding line-worker positions was 76 percent; the proportion of men holding line-worker positions was 55 percent. The proportion of men holding warehouse and maintenance positions was 20 percent; the proportion of women holding warehouse and maintenance positions was 3 percent.[29]

Returning for a moment to the Bataan EPZ, the number of firms grew from a low of 12, during the period of labor strife in the early 1980s, to 34 in 1986, 44 in 1993, and 70 in 1998. The composition of activities changed somewhat as well. While 46 of the 70 firms were in the textile, apparel, footwear, or sporting goods sectors, 24 (33 percent) established more sophisticated operations, including 18 firms in electronics, automotive parts, chemicals, plastics, optical equipment, metal fabrication, and heavy equipment.[30]

Testimony from workers indicates that improvement in the treatment of workers in the Bataan EPZ was not limited to plants with more sophisticated operations. In contrast to the surveys in the early 1980s, which found that the wages of a significant percentage of the Bataan work force were less than or just equal to the statutory minimum, by the mid-1990s nearly all the enterprises in the Bataan EPZ respected the prescribed rates for the minimum wage and overtime, and many paid more than the minimum. In the Bataan zone the proportion of workers who reported that their earnings were higher than they needed to meet living expenses (56 percent) was larger than the average across all Philippine zones. Interviews with zone workers and trade-union leaders confirmed that employees received social security, medical care, paid vacation, sick leave, and maternity leave, and had free uniforms, adequate protective gear, and access to canteen facilities; monitoring procedures and health and safety conditions also improved.[31] Firms engaging in lower- as well as in higher-skill operations got high marks for their treatment of workers. In 1997, Reebok and Mitsumi, for example, won national awards for labor-management relations in their Bataan plants.[32] In 1998 the ILO singled out the Bataan EPZ, noting that "the Bataan zone, previously wracked by labor-management conflict, is now setting an example for labor-management cooperation."[33] A local labor lawyer with the Philippine Bureau of Labor Relations referred to this evolution as "the fall and rise of Bataan."[34]

Overall, therefore, as the number of EPZ firms has grown and the composition of investment has shifted toward more sophisticated operations, the evidence from the Philippines suggests not only that the treatment of workers improved in individual plants but that widespread patterns of labor suppression gave way to new forms of worker-management relations.[35] This transformation has occurred across the board: in both higher- and lower-skill operations in newer EPZs, in higher-skill operations in older EPZs, and indeed even in lower- and lowest-skill operations in the oldest EPZs. Improvements have taken place in OECD firms, non-OECD firms, subcontractor firms, and local Philippine firms (which made up 20 percent of the companies in the zones at the end of the 1990s).

In 1993, drawing on the successful experiences of the Mactan, Baguio City, and Cavite zones—and aiming to avoid the labor strife associated with the Bataan EPZ—the Philippine Department of Trade and Industry set up the Center for Labor Relations Assistance to promote the creation of labor-management councils in all zones and zone enterprises. Labor organizations initially feared that this effort reflected an antiunion strategy on the part of the central government.[36] But the Department of Trade and Industry reassured the Department of Labor and Employment that the labor-management councils would not substitute for unionism or collective bargaining, and by the end of the 1990s the councils had spread to almost one thousand unionized and nonunionized plants. At the same time that they were promoting the labor-management councils, the Department of Trade and Industry and the Department of Labor and Employment launched joint training programs to educate workers and management about modern human-resource policies and dispute-resolution techniques, and about the relationship between good working conditions and enhanced competitiveness.[37]

To be sure, reports of abuse and of violations of labor statutes and disagreements about the handling of labor relations by no means disappeared from the Philippine EPZs. Compulsory overtime remained a controversial issue. Reports of casualization—the practice of firing employees before their probationary period is up and then rehiring them—persisted. Employees continued to object to the lack of air-conditioning, and to file individual complaints about arbitrary dismissals and failure to pay social security benefits. And the ILO continued to receive reports of blacklisting, antiunion discrimination, and harassment and firing of union organizers.[38]

As will be found in the two examples that follow, union representation in EPZs is the subject of continued controversy. At issue is whether such representation is essential for meeting core labor standards, or whether the same ends can be achieved through nonunion worker-management organizations. In the Philippines, for example, the Bataan EPZ started out as, and remains, the most highly unionized zone, with approximately one-third of all firms operating with union workers. Organizing efforts have achieved a small degree of success in the Cavite EPZ, but neither the Baguio City nor the Mactan zones have trade unions: employers assert that their labor-management initiatives have precluded the need for unions. Trade-union representatives complain, however, that the employers use their internal labor-management mechanisms to thwart union organizing. In the view of some observers, organizations such as the Philippine labor-management councils constitute an "inauthentic" expression of freedom of association, or reflect "interference" in freedom of association. Debate over various forms of worker representation will arise again in the discussions of the Dominican Republic and Costa Rica.

*The Dominican Republic: On-the-Job Training, Increased
Productivity, and the Search for "Social Peace"*

With respect to foreign investment in higher-skill operations and
improvements in the treatment of workers, the Philippines and the
Dominican Republic share important similarities despite many differences in their economic histories. The Dominican example also provides
an unusually close look at the effects of rather elemental amounts of on-
the-job training—and subsequent learning-by-doing—on the growth of
productivity among EPZ line workers in various sectors.

The history of EPZs in the Dominican Republic dates from 1969,
when La Romana was set up to accommodate the needs of a single
multinational company, the Gulf & Western Corporation. But high
inflation and an overvalued exchange rate limited export growth
throughout the 1970s. After macroeconomic reforms in the early 1980s,
however, foreign investment expanded, and by 1987, 178 firms—confined largely to clothing and shoes—employed 85,000 workers in five
zones. During the early 1980s the objective of the Dominican government's strategy was to create employment in the poorer regions, in the
provinces and along the border with Haiti. Dominican labor law did not
impose the minimum wage on EPZ firms during this period, and the
enforcement of other worker-protection statutes was not noticeably rigorous. As did some regions of the Philippines, Dominican EPZs experienced repeated bouts of labor unrest.[39]

In an effort to upgrade and diversify exports, Dominican authorities,
like their counterparts in the Philippines, began in the second half of the
1980s to license new zone franchises to private developers. The Dominican innovation was to allow international companies with higher-skill
operations to act as both investors and promoters. The Itabo zone, for
example, included Westinghouse as both a zone owner and an exporter.
Led by Westinghouse, Itabo targeted other Fortune 500 firms to join in
setting up plants in the zone. The San Isidro zone grew up around the
operations of GTE (now Verizon), deploying that company's connections in the electronics sector to attract similar firms. The Las Americas
zone concentrated on information services.

Instead of searching for the cheapest sources of labor, the investors
whose operations were devoted to more sophisticated products chose to
be located near the capital, Santo Domingo, where they had access to
more skilled or more easily trained labor. To meet the needs of such
investors, private zone developers in the Dominican Republic, like their

counterparts in the Philippines, began to offer assistance with—and charge fees for—worker recruitment, worker transportation, and worker health services; the developers also provided business services and round-the-clock customs administration. The average rents charged by the private zone developers rapidly grew to more than three times the rates charged in the public zones.[40] Despite the added cost, survey data indicate that the foreign firms were willing to pay the premium rents because the better working environment served their "production needs" or better reflected their "corporate image."[41] In the manufacture of pharmaceuticals, for example, production facilities in the private zones were designed to meet the inspection standards required by the U.S. Food and Drug Administration.

Over the course of the 1990s, electronics, electrical equipment, medical equipment, metal products, and data processing became the largest new sectors represented in the EPZs, totaling 21 percent of all zone firms and 36 percent of all zone investment in 2000.[42] Textile and garment investors still had a significant presence, however, representing 57 percent of all zone firms and 73 percent of all zone employment in 2000. In almost all the zones Dominican companies mixed with foreign investors, making up 35 percent of all zone firms (166 of 481 firms).

As in the Philippines, the leading export companies in the Dominican zones took the initiative in trying to improve worker-management relations, but in the Dominican case they had difficulty persuading a majority of their colleagues that zone workers should be allowed the same treatment as workers elsewhere in the economy.[43] In 1992 the ILO provided advisory services to Dominican authorities to assist with the development of a new labor code that would be applicable across the country, including the EPZs. Six workers' federations and the directors of the association of zone employers signed an implementing document—the Agreement for Social Peace and Productivity—which acknowledged freedom of association as "an inherent right of workers." But the broader membership of zone employers failed to ratify the agreement. Two years later, the zone employers' association, the trade unions, and the government called upon the Catholic Church to serve as mediator in brokering a new agreement to harmonize labor relations in the zones. This time, ratification was successful, with all parties pledging to resolve conflicts through mediation.

By 1998 fourteen trade unions were operating in the zones, and some seven collective bargaining agreements were in effect. The provision of health-care and day-care facilities became mandatory in all zones. The

ILO *Global Report 2000* singled out the Dominican Republic as a "positive example" of a country that was taking steps to improve labor relations and protect freedom of association in its EPZs.[44] As was the case in the Philippines, host-country programs in the Dominican Republic to train labor leaders, employers, and inspectors in the basics of human-resource policies, conflict management, and dispute resolution—often with ILO participation and assistance—appear to have played an important role in promoting cooperative outcomes to labor disputes. Most zone plants in the Dominican Republic remained nonunion, however, and wages were determined outside of collective bargaining contracts.

Data from EPZ firms in the Dominican Republic provide an unusually detailed look at the impact of on-the-job training and learning-by-doing on a labor population that was considerably less educated than that of the Philippines.[45] Of the work force with which the EPZ firms began, 85 percent came directly from the country's unskilled labor pool. Within thirty-three U.S. firms and eleven Dominican firms, productivity increased 44 percent in the second year after the start-up of operations and 10 percent in the third. Within twelve Korean, Taiwanese, and Hong Kong firms, productivity increased 67 percent in the second year after the start-up of operations and 13 percent in the third. Achieving these large productivity increases did not require heroic measures on the part of zone employers: the typical pattern involved 2.3 months of on-the-job training for unskilled workers, followed by a period of learning-by-doing that continued for the rest of the first year.

By the end of the first five years of operation the Dominican employees in the U.S. affiliates had reached 76 percent of best-practice labor productivity in the United States. At the end of the first six years of operation, Dominican employees in the Korean, Taiwanese, and Hong Kong affiliates had reached 62 percent of best-practice labor productivity in the home countries of the investors.[46]

Of workers who had achieved the status of skilled worker by the end of the first year, 85 percent of those in the U.S. firms and 80 percent of those in the Korean, Taiwanese, and Hong Kong firms reported that they had developed their skills exclusively at their current company at the time of the survey. Without the opportunity to develop these skills, these zone workers would most likely have either been unemployed or earning approximately 60 percent of their current wages.[47] During the period of strong EPZ expansion between 1986 and 1993, the availability of jobs in the apparel and footwear industries in the zones helped reduce the proportion of poor women in the population from 23 to 16 percent.[48]

These results are all the more remarkable given that the firms in the Dominican zones—like employers in zones elsewhere—had to contend with cherry-picking on the part of other companies, high turnover, and job-hopping. Uncertainty about worker retention tends to reduce the incentive of any individual corporation to engage in training for its employees, leading to underinvestment in human-resource development. One solution is for the host government to step in, to the extent possible, to provide vocational education and training programs whose graduates are available to employers at large. The next example—Costa Rica—shows an imaginative effort in this direction.

By 2000, 481 firms had invested more than $1 billion in 46 zones, creating 196,924 jobs.[49] Zone exports of $4.7 billion represented more than 80 percent of the country's total exports, and virtually all of its manufactured exports. Average compensation for production workers in the zones increased from $0.57 an hour to $1.36 an hour between 1993 and 2000; the minimum wage for private sector employees was $0.78 in 2000.[50] Wages and benefits for production workers at some of the newer private zones (such as the Palmarejo zone), where there was a large concentration of more sophisticated operations, amounted to two to three times the minimum wage, with an average of $2.01 an hour in 2000. But the growth in compensation was not confined to the newer zones: wages and benefits for production workers in some of the older zones (such as the La Romana zone) actually exceeded the national average for the zones, perhaps because firms requiring higher-skilled workers settled alongside garment and footwear producers.

Between 1993 and 2000 the proportion of the zone work force classified as "technicians" increased, and the average compensation for technicians rose by more than 150 percent, from $1.23 to $3.21 an hour. Skilled workers earned premium wages at older as well as newer zones: at the La Romana zone, for example, the average compensation for technicians was $4.21 an hour in 2000. Across all zones, 10 percent of male workers and 6 percent of female workers qualified as technicians in 2000. Dorsati Madani reports, moreover, that a growing number of women hold supervisory positions on the production floors in the Dominican EPZs.[51]

As in the Philippines, however, labor relations in the Dominican Republic are not without controversy: there have been ongoing complaints to the ILO that wages are set by direct interaction between management and employees in individual plants, and that disputes are resolved through mediation, without formal collective bargaining.

Costa Rica: Marketing the Country to Investors in Higher-Skill Operations

During the early years of investment in textile and garment plants in Cost Rica, there was little evidence of labor suppression or worker unrest of the sort that had occurred in the Philippines or the Dominican Republic; however, the transition from lowest-skill to higher-skill operations in the Costa Rican EPZs does show the same pattern of employer-led initiatives to promote stability and loyalty within the work force that was prominent in the Philippine story. The Costa Rican example also illustrates how important highly proactive investment-promotion strategies are in the attraction of sophisticated international investment: Intel's catalytic investment in a semiconductor assembly and testing facility provides a particularly vivid example of the value of such efforts.

Intent on attracting foreign firms engaging in labor-intensive operations, Costa Rica launched its first EPZs in 1981. But an overvalued exchange rate and the lingering effects of the Latin American debt crisis hindered inward investment until the second half of the 1980s. Between 1986 and 1992 business-friendly domestic reforms and the adoption of a more realistic exchange rate enabled Cost Rica to pull in some $368 million in investment and create 37,000 EPZ jobs, almost exclusively in the clothing industry.

As part of its early strategy, Costa Rica offered special preferences and incentives to firms willing to locate in the less developed parts of the country.[52] Like other host countries, however, Cost Rica encountered difficulties with its efforts to use EPZs to generate jobs in the country's poorest, lowest-wage regions.

With sluggish growth in established exports, Costa Rican authorities began to fear that their country was losing its ability to compete in the manufacture of labor-intensive products, and decided to change the course of their development strategy: instead of relying on the attraction of low-cost labor, the authorities chose to build upon the cumulative national investments in education, which had yielded a 94 percent literacy rate. To accomplish this goal, Costa Rica fundamentally restructured and reoriented its investment promotion and development agency (la Coalicion Costaricense de Initiativas para el Desarrollo, or CINDE) in 1992.

Modeled on the Economic Development Board (EDB) of Singapore, CINDE was charged with playing the role carried out by private zone developers in the Philippines and the Dominican Republic.[53] Costa

Rica's application of the Singapore approach to investment promotion offers an opportunity to view the transformation that occurred in the 1990s: as the spread of more advanced industrial operations gained speed, a fundamental shift occurred in how the challenge of attracting higher-skill operations was conceptualized. During the early years of the globalization of industry—from the 1970s into the 1980s—most developing countries viewed multinational corporations as omniscient actors, scanning the globe for profitable opportunities, eager to pounce when any occasion presented itself. Thus, until the late 1980s and early 1990s, a majority of host-country agencies with responsibility for foreign direct investment dedicated their energies to screening applicants and imposing conditions on the foreign investors that showed up.[54] As will be discussed in chapter 7, as long as investment-promotion agencies were charged with using manufacturing investors primarily for import substitution in the domestic economy, the prospect of high profits in tightly protected markets was sufficiently attractive to potential investors—at least in the case of larger economies—that host-country authorities had little reason to subject their view of the motivations and behavior of multinational investors to critical scrutiny.

However, for host countries, or would-be host countries, that wanted to attract export-oriented investment within a manufacturing corporation's regional or global sourcing network—in electronics, automotive parts, and other industrial equipment, for example—the foreign investors' decisionmaking process did not resemble the pouncing of omniscient supercorporations. Even under the pressures of global competition, international companies were cautious about making "irreversible commitments" by building capital-intensive plants in new and untried locations, especially when the foreign investors depended on those plants to play an integral role in the parent companies' strategy to bolster their competitive position worldwide.[55] Development authorities that wanted to break into the relatively small circle of nations that hosted the more advanced foreign industrial operations had to demonstrate the attractiveness of their economies by actively and persuasively marketing their countries; the process was akin to one in which risk-averse buyers must be persuaded that they can safely sink a lot of money into something they need to rely on—and not be stuck with a lemon.[56]

Like the EDB of Singapore, CINDE combined careful investigation of the needs of companies (in electronics, medical devices, pharmaceuticals, and telecommunication services, for example) with a newfound aggressiveness toward potential investors.[57] Unlike many other developing countries, where the slogans changed, but the attitudes—and the investment-agency staff—remained the same, Costa Rica thoroughly embraced a fresh, proactive stance.

Between 1992 and 1995 CINDE achieved some degree of success, attracting international companies to its EPZs that included Baxter Healthcare, DSC Communications, and Motorola. A qualitative breakthrough in Costa Rica's new EPZ strategy came in 1996, however, with the successful culmination of its effort to attract Intel to the country.[58] From the very inception of CINDE's new strategy, Intel had figured prominently among the targets within the international electronics industry. But Costa Rican authorities discovered that the country was not even on Intel's "long list" of potential sites for a new assembly and testing plant—a list that included Chile, Puerto Rico, Singapore, Taiwan, Thailand, and Ireland. During the first two years of the courtship, despite repeated requests, CINDE could not even gain an invitation to visit Intel's headquarters.

The agency nonetheless took the initiative to prepare a comprehensive proposal designed specifically for a semiconductor assembly and testing plant; the proposal covered export-zone regulations, ownership policies, educational facilities, human-resource opportunities, taxation, environmental regulations, and various permits. In 1995 Costa Rica finally broke into the ranks of Intel's long list, and offered its customized proposal. According to Debora Spar's study of the Intel investment decision, Costa Rica's long tradition of political democracy, strong commercial-law institutions, and high transparency and low corruption ratings helped put Costa Rica into contention.[59] Union-free throughout its manufacturing facilities, Intel was also searching for a location where it would have the option of establishing a nonunion plant without asking for a special exception.

As Intel neared its final decision on site selection, three factors played a strong role in fostering the company's growing interest in Costa Rica: First were the favorable comments of foreign investors already in place—in particular, DSC Communications and Motorola, whose smaller electronics operations offered a credible view of how trainable the work force might be; and Baxter Healthcare, whose expertise with clean-room facilities Intel respected.[60] Second was Costa Rica's commitment to fund a separate substation of the national electric utility as a backup to ensure Intel dependable access to 5 percent of the country's entire power supply. Third was the fact that, as the final decision on the plant site approached, a united front of Costa Rican agencies offered Intel fast-track approval of all necessary permits.[61]

But one "most pressing concern" remained. Intel had concluded that Costa Rica lacked the vocational-training infrastructure that was required to support the company's personnel needs, despite superior levels of general education among the population. To overcome what would otherwise have been a "deal breaker," the Costa Rican Ministry of Education and Ministry of Science and Technology worked jointly with Intel's human-resource staff, with teachers from Costa Rica's Institute of Technology, and with local technical high schools to design special one- and two-year postsecondary technical-training programs for potential new semiconductor assembly employees.

Once President Jose Figueres had signed off on the team's proposals, the two sides shook hands. In 1996 Intel announced its decision to locate the company's new $300 million semiconductor assembly and testing facility in Costa Rica, adding this new host country to its overseas plants in China, Malaysia, the Philippines, Ireland, and Israel.

The plant, which employed 3,500 workers to produce the Pentium II processor, represented the largest single investment yet made by any firm in Central America. Within two years of construction, Intel's operation had achieved the capacity to generate some $700 million in annual exports, potentially surpassing coffee and bananas—Costa Rica's two main traditional products—combined. In 1999 employee wages in the Costa Rican manufacturing sector averaged $2.21 an hour, and averaged $3.36 an hour at Intel.[62]

With the Intel investment, Costa Rica established itself as a pioneer in the use of vocational-training support to attract foreign investment. The one- and two-year technical training programs launched with Intel were expanded to other industrial sectors as well. Between 1997 and 1999 enrollment in engineering studies at Costa Rican universities doubled; by 2000 874 students were enrolled in the engineering program at the Institute for Technology.[63]

As part of their investment-promotion package, Costa Rican authorities offered foreign investors three months of reimbursement for the salaries of new EPZ production workers while the workers received free, on-site training from the National Institute of Apprenticeships. Costa Rica's Institute for Technology also began to provide intensive language training in English for Costa Rican technical students, and in Spanish for foreign expatriates.

Between 1996 and 2000 the new CINDE strategy had more than tripled the level of foreign direct investment in Costa Rica's EPZs, to $1.3 billion. Annual exports were more than $3.3 billion, and the job base was 57,000 workers.[64] Costa Rican EPZs housed eighty-five Fortune 500 companies, including regional headquarters for both Procter & Gamble and Western Union. In a 1999 survey of sixty-one foreign investors, some 72 percent of the firms (thirty-six in the electronics industry, thirteen in medical devices, three in business services, and nine in other sectors) indicated that the presence of the Intel plant had had an important "signaling effect" on their own investment-decision process.[65] In 2000, overtaking Chile, Costa Rica became, on a per capita basis, the most export-intensive economy in Latin America.

As in the Philippines, investors in Cost Rica's EPZs took the initiative at the plant level to establish mechanisms to help preserve stability and instill a measure of loyalty within the work force. In Costa Rica, "solidarity associations" became the vehicle for fostering improved labor-management relations. These associations typically offer workers subsidized credit and housing loans, as well as a savings program funded by joint contributions from workers and their employers.

The solidarity associations have been the focus of persistent complaints, however, on the part of local and international trade-union organizations. At their request, the ILO undertook two missions to Costa Rica, in 1991 and 1993, to help prepare labor statutes that would "protect against any infringements of trade-union rights."[66] In 1993 the Costa Rican legislature passed legislation prohibiting any activities that hindered the formation and operation of trade unions, in the zones or elsewhere, and barring solidarity associations from signing collective agreements.

During the 1990s support for solidarity associations among zone employers grew as the number of foreign investors increased, and as the proportion of companies whose home-country operations were not highly unionized expanded. As was the case in both the Philippines and the Dominican Republic, disputes have arisen in Costa Rica about what constitutes "authentic" worker-management interaction. For its part, the ILO has complained that the solidarity associations are dependent on employers' financial contributions, include supervisors and managerial-level staff among their members, are often formed at the employer's initiative, are responsible for the relatively weak presence of trade unions in the zones, and have often replaced collective bargaining with a system of "direct settlement."[67] In defense of the solidarity associations, the zone employers claim that the associations offer a means of promoting harmonious relations, and of "obviating" the need for trade unions.[68]

Improving the Treatment of Workers at Lower and Higher Skill Levels Together

For all their differences, there are a number of common themes in the experiences of the three host countries examined here. As the Philippines, the Dominican Republic, and Costa Rica attracted larger numbers of foreign investors and higher-skill operations, the labor-management regimes in the foreign plants underwent fundamental changes. The situations are too complex to provide a perfect social science "experiment" showing precisely which factors produce exactly which results in the evolution of labor-management relations. Many important changes were taking place simultaneously. Nevertheless, a number of patterns are clear.

In each country, foreign investment was moving from isolated and poverty-stricken local labor markets, where workers had little experience in the formal sector and limited knowledge of other options, to more competitive labor markets with a more knowledgeable labor force. Successive waves of foreign direct investment included increasing numbers of firms that had to meet international standards for the dependability and precision of their manufactures, which included electronic, electrical, automotive, industrial, pharmaceutical, and medical products.

As foreign investment moved beyond garments, footwear, toys, jewelry, and similar products, certain trade-offs became increasingly clear to employers: lower wages, poor working conditions, and rote production were associated with employee dissatisfaction, whereas higher wages, better working conditions, and more job flexibility were associated with greater employee satisfaction. Purely as a matter of self-interest, investors with more skill-intensive operations showed signs of becoming more attentive to the need to attract and maintain a more contented and better-trained work force. These investors sought out worker-friendly services in worker-friendly environments, paying zone rents that were triple those elsewhere for the superior conditions.

With time, increasing numbers of influential investors found that the costs of labor unrest were intolerable, and became willing to increase wages and benefits—and to make institutional changes—in order to head them off. When international companies with needs for higher-

skilled workers settled in the same EPZs that housed international firms
with needs for lower-skilled workers, and the two types of firms joined
together in employers' associations to help set the terms for the treatment of workers, the firms conducting lower-skill operations were
pulled toward the standards set by the firms conducting higher-skill
operations.[69]

These host-country examples reinforce the observation made in the
first chapter—that simply providing access to lowest-wage, lowest-
skilled workers is a weak inducement for foreign investors. To the contrary, the experiences of the Philippines, the Dominican Republic, and
Costa Rica all demonstrate that host countries' investment in education
(including even high school and vocational programs) offers highly valuable returns: an educated work force not only attracts foreign investors
in general but helps move the composition of foreign investment from
lower- to higher-skill operations. Thus, developing countries that want
to take optimal advantage of foreign direct investment clearly need to
adopt a build-up rather than a trickle-down strategy—that is, to
strengthen the development of skills in the labor population rather than
to simply hope that the presence of foreign firms will eventually have
favorable effects that spread to the host economy at large.[70]

Although the evidence supports its effectiveness, this build-up strategy raises a number of issues. First is the fact that investors who must
participate in extensive employee training in order to have access to an
adequate work force are essentially being required to create public
goods: they invest in workers who are then free to take their skills elsewhere. The build-up strategy also has to find ways to maximize backward linkages, externalities, and positive spillover effects to local firms
and workers in the host economy when these local firms and workers do
not enjoy the favorable production conditions that exist in the zones.
Host-country authorities that wish to follow a build-up strategy will
quickly discover, as a result, the drawbacks of continuing with the zone
approach to development when the general liberalization of trade and
investment offers much greater potential advantages. These issues are
dealt with in chapter 7, in the context of discussing how host countries
can best position themselves along the frontiers of best technology, quality-control, and management practices in globalizing industries.

Overall, the experiences of the three countries described in this chapter, like those of Mauritius and Madagascar in the previous chapter,
demonstrate that the effort to attract larger numbers of investors and to
build a path up from least-skilled to even slightly higher-skilled opera-

tions is a remarkably powerful force for improving the treatment of workers and transforming the labor-management regime of the host country. In the five examples introduced so far, this transformative process touched the lives of hundreds of thousands of workers directly—and of many more indirectly.

The evidence examined here provides a clear answer to whether the growing globalization of production around the world will increase—or decrease—the likelihood of labor suppression and labor abuse in developing countries. The evidence indicates that the growing globalization of production acts to improve the treatment of workers in host countries and helps to remedy the mistreatment that can occur when the flow of foreign direct investment is weak or nonexistent. Nevertheless, the evidence does not show that improvement occurs in each and every case, in each and every plant. The examples reveal both the persistence of old conflicts and complaints and the emergence of new controversies.

What role should the international community play in helping to improve the treatment of workers in foreign-owned and foreign-controlled plants? And when might international initiatives reinforce—or undermine—the processes of improvement in the treatment of workers described here? These are the subjects of the next three chapters.

4 Core Standards for the Treatment of Workers around the World

As demonstrated in chapter 3, a potent method of improving the treatment of workers in foreign-owned and foreign-controlled plants is to complement lowest-skill with relatively higher-skill operations. When this strategy is successful, employers are compelled, by their own self-interest, to adopt measures designed to attract and retain better workers. But even in the countries examined in the last chapter—let alone in larger and more diverse economies such as those of China, Indonesia, India, and Brazil—improvement in the treatment of workers does not, of course, necessarily take place for every worker, or for every plant, or for every export processing zone. What role might the international community play in promoting broader improvement in the treatment of workers, and in preventing mistreatment? This question is the focus of a discussion that begins here and continues in the two chapters that follow.

To set the stage, this chapter begins with an examination of the four core labor standards of the International Labor Organization. These standards, which have acquired the widest legitimacy as the basis for the treatment of workers around the world, address problems of discrimination, forced labor, and child labor, and promote freedom of association and the right to collective bargaining. The chapter then considers two other proposed standards—minimum health and safety standards and the provision of a "living wage." Next, the focus of the chapter shifts to the one core standard that has been the subject of greatest controversy for foreign investment in low-wage, low-skill operations—that is, the standard that addresses freedom of association, the right to engage in collective bargaining, and the formation of trade unions. The concluding section of the chapter considers a formula in which each country simply "enforces its own labor laws"—an approach that is embodied in the U.S.-Jordan free trade agreement—as a possible short-cut for determining when ILO members are in violation of core labor standards.

As this chapter and the two that follow will demonstrate, any effort on the part of the international community to define and monitor compliance, investigate complaints, and impose penalties on violators would be a complex and difficult undertaking. Chapter 5 explores an "authoritative" approach implemented through the World Trade Organization and backed by trade sanctions or fines; chapter 6 examines a "voluntary" option relying on corporate codes of conduct, certification organizations, and compliance labeling.

Defining Core Labor Standards: The ILO's Fundamental Principles

The 1998 Declaration of the International Labor Organization on Fundamental Principles and Rights at Work is the most widely accepted starting point for the discussion of core labor standards. The declaration is based on the Constitution of the International Labor Organization, as reaffirmed at the World Summit for Social Development in Copenhagen (1995) and at the Ministerial Conference of the World Trade Organization in Singapore (1996). The declaration stipulates that "all Members, even if they have not ratified the Conventions in question, have an obligation, arising from the very fact of membership in the Organization, to respect, to promote and to realize, in good faith and in accordance with the Constitution, the principles concerning the fundamental rights which are the subject of those Conventions."[1] The four fundamental principles are

—The elimination of discrimination in respect of employment and occupation (conventions 100 and 111).

—The elimination of all forms of forced or compulsory labor (conventions 29 and 105).

—The effective abolition of child labor (conventions 138 and 182).

—Freedom of association and the effective recognition of the right to collective bargaining (conventions 87 and 98).

At first glance, each principle appears to be simple and clear-cut. But how easy—or difficult—would it be to determine when an ILO member state is in compliance with, or in violation of, these core labor standards?

ELIMINATION OF DISCRIMINATION IN EMPLOYMENT AND OCCUPATION. In the case of the elimination of discrimination in employment, the objective is straightforward: to do away with differences in treatment and remuneration that are based on ethnicity, religion, or gender. Determining what might constitute a violation, however, is much more complicated. Whether an ostensibly simple standard—such as equal pay for equal work—is being observed depends upon a variety of factors—including, for example, how national job-classification systems are constructed, how frequently reclassification occurs, whether there is equal access in hiring, and whether promotions are merit-based.[2] Moreover, the definition of compliance would require agreement, across borders and cultures, that particular workers can or cannot be excluded from certain jobs because of the nature of the work involved (for example, heavy exertion or danger).

Enforcement typically depends upon complaints (or lawsuits) brought by those who are discriminated against. Yet women or minorities who might find themselves the objects of discrimination may judge themselves too vulnerable to file a complaint, may lack the resources to pursue a legal remedy, or may not even know for sure that discrimination has occurred. Setting standards for enforcement may hinge, therefore, on international agreement about the obligation of local or national authorities to provide not only well-functioning labor courts but also public legal services.

Adding a further controversial dimension, some countries (including India, Malaysia, and the United States) have adopted affirmative action plans at various points in time to assist in overcoming barriers to nondiscrimination; such plans, which specify targets and timetables for the hiring and promotion of members of specified groups, have given rise, in turn, to complaints of reverse discrimination.

ELIMINATION OF ALL FORMS OF FORCED OR COMPULSORY LABOR. The objective of the ILO principle that calls for the elimination of forced labor also appears simple: to prohibit all labor that is coerced or bonded, or that includes elements of servitude or slavery. In practice, however, determining compliance with this standard is complex: it would be necessary to distinguish, for example, between instances in which employers' offers of advances in pay involve deception or entrapment, and those in which workers misjudge an employer's intent or have second thoughts about earlier agreements. The definition of compliance would also have to take cultural differences into account: in some countries, unpaid apprenticeships would be regarded as the equivalent of indentured servitude; in others, they are an established part of the traditional economy. Similarly, it is acceptable in some cultures, but not in others, for employers to provide loans or travel funds that are then repaid through the labor of the recipient.

Whether freedom from forced labor should apply to the use of prison labor adds further complexity to the issue. Prison labor may provide training that will be useful to prisoners after they have served their sentences, and can thus encourage rehabilitation. Determining whether participation in prison work programs is voluntary, however, is complicated by the fact that it is often a condition of parole. In the United States, for example, some states require all able-bodied prisoners to accept jobs in prison. Both within and outside the United States, the work of convicts is usually paid, though often not at market rates. The U.S. Bureau of Prisons operates some one hundred factories where prisoners, according to management, are "not covered by the Fair Labor Standards Act or minimum wage laws. They don't get retirement benefits, unemployment compensation, etc. They're workers, but they're not employees."[3] To take prison labor into account in determining compliance with the ILO principle would require nations to agree on two main issues: what constitutes forced or compulsory participation, and how the treatment of convicts may diverge from the treatment of employees.

EFFECTIVE ABOLITION OF CHILD LABOR. The prohibition of child labor is one of the most widely enacted regulations in the national statutes of countries around the world, yet ILO convention 138—which has the long-term goal of eliminating any employment of children under the age of fourteen that interferes with schooling—has received fewer ratifications than other fundamental conventions. The ILO has estimated that around the world, at some point during the year, more than 120 million children below the age of fifteen take part in substantial economic activity in both formal and informal sectors of the economy. For many, low-cost education is not a realistic alternative to work: because most of these children earn income that is vital to their families, the abolition of child labor in the production and assembly of goods (to the extent that it can be enforced) may well leave such children and their families less well off, and push the children into more hazardous occupations, such as prostitution or street begging.

The effort to determine what constitutes appropriate national regulation of child labor thus devolves quickly into other questions—about a country's performance in alleviating poverty, and in providing universal, low-cost, elementary education.[4] In 2000 ILO convention 138 was supplemented by convention 182, which directs the attention of ratifying nations to eliminating the worst forms of child labor—those that are "likely to jeopardize the health, safety, or morals" of children.

FREEDOM OF ASSOCIATION AND THE RIGHT TO COLLECTIVE BARGAINING. Unlike the other core labor standards, freedom of association and the right to collective bargaining are the source of considerable controversy: experts in public policy and development strategy disagree not only about how to define the operative terms but about whether freedom of association and the right to collective bargaining should be accorded the status of fundamental principles at all. Some development strategists, while endorsing good treatment of workers, nonetheless view the formation of unions as an attempt by a "rent-seeking" labor aristocracy, in the characterization of T. N. Srinivasan, to interject monopoly power into the economy, "promoting the interests of a small section of the labor force at the expense of many."[5] In this view the ability of particular groups of workers to levy restrictions on numbers and kinds of jobs— thereby creating inefficiencies in the local economy—should be regulated, like other aspects of social policy, rather than endowed with the status of a basic human right. Other development strategists argue, however, that trade unions and other worker and worker-employer organizations can promote efficiency, instill loyalty, and enhance stability.[6]

Even among countries that regard freedom of association and the right to collective bargaining as fundamental rights, there are considerable divergences about what might constitute a violation of the ILO principle that addresses these two issues. Some national labor-relations systems, for example, allow labor organizations at the firm level, others at the industry level, and others at the national level—and there is considerable controversy about which approach best promotes growth, efficiency, and equity.[7] Similarly, some systems allow a closed shop, which allots considerable power to a given union, arguably at the expense of more general employee rights; others endorse right-to-work laws, which allow individual workers to enjoy the benefits obtained by union negotiations without having to join the union or pay dues. Some countries, including the United States, allow employers to hire permanent replacements for striking workers, a practice that constitutes a considerable limitation on the exercise of collective bargaining.[8] Under various conditions, both developed and developing countries often limit the right to strike.

Other Proposed Standards

In addition to the four fundamental principles espoused by the ILO, a number of other standards are often proposed as minimal requirements for the treatment of workers. These include health and safety standards and a minimum wage or living wage. Like the four fundamental principles, however, both of these "simple" standards give rise to their own complexities.

In the case of minimum health and safety standards, for example, it would seem that the general goal of protecting workers' health and safety could be translated into straightforward rules that would prohibit certain behavior, such as the blocking of fire exits or the unprotected use of carcinogenic chemicals. Once again, however, the question of how to establish a core of prohibited practices—while allowing production processes, building codes, and zoning laws to vary considerably across countries—is not as simple as it might at first seem. The criteria for determining what constitutes a violation would have to address a number of variations—in income, infrastructure levels, production processes, building codes, and zoning laws, for example—across countries and in different regions of the same country. Because of the complexity and difficulty of addressing such variations, health and safety conditions are usually not included in the list of core standards that might be subject to international enforcement.[9]

While the analysis of the issues surrounding the most widely endorsed standards for the treatment of workers could be amplified in much more detail, it is safe to say that countries diverge widely in their perceptions of what each core principle demands; moreover, within any given country, there are complex and somewhat idiosyncratic chains of interpretation about how to go about implementing such standards at the national, provincial, or municipal level. The divergences are likely to be particularly pronounced on the subject of freedom of association, collective bargaining, and union organizing—the precise areas in which most controversies involving foreign direct investment in labor-intensive operations have arisen. Before the issues surrounding freedom of association, collective bargaining, and union organizing are considered in more detail, the question of whether some kind of minimum wage or living wage should be added to the list of core labor standards requires special consideration.

Providing a Minimum Wage or a Living Wage

To outsiders, wages of a few dollars a day paid to workers in lowest-skill factory jobs appear abysmally low, even when these wages are substantially higher than what would be available in agricultural or domestic work. In order for the external world to consider the products acceptable in international markets, should a minimum compensation package be established for workers in export plants? Arriving at an answer that serves the interests of low-skilled workers in the developing world, without damaging their prospects, requires careful investigation.

Standard economic theory has traditionally warned that setting a minimum wage, and raising it in real terms, will hurt workers by reducing the demand for their labor. Although recent studies from the United States have called into question the universality of the relationship between higher wages and lower demand for labor, documenting cases in which small increases in the minimum wage did not hurt the employment of relatively low-skilled workers,[10] the likelihood that minimum wages could be enforced and increased without causing unemployment in developing countries would appear to be rather slim.

In many countries the disparity between the legal minimum wage and average income is much greater than in the United States; and the disparity is larger in poorer countries than in middle-income countries.[11] The World Bank reports that in some sectors in Bangladesh, for example, minimum wages are more than double the per capita gross national product. In practice, legal minimum wages are often not enforced, obscuring the negative impact they might otherwise have on employment. In some countries surveys of employees in the formal sector show that more than half receive less than the minimum wage. Outside of the formal sector (and in nearly all rural occupations), most workers are not covered by minimum wage regulations at all.

A hypothetical scenario in which minimum wages in developing countries were suddenly enforced with rigor—or increased and then strictly enforced—would be unlikely to leave employment levels unaffected. Within any given country, an externally imposed minimum wage that singled out the operations of foreign direct investors and their subcontractors, and thereby raised the relative costs associated with foreign direct investment, would shift the composition of activities within the economy away from those engaged in by foreign investors and back toward other sectors, such as traditional exports and subsistence agriculture.

Across countries, an externally imposed minimum wage for foreign investors and their subcontractors would lead investors to relocate production facilities to higher-productivity sites. As the next chapter will show, for a supplier making jeans or athletic shoes for export, labor costs at the production stage may range from 20 to 46 to 250 percent of the profit margin. Management at the production stage is therefore likely to be under considerable pressure to keep labor costs low at current production sites, and to be on the lookout for new production sites where the combination of wage and productivity levels might be more favorable.

A mandatory global minimum wage for export workers that was uniform throughout the developing world would hit the poorest countries with the lowest-skilled workers the hardest, by depriving them of the opportunity to use their cheaper labor to penetrate external markets. For example, a mandatory global minimum wage of $2.31 an hour (in 2000 dollars), which is the average wage in export zones in Costa Rica, would lead foreign investors to abandon the Dominican Republic, where the average wage is less than $2.00 an hour (in 2000 dollars), in favor of more productive labor at the same price in Costa Rica—and never even to consider pools of cheaper (but also less productive) labor in El Salvador, Haiti, or Nicaragua, let alone Bangladesh or Indonesia, at all. Thus, by cutting off access to jobs that would otherwise be available to their workers, a uniform minimum wage would create disadvantages for the very countries for which foreign investors with labor-intensive operations constitute the greatest relative opportunity.[12]

Within countries, a mandatory minimum compensation package would similarly place lower- or least-skilled workers at a disadvantage. In a pattern known as the displacement effect, employers required to pay the mandatory minimum wage would fill their labor force with workers whose skills qualified them for payment at that level, and the less qualified—but still adequately skilled—workers would be left behind. So, for example, a mandatory minimum wage of $2.76 an hour in the Philippines (in 2000 dollars), the average wage in the Baguio City EPZ, would divert to Baguio, which has a relatively higher-skilled labor force, investment that would otherwise be destined for the large labor pools of modestly skilled and demonstrably trainable workers around the Cavite and Bataan zones.

Across developing countries and within each developing country, therefore, compensation must be permitted to vary with productivity, in order for each nation to be able to exploit the comparative advantages of its own economy. The examples of Mauritius and Madagascar in chapter 2 showed that in deciding whether to expand or contract employment, labor-intensive investors are quite sensitive to changes in relative wage levels (there did not appear to be a strong propensity to substitute capital for labor as labor costs rose, however).[13] Similarly, evidence that assembly-plant owners have shifted production patterns in Southeast Asia in response to rising wages indicates that host countries need to avoid setting a minimum compensation package for export occupations that might price the country's workers out of the market.[14]

In an attempt to allow poorer countries to maintain their relative advantage as production sites, the living-wage movement has proposed that minimum compensation levels be established for workers on a country-by-country basis; such wages would be high enough to support an individual or family over the course of a year, but would be calculated to reflect purchasing power in each individual economy. Debates among the proponents of this idea show, however, that the task of determining a living wage is extremely complex, and must take into account a range of factors, including nutritional standards; housing types; expenditures on water, energy, clothing, transportation, health care, education, and savings; and provision for contingencies.[15] Moreover, alternative methods of calculation and subtle differences in estimating "purchasing-power parity" would inevitably favor one country over another. Legitimate disagreements about how purchasing-power parity should be calculated and about how host authorities should manage macroeconomic and exchange-rate policies would lead to large divergences, across nations, in what might be considered a proper definition of a minimum compensation package. Such divergences would offer a rather large opportunity for outsiders to use calculations of minimum compensation packages to protect themselves against more competitive imports. Adding to the difficulties, there is no convincing reason to extend living-wage calculations across national markets when regional conditions differ significantly. In large economies such as those of Brazil, China, Indonesia, India, or South Africa, a national minimum compensation package would unavoidably benefit some locations at the expense of others.

The estimate of the family size that a worker is assumed to support, moreover, is inherently arbitrary and unavoidably discriminatory. On the basis of its experience in Mexico, Haiti, and Indonesia, for example, the Center for Reflection, Education, and Action has recommended that the living wage be calculated to support one adult and one minor child.[16] The National Labor Committee has proposed, in contrast, that the living wage be set to support a family of 4.3 people, which is the average family size in El Salvador.[17] Researchers from Columbia University, however, have pointed out that some garment and footwear workers in El Salvador return to rural households—where the average family size is 5.2—at the end of the day or week.[18]

Whatever number for average family size might ultimately be chosen as the basis for computing a living wage, the calculation would penalize countries, or regions of the same country, where families are relatively large—that is, where new employment opportunities for low-skilled workers are likely to be most scarce and most valuable. Moreover, it is in precisely such areas that personal benefits and externalities (including increased agency for female employees) and host-country benefits and externalities (including reductions in fertility rates and in the intergenerational transmission of poverty) might be greatest. On the basis of the Columbia University researchers' data from El Salvador, an investor bound by living-wage obligations (all other things being equal) would locate a labor-intensive plant in a country where the average family size is less than 5.2 people—and where, consequently, the living-wage computation would be lower—and would shun El Salvador, especially rural El Salvador.

In determining a living wage, the risk of arbitrariness and discrimination would not be limited to decisions about which figures to use in the calculation. More fundamentally, determining a living wage would require apportioning compensation packages among workers of different ages and with different familial responsibilities, without engaging in any of the forms of discrimination proscribed by the ILO's core principles. Survey evidence introduced in chapter 2 showed that among employees in the garment, footwear, and toy industries, women are usually in the majority, and that the mix of female employees includes widows, divorcees, and heads of households as well as younger women; among the latter group, some provide the majority of the income for nuclear families back in their village, and others use their income for the clothes and other appurtenances that teenagers purchase when they are first living away from home.[19]

Requiring all workers to receive a full, family-based living wage would discriminate against workers who are younger, less experienced, entry-level, or self-supporting. But a living wage separated into various levels—for those who live with and support nuclear families, those who support families in their home village, and those who support only themselves—would, in addition to being hopelessly difficult to administer, discriminate against those with larger family responsibilities. In a complicated version of the displacement effect, workers with larger family responsibilities might be inclined, in the face of possible unemployment, to conceal those responsibilities in order to compete for the less well-paid jobs available to workers in the self-supporting category. Wendy Diaz, the fifteen-year-old Honduran orphan who is supporting three younger brothers, would thus be competing against a cheaper, hypothetical Maria Diaz who supports no one but herself. To protect her job, Wendy will likely neglect to mention her three younger brothers.

The more generous the formula for calculating the living wage were to become, the greater the impact. At the margin, jobs would move from developing to developed countries, where goods such as garments, footwear, and toys would be protected against imports by the high wage requirements imposed on producers. (The T-shirts emblazoned with the logo of the United Students Against Sweatshops are produced in Bangor, Pennsylvania.) As many of those who are working to improve employment opportunities for low-skilled workers in the developing world would acknowledge, this is hardly a desirable outcome for their efforts.[20]

The preceding analysis militates against attempting to include a minimum wage or an arbitrarily defined living wage in the list of core labor standards. Does this mean, however, that the international community should take no steps to try to improve the wages of low-skilled workers at foreign-owned and foreign-controlled plants in developing countries? Quite the contrary.

As will be shown in chapter 6, public pressure on international investors and retailers to use some of their earnings to live up to their professed willingness to provide good working conditions to employees throughout their supply chains may turn out to be a more potent tool than is conventionally assumed. In contrast to the production stage, where market conditions are highly competitive, international investors and retailers have greater potential to earn substantial profits. These firms devote tens of millions of dollars to building up a brand image; part of that investment usually involves creating a reputation for socially responsible behavior on a range of race, gender, and labor issues. International investors and retailers can mobilize tens of millions of dollars to avoid denunciations that threaten their accumulated investment in brand image. For them, unit labor costs at the production stage are a small portion of the final price (1 percent or less for branded garments and footwear; 1 to 3 percent for unbranded garments and footwear); thus, higher wages for low-skilled workers need not raise the final price by a large amount.[21] Moreover, consumer demand for branded footwear and garments is relatively inelastic, meaning that a price increase will not lead to much of a fall in demand. Consumers testify that they would be willing to spend more—$1 to $5 additional for a $20 item— for products manufactured under good working conditions.[22] It is not unreasonable to conclude, therefore, that most, if not all, of the extra expenses associated with better treatment of workers could be absorbed by investors, retailers, and consumers in the developed world without producing a large reduction in employment (or substitution of capital for labor) in developing countries. The international investors and retailers that control the supply chains could reward—or compensate— the low-skill production stage with premium prices and more assured outlets for their products. Simply imposing higher labor costs on competitive suppliers whose profits are much more sensitive to changes in the wage bill, in contrast, is more likely to induce them to take labor-saving actions that minimize the burden, or to move to lower-cost sites.

Chapters 2 and 3 showed employers—both foreign and indigenous— discovering that it was in their own self-interest to raise wages and provide some of the most widely desired benefits (transportation, free meals, training, day care) in order to ensure a reasonably stable and satisfied work force. They appeared to want to avoid some of the costs associated with the "war of attrition"—David Card and Alan Kreuger's term for the high rates of labor turnover that can occur in low-skill operations.[23] As a result, the burden of socially responsible behavior may thus prove to be much lighter than expected, especially if the international garment, footwear, and toy companies—and their retailers—help supplier firms develop worker-friendly human-resource policies instead of simply threatening to terminate their contracts if abuses are uncovered. Thus, encouraging the international community to push international investors and retailers to devote a greater proportion of their oligopoly rents, their branding expenditures, and their advertising budgets to create a supply chain of plants (owned by themselves and others) that can stand the light of public scrutiny may well be a feasible means of improving the treatment of workers in developing countries.

Freedom of Association, Collective Bargaining,
and Union Organizing in EPZs

The brief analysis of the four ILO core labor standards at the beginning of this chapter concluded that even the three most straightforward objectives—preventing discrimination in the workplace, limiting child labor, and eliminating the use of forced labor—raise complex issues that are difficult to interpret, let alone achieve consensus on, across countries. As noted earlier, the most contentious debates surrounding foreign direct investment in low-wage, low-skill jobs in developing countries concern the fourth core labor standard—freedom of association and the right to collective bargaining. Given the legacy of hostility to union organizing in EPZs, the level of controversy is understandable. The discussions of the Philippines, the Dominican Republic, and Costa Rica in the previous chapter identified fundamental issues that are sure to arise in any multilateral effort to enforce global core labor standards; such issues include the appropriate representation of workers, antiunion discrimination, the right to strike, and the threat to close plants that form unions.

REPRESENTATION OF WORKERS AND ANTI-UNION DISCRIMINATION. Looking first at representation of workers and antiunion discrimination, disputes about whether employer-initiated worker-management associations constitute an authentic and acceptable forum in which workers can pursue their interests arose repeatedly in all three of the countries examined in chapter 3. The ILO has singled out the management-sponsored labor-management councils in the Philippines and the solidarity associations in Costa Rica as constituting "blatant forms of interference" with freedom of association that were "linked to acts of discrimination aimed at ending union representation."[24] The Dominican Republic has only recently ceased to be the focus of persistent ILO criticism along the same lines.

The zone employers, in contrast, have taken pride in their employer-initiated worker-management organizations, crediting them with fostering good employee-employer relations and with eliminating the conflict that reigned elsewhere in their absence. And, the EPZs in which multinational employers were most determined to establish worker-management committees that would "obviate" the need for unions—at plants in Baguio City, in the Philippines; in Itabo, in the Dominican Republic; and at plants in the semiconductor, medical products, and data-processing sectors throughout Costa Rica—recorded the highest wage levels and the best treatment of workers of all EPZs (these high standards applied as well to the garment and footwear plants located in the same zones).

The complaints to the ILO that are directed against plants where worker-management councils were established have not focused on outcomes, however. Instead, the complaints have combined abstract arguments about what constitutes authentic representation of the interests of workers with claims that employers use plant facilities and paid work time to mobilize support for the kinds of worker-management associations that they favor, but deny trade-union organizers the use of plant facilities and paid work time. The complaints have also alleged that management made threats against union representatives and dismissed workers who were involved in union organizing.

Such controversies are by no means limited to developing countries. In "observations" accompanying the annual report that the U.S. government submitted to the ILO in 2000, for example, the International Confederation of Free Trade Unions asserted that

in nine out of ten union representation elections employers use mandatory closed-door meetings conducted on their own property during work hours to campaign aggressively against collective bargaining and trade unions. . . . Except in rare circumstances, trade union representatives are denied access to the employer's property to meet employees during non-working time. During organizing campaigns, threats of arrest against union representatives and their expulsion from the employer's property deny workers any reasonable opportunity to consider freely the advantages of union membership.[25]

A multilateral effort to determine whether labor practices in EPZs were in violation of the ILO's core labor standards would have to begin with a common understanding, among developed and developing nations alike, of the obligations imposed on all member states by ratification of ILO conventions 87 and 98 (or by implicit ratification, via membership in the ILO, since many countries—including the United States—have not ratified conventions 87 and 98), with respect to the forms of, and procedures for, worker representation.

RIGHT TO STRIKE. One of the most frequent complaints investigated by the ILO's Committee on Freedom of Association is that workers both within and outside EPZs have been dismissed for participating in strikes.

The history of EPZs in the Philippines and the Dominican Republic is filled with assertions of this kind, and the record in other countries is no different: in 1999 alone, the Committee on Freedom of Association examined the cases of workers from Brazil, Colombia, Mexico, Nicaragua, and other developing countries, who had lost their jobs in the course of strikes. Some developing countries permit replacement workers to be hired when a plant goes on strike: in 2000, the ICFTU submitted a complaint (called an "observation") about this practice in Thailand.[26] In El Salvador in the same year, an employer was accused of wholesale dismissals of workers who had organized a union—locking them out of the plant, withholding their wages, and hiring replacement workers to do their jobs.[27]

To underscore the seriousness of such complaints, the director-general of the ILO argued in the organization's *Global Report* for 2000 that "the right to strike is the logical corollary of the effective realization of the right to collective bargaining. If it does not exist, bargaining risks being inconsequential—a dead letter."[28] Addressing this same issue—recognition of the right to strike—among developed countries, the ICFTU reported to the ILO that in the United States,

> recent surveys of employers with impending negotiations have found that upwards of 80 percent are committed to, or contemplating, replacing workers if they cannot get a deal they like. Under the law, employers can hire replacement workers during an economic strike. Although the dismissal of strikers is banned, the use of permanent replacements is, in practice, virtually indistinguishable from dismissal. More and more employers have deliberately provoked strikes to get rid of trade unions. Unacceptable demands are made of workers ["demanding big cuts in existing wages, working conditions and benefits in contracts established through collective bargaining"] and are often accompanied by arrangements for the recruiting and training of strike-breakers. Permanent replacement workers can vote in a decertification election to eliminate union recognition. Should the company and the union reach an agreement during a strike, striking workers do not automatically return to work. The law only gives strikers the right to return to work as jobs become available.[29]

The ICFTU also asserted that "at least one in ten union supporters campaigning to form a union is illegally fired."[30]

As was the case with representation of workers, the right to strike gives rise to fundamental debates about what constitutes acceptable conduct within the context of ILO core labor standards, and such debates run in parallel in developed and developing countries.

THREATS TO CLOSE UNIONIZED PLANTS. In both the Philippines and the Dominican Republic the history of EPZs shows repeated complaints of threats to close down plants that accept union representation. A conflict that has gained more recent worldwide prominence, however, occurred between Phillips–Van Heusen and workers who voted to form a union at a plant in Guatemala.[31] In 1997, in the face of internationally orchestrated pressure, Phillips–Van Heusen finally acknowledged the results of a successful union-organizing campaign, entered into collective bargaining, and signed a contract with the workers. One year later, however, citing excess capacity and the need for more flexibility, the company cut back on its purchases from the unionized plant, leading it to close.

With respect to this category of complaints to the ILO, the ICFTU has observed that in the United States,

> although it is illegal for employers to threaten to close or move their operations in response to union organizing activity, a study released in 1996 found that employers threaten to close their plants in over half of all organizing campaigns, and in industries such as manufacturing where this threat is most credible, this violation occurs in over 60 percent of all campaigns. Where collective agreements are negotiated for the first time 18 percent of employers threaten to close their facilities and 12 percent of the employers actually follow through with their threats.[32]

To address complaints about freedom of association and collective bargaining, workers in the United States have recourse to the National Labor Relations Board (NLRB)—but whether NLRB interpretations of U.S. law are consistent with the core ILO conventions, and whether NLRB enforcement procedures adequately protect freedom of association and collective bargaining—are both subject to controversy. In 2000 the ICFTU submission to the ILO about labor practices in the United States asserted that

> the procedures of the National Labor Relations Board (NLRB), the body which governs industrial relations in most of the private

sector, do not provide workers with effective redress in the face of abuses by employers. Many workers, including those fired illegally, do not use available legal procedures because they take too long and fail to provide adequate compensation or redress the wrong done to them. It takes an average of 555 days for the NLRB to resolve a case. In 1998, 62 workers illegally fired during a union organizing campaign that took place 19 years earlier finally received a financial settlement arising from the illegal activity of their former employer. One study found that, where employees are ordered reinstated, only 40 percent actually return to work and only 20 percent remain employed for more than two years. The workers that do quit give unfair treatment as their main reason for leaving.[33]

Employers' associations from the United States did not submit their own observations or rebuttals to the ICFTU charges to the ILO.

These areas of conflict—representation of workers and antiunion discrimination, right to strike, and threats to close plants—by no means exhaust the controversies about what the ILO core standards require of member states, or what constitutes adequate enforcement on the part of member states.[34] Whatever the merits of these or other particular complaints, interpretations of what is and is not permissible under the ILO conventions vary widely, and achieving agreement on what constitutes actionable violations would require painstaking negotiations across developed and developing countries.[35]

An optimistic view would hold that such an exercise could bring labor practices in all nations—including the United States—up to a higher level. To accomplish this goal, however, would require exposing U.S. labor practices to much more thorough scrutiny than American authorities have so far been willing to permit. The side-agreement on labor included as part of the North American Free Trade Agreement (NAFTA), for example, does not require the national labor laws of the participants to meet any agreed-upon minimum or to be consistent with ILO core labor standards.[36] Further, the side-agreement excludes certain complaints—regarding freedom of association, the right to collective bargaining, the right to organize, and the right to strike—from being submitted to any outside review by experts or arbitrators. A less optimistic view would be that such an exercise—as a prerequisite to creating an international system to identify and enforce violations of core labor standards—would be lengthy, contentious, and extremely difficult to complete. Progress would be slow, not least because the participants would have to determine how to harmonize labor regulations and enforcement procedures among subnational entities, including states and municipalities, that have jurisdiction over such matters in many constitutional systems. For example, in explaining why the United States has ratified only two of the seven major conventions of the Declaration of Fundamental Principles and Rights at Work, William Daley, then secretary of commerce, pointed to the fact that "much of our labor law is state law."[37] In 2000 the President's Committee on the ILO had a standing rule that "no ILO convention will be ratified unless U.S. law at both the federal and state level is already in full conformity." It would be surprising indeed to discover that the international community could create a framework to address the labor disputes that arise in EPZs in developing countries without at the same time requiring extensive revision of U.S. labor codes and standards.

A Possible Shortcut?

Might the U.S.-Jordan Free Trade Agreement—the first U.S. trade agreement to include labor standards within the text of the agreement—offer a way around the difficulty of requiring that the parties first agree on their national obligations under the ILO core labor standards?

According to the U.S. Trade Representative, the U.S.-Jordan Free Trade Agreement "will not require either country to adopt new laws, but rather requires each to enforce the laws it currently has."[38] According to the language of the agreement, however, the determination of the content of national statutes, and of the adequacy of local enforcement procedures, takes place within the context of ILO "obligations." In the section on labor (article 6.1), "the Parties reaffirm their obligations as members of the International Labor Organization ('ILO') and their commitments under the ILO Declaration on Fundamental Principles and Rights at Work and its Follow-up. The Parties shall strive to ensure that such labor principles and the internationally recognized labor rights set forth in paragraph 6 are recognized and protected by domestic law." Under article 6.4a, each party then promises that it "shall not fail to effectively enforce its labor laws, through a sustained or recurring course of action or inaction, in a manner affecting trade between the Parties."

Should a dispute about the enforcement of labor standards arise, the complaining party may request consultations. If consultations fail to resolve the matter, either party can refer the matter to a joint committee. If the dispute is not resolved there, either party can refer the matter to a three-person dispute-settlement panel consisting of one member appointed by each of the parties individually, and a third member, who serves as chairman, appointed jointly by the two other appointees. The dispute-settlement panel prepares a report containing findings of fact and "its determination as to whether either Party has failed to carry out its obligations under the Agreement." The report is nonbinding. The joint committee then makes a second attempt to resolve the dispute, "taking the report into account, as appropriate." If this measure fails, "the affected Party shall be entitled to take any appropriate and commensurate measure." The U.S.-Jordan Free Trade Agreement does not provide guidance, however, about how the joint committee or the dispute-settlement panel might determine whether a party is enforcing its own laws adequately in light of the obligation "to recognize and protect" the ILO core standards.

In the context of an intimate bilateral relationship, such as the one between the United States and Jordan, in which potential disputes over trade or labor practices would be well buffered by deep security links between the two parties, and penalties would be limited to the extra benefits provided under the free trade agreement and would not affect trade privileges more generally, certain issues—such as differences in how the two countries might interpret ILO core labor standards, or the lack of specific guidance for dispute-settlement panels attempting to identify violations—might never rise to prominence. But the same could not be said of an international system to identify and punish violations of labor standards among more than 140 nations, especially if the punishment allowed the entire world trading community to impose trade sanctions or fines, as in the hypothetical WTO-based system considered in the next chapter.

Given the previous discussion of complaints regarding the representation of workers and antiunion discrimination, the right to strike, and threats to close plants, it is difficult to understand how dispute-settlement panels could evaluate complaints and identify actionable violations, or how appellate boards could settle appeals, without being instructed in the relationship between the enforcement of national laws and the obligation "to recognize and protect" ILO core labor standards. Dispute-settlement panels and appellate boards could hardly determine whether enforcement is adequate without knowing what is to be enforced.[39]

The issue of enforcement, moreover, raises a new set of problems. How might dispute-settlement panels and appellate bodies distinguish between intent and ability to comply? Should the standards for enforcement differ across nations or across regions within a single country? Should poorer nations or poorer regions be held to a lower standard than richer nations or regions, or to the same standard? However these questions are answered, the issue of enforcement is likely to magnify developing countries' sense of vulnerability. Even among those with the most worker-friendly intentions, preventing discrepancies in the treatment of workers in individual plants at the provincial and municipal levels is one of the most daunting tasks imaginable. And the thought of facing penalties for violations at these levels—over which developing countries have the least confidence of being able to exercise control—is sure to constitute, for many developing countries, their worst nightmare. Moreover, if a guilty verdict depends on the outcome of a duel between well-equipped legal outsiders documenting shortcomings in a developing country's national and subnational court systems, regulatory agencies, and local inspectors—even repeated and persistent shortcomings—and beleaguered host authorities attempting to reconcile actual enforcement with the (often quite lofty) demands of domestic labor statutes, few developing countries will be persuaded that they can consistently be on the winning side.

In sum, the more closely one examines the prospects for reaching agreement on what constitutes actionable violations of core labor standards—or for creating an international system to monitor and punish poor treatment of workers without such agreement—the more arduous the task appears. The inherent difficulties of such an effort may cloud the prospects for the authoritative WTO-based system, backed by trade sanctions or by fines, considered in chapter 5. But, curiously, the same difficulties may brighten the appeal of so-called voluntary mechanisms for the enforcement of labor standards, considered in chapter 6.

5   WTO-Based Enforcement of Core Labor Standards

The World Trade Organization is the repository of obligations on trade issues accumulated by member states since 1948, in the course of eight rounds of multilateral trade negotiations conducted under the General Agreement on Tariffs and Trade (GATT). Through a process of trial and error, and often at a pace considered too slow by some of its members, first the GATT and then its successor, the WTO, has increasingly circumscribed the ability of individual states, especially large states, to take arbitrary and unilateral actions that conflict with the multilateral GATT/WTO agreements.

Although the internal operating procedures of the WTO have been the subject of criticism (especially with regard to transparency, accountability, and access), both rich and poor countries have a great interest in protecting and sustaining widespread acceptance for the institution's work. Debates about whether the WTO should take on specific new responsibilities regarding labor and environmental issues, for example, cannot occur in isolation from this larger context.

The analytic appeal of choosing the WTO to enforce core labor standards around the world, rather than relying on the voluntary mechanisms considered in the next chapter, derives from the fact that the WTO occupies a powerful and authoritative position in adjudicating disputes and imposing penalties on its members. Thus, in the area of labor standards, it could play the role of a benevolent dictator, acting on behalf of the common good and overcoming the collective-action problems—cheating and free riding—that plague voluntary mechanisms.

But the power and authority of the World Trade Organization derive from, and rely upon, the consent of WTO members from both the developed and developing worlds. To gain the support needed to enforce labor standards, any new WTO-based system would have to demonstrate its effectiveness as a mechanism for improving the treatment of workers—and further demonstrate that it posed no significant threat to the self-interest of members.

The first portion of this chapter focuses on how the insertion of core labor standards into the WTO, backed by potential trade sanctions, might function. The two principal means of enforcing core labor standards within the context of a WTO-based system are trade sanctions and fines. In the case of trade sanctions, the primary concern is how broadly, or narrowly, the enforcement mechanism is allowed to operate—that is, on a plant-by-plant basis, against an entire EPZ, against all EPZs within a given country, or against exports from throughout the economy of the given country. The breadth of enforcement is important because it can largely determine the extent of potential damage to developing countries: the broader the enforcement mechanism, the more likely it is to undermine the transition from lowest-skill to higher-skill operations—and to offer protectionist interests in the developed world an opportunity to turn dispute-settlement procedures to their own ends.

The chapter then considers the alternative of using fines—specifically, whether the North American Free Trade Agreement or the Canada-Chile Free Trade Agreement might offer a useful model for "monetary assessments" under a WTO-based system.

The chapter next turns to a related but analytically distinct proposal: that the WTO mandate should be expanded not just to enforce core labor standards but to prevent countries from using substandard treatment of workers to gain "unfair advantage" for their exporters that might "injure" firms and workers elsewhere. At issue here is whether low labor standards appear to act as a kind of subsidy for attracting investors or supporting exports.

The concluding section of the chapter explores how the goal of preventing race-to-the-bottom competition among alternative production sites fits into the larger challenge of creating a level playing field for trade and investment around the world.

The assessment, in this chapter, of a potential WTO-based authoritative system provides a contrast to the alternative of voluntary measures—including corporate codes of conduct, certification mechanisms, and compliance labeling—considered in the next.

Designing a Hypothetical WTO-Based System

Proposals to enlarge the WTO's work to include the enforcement of core labor standards have not yet come with detailed architectural plans. How a hypothetical WTO-based system, backed by trade sanctions, might work is thus a matter of considerable conjecture.

In its basic form, however, a new WTO-based system might permit a member state to file a complaint against another state for failure to observe one or more of the core labor standards (or, most likely, for a "persistent pattern of failure to observe or enforce" one or more of the core labor standards); this would lead to an investigation and dispute-settlement procedure similar to that used in other WTO trade actions. Since the WTO has no particular competence in investigating or adjudicating workplace disputes, the new system might rely on the ILO for assistance with investigation and conciliation.

If the investigation confirmed the validity of the complaint and the dispute-settlement process failed to rectify the situation, the country bringing the complaint—or all WTO members, if the action were taken on a multilateral basis—would be allowed to suspend trade obligations incurred under WTO agreements toward the country in violation, and to impose quantitative restrictions or higher tariffs on that country's exports.[1] Before the penalty came into effect, the country against which the complaint had been brought would have an opportunity to appeal the finding.

TARGETING TRADE SANCTIONS. The details of how this hypothetical WTO-based system might work would be quite complex. The scope of the enforcement actions and the nature of the target, however, would be central to the blueprint for the new system. Would the enforcement action be directed at the offending plant? At the EPZ in which the plant was located? At all EPZs in that country? At a retaliation list derived from the entire array of host-country exports?

If the model used in a WTO-based system were derived from the practice that the United States follows with respect to countries receiving GSP treatment (the Generalized System of Preferences offers more favorable market access than that agreed to under the WTO), a guilty verdict would allow the country lodging the complaint to select products for retaliation that are drawn from a list of all host-country exports. If the U.S.-Jordan Free Trade Agreement were used as the precedent, the affected party would be "entitled to take any appropriate and commensurate measure" in response to unresolved complaints of labor abuses.

Of course, the larger the scope of the sanctions, the greater the pain inflicted on the country. But how the sanctions are levied makes a much larger difference than this. There is a well-recognized irony associated with even the most narrowly focused enforcement system—one that limits trade sanctions to exports from the plant where the labor abuses are found. When the exports from the offending plant are blocked, the ill-treated workers at the plant are likely to find themselves laid off or fired: the penalty imposed on the offender thus punishes the victims. But this outcome is not nearly as damaging as the impact of a more expansive enforcement mechanism. If the WTO enforcement system allowed sanctions to be levied against an entire EPZ, plants operating with higher labor standards would be among those whose exports would be blocked. Attempting to force plants with substandard labor practices to improve their behavior by blocking exports from an entire EPZ not only multiplies the number of labor victims but undermines the strongest mechanism that exists for improving the treatment of workers within and across EPZs.

In the Philippines, an EPZ-wide action on the part of the WTO against a firm with low labor standards in the Bataan EPZ, for example, would cut off exports from the Reebok and Mitsumi plants in the same zone, which have won national awards for labor-management relations. Similarly, an EPZ-wide action against a garment subcontractor in the La Romana zone of the Dominican Republic would cut off exports from foreign-owned electronics plants in the same zone, which pay higher-than-average wages and provide superior working conditions.

Worse still, if the WTO enforcement system allowed sanctions to be levied against all EPZs, or against a retaliation list of exports selected from across an entire host economy, such an action would threaten to block the transition from lowest-skill to higher-skill occupations—a transition that has driven improvement in the treatment of workers in each of the countries examined.

To expand on the examples drawn from chapter 3, a WTO case against the Philippines aimed at rectifying the treatment of footwear workers at an older plant in an older EPZ could be used to block exports of electronics, medical equipment, automotive parts, and data-processing services from the more modern and better-administered EPZs at Baguio City, Cavite, and Mactan. A WTO case targeted at the behavior of a developing-country investor in a lowest-wage EPZ of the Dominican Republic would almost certainly hit the exports of European, Japanese, and U.S. Fortune 500 investors that Dominican authorities have managed, in recent years, to attract to the model Itabo and San Isidro zones. Such examples support the observation made by critics of a WTO-based trade-sanction system—that the big stick of the WTO is a blunt instrument.

But however the enforcement efforts are targeted, the principal problem with a WTO-based approach is not simply that the WTO is a blunt instrument, but that the effort to punish violations by the worst offenders could have such a vastly destructive impact on the cause of improving the treatment of workers more generally. Investor operations in, for example, industrial equipment, electrical equipment, semiconductors, chemicals, pharmaceuticals, and data-processing services would be put at risk to punish violations at plants producing garments, footwear, toys, or other similar products. OECD investor operations would be put at risk to punish violations at plants owned by non-OECD investors. High-profile, branded investor operations would be put at risk to punish violations at low-profile, unbranded investor operations. Multinational investor-owned operations would be put at risk to punish violations at the plants of subcontractors. International firms throughout the developing world—who might otherwise play the role of the companies that pioneered worker-management councils in the Philippines, or persuaded their colleagues to accept the Agreement for Social Peace and Productivity in the Dominican Republic, or instituted the solidarity associations in Costa Rica—would be caught up in the drive to weed out individual violators lingering in the host economy.

The desire for perfection would become the enemy of progress toward the good.

CONFRONTING THE RISK OF CAPTURE BY PROTECTIONIST INTERESTS. An enforcement mechanism that extended trade sanctions beyond single plants might intensify the danger, moreover, that WTO dispute-settlement procedures would be captured by protectionist forces in developed countries. Some critics of working conditions in developing countries are quite forthright about their desire to protect jobs in developed countries (Sir James Goldsmith, Ross Perot); there are, however, proponents of a WTO-based system who endorse free trade, but who downplay the extent to which developed countries could use a WTO-based system to protect jobs at home.[2] They argue that because many low-wage, low-skill, labor-intensive products—such as toys, tools, and garden implements—are no longer widely produced in developed countries, a WTO-based effort to improve working conditions would simply shift the production of such goods among sites in the developing world instead of being used to protect jobs in the importing countries.

But careful consideration of an enforcement mechanism that permitted exports to be blocked—from entire EPZs, from all EPZs, or from the entire host economy—reveals a much more tempting object for capture by protectionist interests in the developed world. Labor organizations representing groups such as auto workers, chemical workers, electronics workers, machine-tool workers, and industrial-equipment workers—along with the firms that employ workers in these sectors—could use WTO actions against abuses in garment, footwear, and toy plants, for example, to defend themselves against competition from an ascending scale of more sophisticated, higher-skill, labor-intensive products from developing countries. This possibility increases the risk that developing countries could face from a WTO-based system, and magnifies the cost to their development prospects should the risk be realized. Even the most worker-friendly developing countries would consider it folly to cooperate in the creation of a multilateral system that had so much potential to block their ability to move their economies up the ladder from lowest-skill to higher-skill activities.

IMPLICATIONS FOR INTERNATIONAL INVESTORS AND RETAILERS. The considerations offered in the two previous sections would necessarily affect the international business community's appraisal of any WTO-based system that allowed sanctions to be applied beyond the level of individual plants. As noted earlier, by far the largest amounts of foreign direct investment in the developing world, outside of natural resources and infrastructure, are destined for plants that employ relatively highly skilled workers whose wages and benefits are substantially above the minimum within their countries. The multinational corporate community that includes automotive, electronics, semiconductor, computer, industrial equipment, chemical, and petrochemical producers has viewed the debate about WTO-enforced labor standards with some skepticism, but without much concern that its interests would be affected—since the firms that make up this community are confident that their labor practices are solidly above the norm. But careful consideration of the implications of a broad—rather than narrow—WTO-based enforcement mechanism would have to alter the calculations of firms that are engaged in higher-skill operations. Enforcement mechanisms that extended to entire EPZs, across EPZs, or throughout the entire economies of developing countries would put investors in higher-skill operations at risk. The multinational investment community is not likely to relish finding its higher-wage, higher-value-added firms included on retaliation lists alongside garment, footwear, and toy producers. To draw on some examples from the countries investigated in chapter 3, the parent companies of Abbot Laboratories, Allied Signal, Intel, Motorola, Philips, Procter & Gamble, Toyota, Volkswagen, and Western Union will certainly not want to have their supply chains interrupted in order to improve the treatment of workers at footwear, garment, and toy plants, let alone at the plants of non-OECD suppliers and subcontractors.

Nor will the "collective guilt" aspect of the hypothetical new WTO-based system appeal to high-profile companies in the garment, footwear, and toy industries that are trying to reinforce their brand image by engaging in socially responsible labor practices. From their vantage point, a sanctions system that punishes exemplary firms along with miscreants is undesirable because it does nothing to publicize the compliance records of the branded firms, no matter how arduous their efforts, or to help them differentiate themselves (and their products) from less committed rivals. On the contrary, under a broadly focused enforcement regime, branded firms may find their above-standard plants, with their above-standard working conditions, shut down in order to force the plants of their less assiduous competitors into compliance.

A yet more perverse impact may extend to retailers as well. Companies like J. C. Penney, Nordstrom, and Wal-Mart, as well as Nike, Reebok, and Mattel, already have difficulty ensuring the good treatment of workers at the hands of suppliers whose plants number in the thousands and sometimes tens of thousands. A major source of leverage over these suppliers is the promise that adherence to fair labor standards will ensure the continuity of the buyer-supplier relationship. If that incentive should disappear—that is, if the buyer-supplier relationship could be disrupted to punish poor behavior at other plants in the same EPZ or in neighboring EPZs—the parent retailers' ability to exercise control over their own subcontractors would diminish correspondingly.

Because it would pose such fundamental threats to the interests of both developing countries and the international business community, any proposal for a WTO-based system that permitted enforcement mechanisms to extend beyond the level of the individual plant or company could expect hardy—and well-justified—opposition. A proposal that limited WTO-backed enforcement to exclusion orders against the goods produced in a specific plant or company, however, might garner more widespread support.

The dangers associated with using trade sanctions to enforce core labor standards have led to increasing interest in the idea of using fines (monetary assessments) to accomplish the same objective.[3] The examination of the NAFTA and the Canada-Chile Free Trade Agreement as potential models for a WTO-based system, which follows, suggests that this approach would avoid some of the larger collateral damage associated with the use of trade sanctions. But it also underscores the fact that fundamental difficulties—defining obligations under the core labor standards, determining when violations have occurred, and developing an effective and broadly accepted system for punishing those violations—would nonetheless remain.

USING FINES TO ENFORCE LABOR STANDARDS: POTENTIAL MODELS. Both the NAFTA and the Canada-Chile Free Trade Agreement provide for fines to be levied when one of the parties shows a "persistent pattern of failure" in enforcing its own labor laws. The WTO system could be designed, similarly, to use fines, or the threat of fines, to punish labor violations at individual plants or companies.

In the labor side-agreement to the NAFTA, and in the Canada-Chile Free Trade Agreement, private individuals or NGOs in a given country can report to the national administrative office (NAO) of their own country about alleged trade-related enforcement problems in eleven areas: freedom of association and right to organize, right to bargain collectively, right to strike, prohibition of forced labor, protection of children, minimum employment standards (including wages and overtime), nondiscrimination, equal pay for men and women, prevention of occupational injuries and illnesses, compensation for occupational injuries, and protection of migrant workers. Complaints can be lodged only with regard to practices covered by "mutually recognized labor laws." Out of respect for national sovereignty, the agreements do not require performance in any of these categories to be consistent with ILO conventions or to meet any agreed-upon minimum standards.[4]

If the NAO agrees that there may be a problem, it initiates consultations with its counterpart NAO in the trade partner (called the national secretariat in the Canada-Chile Free Trade Agreement). If those consultations do not prove satisfactory, the NAO bringing the complaint can request consultations between ministerial-level officials. These consultations can lead to the formation of an experts' committee, which would make an evaluation and offer "practical recommendations" for consideration by the parties' joint commission for labor cooperation (CLC). If the dispute persists, an arbitral panel may be appointed to review the remedial efforts, determine whether a persistent failure exists, and, if necessary, impose a "monetary enforcement assessment."

In both the NAFTA and the Canada-Chile Free Trade Agreement, disputes concerning freedom of association and the rights to organize, to bargain collectively, and to strike are precluded from going beyond ministerial consultations.[5] Thus, allegations of violations in these areas cannot be reviewed by any dispute-settlement structure external to or independent of the individual governments, cannot be submitted to a committee of experts chosen by the parties, cannot be submitted to arbitral panels, and cannot be subject to punishment by fines or by any other measure.

The fines collected for labor violations in other areas are deposited in a fund established by the parties' CLC, and expended at its direction to improve the enforcement of labor law in the country where the violation occurred. The NAFTA caps fines at 0.007 percent of the total trade in goods between the disputants (in 2000, approximately $17 million for the United States and Mexico, and $29 million for the United States and Canada).[6] In the Canada-Chile Free Trade Agreement, fines cannot exceed $10 million. Although few fines have actually been imposed, the Mexican government did levy a $9,000 fine against the Han Young plant for health and safety violations, indicating that enforcement actions are likely to be carefully targeted. (The case was brought by the U.S. NAO in response to a complaint by the Support Committee for Maquiladora Workers, et al.)[7] In the event of failure to pay a duly authorized fine, the United States or Mexico can suspend obligations under the NAFTA to the extent needed to collect the value of the monetary assessment (by raising tariff rates, for example). The U.S.-Mexico part of the NAFTA thus authorizes trade sanctions as the ultimate method of enforcing the side-agreement on labor. Canada, however, refused to permit the use of trade sanctions on labor (or environmental) issues under any circumstances, and insisted that external complaints be enforced via submission to federal or provincial courts, depending upon where jurisdiction for the particular segment of labor law resided.[8] The same formula—recourse to host-country courts to enforce fines arising out of labor disputes, with no possibility of trade sanctions at all—became embedded in the Canada-Chile Free Trade Agreement.

USING FINES TO ENFORCE LABOR STANDARDS UNDER A WTO-BASED SYSTEM. The designs of the NAFTA and the Canada-Chile Free Trade Agreement serve to circumscribe the harm that the enforcement mechanisms could otherwise inflict on the victims of labor abuses, on workers in plants where labor standards are exemplary, and on the virtuous cycle in which foreign investment in higher-skill operations improves the treatment of workers in lower-skill operations. A hypothetical WTO-based system, backed by fines, that was comparably careful might enjoy greater appeal among developing countries, and among investors and retail purchasers, than a less narrowly targeted, sanctions-based system. But the consideration of the NAFTA and the Canada-Chile agreement shows that a central challenge remains: the use of fines rather than trade sanctions does not alleviate the need to establish precise standards and procedures for bringing cases, determining when violations have occurred, and punishing violators. Any system agreed to by the 142 members of the WTO could hardly finesse the issue of what constitutes a violation or appropriate enforcement; nor could such a system remove freedom of association and the right to collective bargaining from multilateral scrutiny altogether, as the NAFTA and the Canada-Chile Free Trade Agreement have.

Moreover, the WTO system would have to address how fines would be set and whether they should be capped. The system would then have to determine who would pay the assessment: the national government, the enforcement agency, or the offending firm. Imposing the fine on an agency with a record of lax supervision may simply exacerbate the problem of poor enforcement. A better option might be to require the national government to pay the fine, with the stipulation that the host country would then pass on the fine to the offending company (if the company is still solvent).

What would the WTO system do with the fine? One option would be to turn the funds over to the ILO, which would use them to provide training and assistance to the underperforming enforcement agency in the country where the fine was collected. However, since a record of poor enforcement may bring reward, whereas a record of good enforcement would eliminate an agency from consideration for ILO support, this approach raises the possibility of creating perverse incentives for hard-pressed regulatory agencies that need larger budgets to do their jobs.

Finally, how would the WTO enforce the payment of fines? One approach, modeled on the segment of the NAFTA that governs labor violations in Mexico, would permit members to suspend their trade obligations toward the offending country—effectively shifting the fines-based system back to the use of trade sanctions to enforce compliance with core labor standards. An alternative approach, modeled on the U.S.-Canada segment of the NAFTA and the Canada-Chile Free Trade Agreement, would be to secure payment through the national courts in the country where the violation occurred.

Overall, therefore, the use of fines in a hypothetical WTO-based system might avoid some of the more severe dangers of relying on trade sanctions, but many of the fundamental difficulties associated with using the WTO to enforce labor standards would remain.

Labor Standards and "Unfair Advantages" for Exporters: Creating a Level Playing Field for International Investment and Trade

A humanitarian desire to place a floor under the treatment of workers around the world is the principal stated objective of those who urge that labor standards be added to the responsibilities of the WTO, adjudicated via WTO dispute-settlement procedures, and ultimately enforced through the use of trade sanctions or fines. There is a related, but analytically separate, justification for including labor issues within the mandate of the WTO: namely, that the special treatment of firms (usually, but not exclusively, in export processing zones)—including interference with union organizing or other violations of workers' rights—constitutes an unfair advantage that injures the interests of other firms, other workers, and other countries. According to this argument, those firms, workers, or countries that are harmed by the particular treatment of exporters in EPZs or elsewhere should be permitted to deploy trade sanctions, or to impose countervailing duties, to offset what might be considered a subsidy to exporters in developing countries.

To evaluate the merits of this rationale for bringing labor standards into the work of the WTO, one must first ask whether poor treatment of workers and weak enforcement of core labor standards provide an unfair advantage to firms in export processing zones or other industrial parks that offer preferential treatment to exporters. The theory and evidence introduced in chapter 3 suggest that the answer is at odds with what is commonly supposed.

Looking first at theory, it was observed in chapter 3 that a monopolistic employer or a collusive set of employers might well be able to gain extra profits by holding wages artificially low (below the value of what the workers produce), and by using a portion of these extra profits to lower the price of exports. Evidence from the early experience of the Bataan EPZ, in the Philippines, and the La Romana EPZ, in the Dominican Republic, did show incidents of labor suppression, as do contemporary instances in which the owners of lowest-skill operations take advantage of tentative and inexperienced entrants to the formal sector by paying the lowest possible wages, firing and rehiring workers in order to deny them benefits, and compelling workers to operate under uncomfortable and sometimes dangerous conditions.

But theory also predicts, and the case examples confirmed, that as these conditions disappear—as workers acquire more skills and more alternative sources of employment, as labor markets become more national, and as employers face the necessity of meeting international standards of quality and reliability—the strategy of suppressing wages and skimping on workers' comforts becomes less and less viable. By limiting a firm's ability to attract and retain good workers, poor labor practices ultimately reduce both productivity and profits, and erode rather than strengthen its competitive position in the marketplace. In all three countries considered in chapter 3—the Philippines, the Dominican Republic, and Costa Rica—the self-interest of many employers eventually led them to take pains to avoid seeing the more valuable workers leave.

More generally, as noted in chapter 3, periodic surveys undertaken by the ILO confirm that wages, benefits, and working conditions within EPZs compare favorably with those outside the zones. Among EPZ investors, firms with more capital-intensive operations, requiring more highly skilled workers, and producing more sophisticated products—in electronics, automotive parts, industrial equipment, and chemicals, for example—tend to have better records in employee relations than companies with more labor-intensive operations. But even among the latter, however, a growing number of firms have concluded that progressive rather than oppressive labor practices (that is, "work smarter" strategies, which involve training in multiple skills, teamwork, and on-the-job training, rather than "work harder" strategies, which involve regimentation and discipline) better serve their purposes.[9]

Thus, evidence is consistent with theory: only within very narrow margins can export companies employ labor suppression to obtain extra profits, lower their export prices, and expand their market share abroad. As EPZs move into more sophisticated, higher-skill activities, the dynamics of the employers' own self-interest push them away from the strategy of labor suppression, and in the direction of strategies that improve both morale and productivity.

But what about labor-intensive operations at the very bottom: how large a competitive advantage might be gained through labor suppression in the lowest-skill operations, where the potential for abuse is greatest and the number of complaints largest? Even here, the evidence suggests that the "subsidy" that might be derived from "squeezing" the wages of low-skilled export workers is rather tiny. In one of the earliest contemporary studies of unit labor costs among suppliers to foreign retailers, the Asian Productivity Organization found that in the mid-1980s, fourteen person-minutes were needed to make one men's shirt in the United States, whereas twenty-five person-minutes were required to make a comparable shirt in Bangladesh.[10] At the time of the study, the average wage for a garment worker was $0.25 an hour in Bangladesh, and $7.53 an hour in the United States.[11] Thus, the unit labor cost of a shirt made in the United States was $1.76, and the unit labor cost of a shirt made in Bangladesh was only $0.10. A hypothetical squeezing of the Bangladeshi worker's wages by one-third would therefore lower production costs by no more than three to four cents per shirt.

More recently, in 2000, the National Labor Committee provided detailed information on the unit labor costs of unbranded jeans at the Taiwanese-owned Chentex factory, in Nicaragua, which are sold at Kohl's and other U.S. retail chains.[12] In this breakdown, the piecework rate used to pay sewers amounted to $0.36 for each pair of jeans; benefits—social security, contribution to the National Technical Institute, holidays, vacation time, and the traditional Christmas "thirteenth month" bonus—added $0.30, for a total of $0.66 per pair of jeans. The retail price for the jeans was $21.99, so the unit labor cost equaled approximately 3 percent of the final sales price. In this case, a hypothetical one-third reduction in wages and benefits would lower production costs by $0.22 per pair of jeans.

Comparable calculations for brand-name products show that the percentage of the final retail price represented by the unit labor cost at the production stage is even lower. In China, in 2000, the National Labor Committee interviewed a subcontractor to the Hong Kong firm that supplied two-piece skirt-and-blazer outfits to Spiegel.[13] The unit labor cost for the jacket, including social security benefits, amounted to $0.84. Since the blazer retailed for $99 in the Spiegel catalogue, the unit labor cost amounted to 0.8 percent of the final sales price. A hypothetical one-third compression of the Chinese worker's wages and benefits would thus reduce production costs for the blazer by $0.28.

In the case of footwear, the Clean Clothes Campaign reported a breakdown of the price components for a $100 pair of sports shoes made in Indonesia.[14] Local production costs were 2 percent of the final retail price, with the unit wage component equal to 0.4 percent of the final retail price, or $0.40. A hypothetical squeezing of the wages of the Indonesian worker by one-third would reduce production costs by $0.13. Nike's Web site provides a cost breakdown for a pair of shoes that retails for $65. Without indicating where the factory might be located, the company lists the labor cost per pair at $2.43, or 4 percent of the final sales price.[15]

The same set of studies show, however, that strong competitive pressures—especially on independent subcontractors—can still push firms to shift production among alternative production sites in developing countries. In the case of the subcontractor producing footwear in Indonesia, for example, the local wage bill constituted 20 percent of the firm's pretax profit. For the Chentex supplier in Nicaragua, the unit labor cost for a pair of jeans was 46 percent of the firm's pretax profit on each pair. In the Nike analysis, the unit labor cost for a pair of shoes was 150 percent of the factory profit for each pair of shoes. Thus, even though shaving the wage rate has only a minuscule effect on a plant's competitive position in international markets, decisions on where to locate individual plants can be quite sensitive to a combination of wage levels, productivity levels, and quality.

This paradox was highlighted in the previous chapter, in the context of including a living wage among core labor standards: managers of production-stage plants are under strong pressures to keep labor costs low, whereas the executives at the headquarters of international producers and retailers are much less so. From the perspective of these executives, the margin for gaining competitive advantage through labor suppression is extremely small; hence, the likelihood that firms and workers in developed countries could show that they were being "injured" by labor suppression in the developing world is faint.

This conclusion is supported by statistical investigations that have generally failed to show any significant positive relationship between low labor standards and the competitiveness of exports, whether shipped by foreign-owned, foreign-controlled, or autonomous firms. A study conducted under the auspices of the OECD, for example, grouped countries according to their degree of observance of freedom of association and the right to collective bargaining, and tracked changes in the countries' share of exports (both in the aggregate and for manufactured goods) in world markets over the period 1980–90. The investigators could find no relationship between trade performance and adherence to these core labor standards.[16] In a separate test, the OECD study examined the prices of textile products imported from developing countries categorized as having either high or low labor standards, to see whether the suppression of freedom of association gave exporters an advantage. Despite substantial variation in the degree of enforcement of freedom of association, the investigators found that the prices of textile imports from developing countries were "rather uniform," and concluded that enforcement or suppression of freedom of association played little role in the determination of export prices.[17]

Along the same lines, in 1994, Mita Aggarwal, of the U.S. International Trade Commission, examined the relationship between labor standards and U.S. imports from ten major developing countries (China, Hong Kong, India, Indonesia, Malaysia, Mexico, the Philippines, Singapore, South Korea, and Thailand).[18] Aggarwal found that those countries with lower labor standards did not exhibit higher rates of import penetration than countries with relatively higher labor standards. Moreover, those countries with strong export performance could not trace their success to cost advantages derived from suppressing wages; the data showed that in the countries with strong export performance, the rate of increase in average real wages was comparable to, or faster than, the average rate at which real value was added. Thus, the evidence indicated that export success and higher labor standards went hand in hand.

In a study of thirty-six developed and developing countries, Dani Rodrik found that after controlling for productivity differences, various measures of civil rights, political rights, democratic institutions, unionization, and the enforcement of labor rights were correlated with higher labor costs.[19] As for whether low labor standards might create a comparative advantage beyond what one would expect from natural endowments, however, the sole statistically significant relationship in Rodrik's data was an association between longer statutory hours and greater comparative advantage in textiles and clothing. When Rodrik omitted high-income countries from the analysis, longer statutory hours remained statistically significant and the indicator for poor enforcement of child labor statutes also became significant; however, the indicators showing weak support for civil liberties, political rights, democratic institutions, ILO conventions, and unionization did not.[20]

Using largely the same data as Rodrik, but different estimation techniques, Peter Morici and Evan Schulz calculated that a one-step decrease in the enforcement of either freedom of association or limits on child labor reduced the average annual wage bill by more than $3,000, and that a one-step decrease in the enforcement of both reduced the average annual wage bill by more than $6,000.[21] However, the meaning of these "very large numbers" for countries such as Indonesia and India, where the average annual manufacturing labor cost at the time equaled only $1,000 (Indonesia) or $1,200 (India) is not clear.[22] The Morici and Schulz analysis also found that when lower labor costs were combined with poor enforcement in the areas of child labor and freedom of association, a country's dependence on textile and apparel exports as a share of manufacturing exports increased significantly. They interpreted this finding to mean that lax labor standards provide developing countries with a competitive advantage in lower-skill, labor-intensive products. But an equally plausible interpretation is that low wages and poor treatment of workers simply make it difficult for a country to create a successful export sector for manufactured products that are more sophisticated than textiles and apparel.

In sum, low labor standards do not appear to significantly enhance the competitiveness of exports; but do they offer an unfair advantage in attracting foreign investors? Aggarwal's study found no association between indicators of weak enforcement of labor standards and the level of U.S. foreign direct investment in developing countries. On the contrary, U.S. firms tended to invest in countries with higher labor standards, and in sectors within countries where labor conditions were similar to, or better than, those in the rest of the economy.[23] Similarly, Rodrik's study also found no correlation between low labor standards and increased foreign direct investment by U.S. firms. Quite the reverse: in nations with low labor standards, levels of foreign direct investment were lower than might be expected on the basis of the country's other characteristics. Rodrik concluded that these results "indicate that low labor standards may be a hindrance, rather than an attraction, for foreign investors."[24]

The Rodrik study also showed a positive, statistically significant relationship between an index for democratic institutions and flows of foreign direct investment. Similarly, Morici and Shulz found that foreign investment was positively correlated with a quality-of-democracy indicator, and that weak enforcement of freedom of association and child labor statutes does not increase foreign direct investment.[25]

These results all point toward a common conclusion: workers and firms in developed countries are unlikely to be able to prove, by any objective measurement, that they are being injured in a substantial way by deviations from core ILO labor standards. The real risk to developing countries, however, is that firms and workers in the developed world, endowed with the right of private action and striving to circumvent normal competitive pressures from lower-wage workers elsewhere, would capture the process for evaluating whether injury had occurred and ensure that the methodology for determining injury would not be objective, as has happened with antidumping procedures.

There is yet another dimension, however, to the relationship between "special privileges" and "unfair advantages." Weak labor standards may not play a strong role in attracting foreign direct investors to the developing world; but that does not mean that individual firms do not demand exceptions in treatment of labor as a condition of investment. Pakistan, for example, in response to an ILO complaint, conceded that it had exempted its EPZs from certain labor laws because of insistent requests from Daewoo.[26] In Bangladesh, the Japanese and Korean ambassadors tried to pressure the government, on behalf of their multinationals, to forbid trade-union organizing in the country's export zones; at the same time, the United States was debating whether to withdraw GSP from Bangladesh because of poor labor conditions in those zones.[27] The ILO reported that Namibia and Zimbabwe seemed convinced, at least in the mid-1990s, that choosing not to apply some national labor regulations would be decisive for the success of their zones.[28] And, as indicated earlier in this chapter, the reduction of unit labor costs in the most labor-intensive sectors, such as garments and footwear, can have a measurable impact on the profitability of independent subcontractors in these industries.

A mix of perception and reality thus fosters a race-to-the-bottom strategy, as would-be host countries conclude that to obtain investment in lowest-skill activities, they must match the low labor standards offered elsewhere. Given the developing world's traditional hostility to the idea of including labor standards within the work of the WTO—and the genuine threat that a new regime to combat "social dumping" could be captured for protectionist purposes, just as economic dumping procedures have been—it may seem fanciful to suggest that developing countries might want to reconsider their position. But if the nature of the competition were presented in the broadest possible context, developing countries might conclude that they have a compelling interest in limiting these race-to-the-bottom dynamics.

Any effort to level the playing field—by, for example, prohibiting nations from lowering their labor standards in an effort to gain competitive advantage in the international marketplace—would inevitably awaken all the familiar controversies, across borders, concerning the obligations that core labor standards impose on ILO member states and the implementation of those obligations by means of national labor laws. But in an unusual twist, both developed and developing countries might find such an endeavor advantageous if a multilateral initiative to set standards for what constitutes fair treatment were not limited to labor rights, but were to consider the much larger race-to-the-bottom tournaments that, increasingly, undermine the creation of a level playing field for trade and investment around the world. These tournaments feature escalating packages of locational incentives that are offered on the part of national and subnational governments and are designed to attract and hold the operations of international firms.

In the developing world, foreign investment zones usually do receive special treatment, including infrastructure, subsidized land and plant facilities, and beneficial tax breaks. In the growing competition among alternative sites around the world, however, the dimensions of the special packages offered by less developed countries pale in comparison to what is offered in the OECD. Developing countries, moreover, are much less adept than developed countries at using these locational packages—especially tax breaks and incentives—effectively.[29]

While much of the literature on multinational corporate strategy suggests that tax breaks and locational incentives do not determine the competitive strategy of foreign direct investors, a growing body of case-study evidence shows that once their larger strategy is set, multinational corporations do try to stimulate "subsidy wars" among roughly comparable plant sites. The resulting incentive packages are used, in the words of General Motors, as "tie breakers" in choosing where to build a given plant.[30]

To be sure, not every plant site competes with every other plant site, and it is difficult to determine in precisely which cases subsidy competition pits sites in developed countries against those in developing countries. But there is clear econometric evidence that the overall responsiveness of international direct investment flows to differential tax treatment and locational incentives is growing stronger—and growing at an increasing rate—over time. In the early 1980s, a change equivalent to raising or lowering the tax burden of international companies by 1 percent yielded a 1 percent change in the location of investment; by the mid-1990s, a 1 percent change in the tax burden yielded a 3 percent change in location.[31] In a study covering fourteen home countries and thirty-four host countries, the impact had grown, by 1997, to 5 percent.[32]

According to John Mutti and Harry Grubert, export-oriented operations show the largest marginal tax effects, and location in lower-income countries (where per capita gross domestic product is below $10,500) is twice as sensitive to incentives that reduce the cost of capital as location in higher-income countries.[33] Depending on the characteristics of the proposed investment (automotive parts, electronic assembly, industrial equipment, or data processing, for example), subsidy wars can affect the location of plants not only within regions but within entire hemispheres. Daniel Chudnovsky and Andres Lopez have shown, for example, how fiscal competition between states within Brazil to capture automotive investment spilled over into the rest of Mercosur, most notably Argentina.[34]

Both developed and developing countries have an interest, therefore, in bringing some multilateral discipline to the competition in incentives. In the course of such an endeavor, it would be indefensible to claim that the locational packages of Ireland, Germany—or, in the United States, South Carolina or Alabama, which are on the order of $100,000 to $300,000 for each job created—have no effect on investment or trade patterns, whereas the incentive concessions of the Philippines, the Dominican Republic, Costa Rica, Argentina, or Brazil, do. If an effort to prevent all "unfair" competition for investment and all "unfair" subsidies for exports were to be launched under WTO auspices, the magnitude of the special advantages derived from substandard labor treatment—to the extent that any might be found—would surely be dwarfed by the impact of fiscal subsidies and incentives, deployed with the largest dimensions by developed countries.

6 Voluntary Mechanisms for Improving the Treatment of Workers

The presumed appeal of using the World Trade Organization to improve the treatment of workers is that, as an authoritative institution, the WTO could compel compliance among actors with varying degrees of commitment to helping workers. Specifically, the WTO could punish producers who might otherwise be tempted to cheat, and could prevent the flow of substandard goods to free-riding or indifferent retailers and consumers. At first glance, voluntary mechanisms, which rely on a blend of persuasion, agreement, cooperation, and pressure (via publicity), are sure to appear less effective.

The discussions in the two previous chapters, however, have demonstrated that transforming the WTO into an entity that can enforce a common set of core labor standards around the world might not be easy—or rapid, or even possible at all, since in order to operate with authority, the WTO itself depends on persuasion, agreement, and cooperation among its members. Despite the problems associated with collective action, it is therefore possible that an apparently weaker approach would produce superior results. As an added benefit, the use of voluntary mechanisms would avoid many of the risks that a WTO-based system would pose to workers and countries in the developing world.

The first portion of this chapter explores the current and potential effectiveness of corporate codes of conduct, certification mechanisms, and compliance labeling—the three principal components of a voluntary compliance system. Specifically, the analysis considers how these elements might be expanded and reinforced in order to achieve a broader and more rapid impact than could be obtained through a WTO-based alternative. The concluding sections of the chapter investigate how the International Labor Organization—an institution that relies largely on cooperation, persuasion, and conciliation, but that might be pushed to play a more active part in multilateral enforcement—can be strengthened.

Corporate Codes of Conduct

Corporate codes of conduct have often been characterized as nothing more than window dressing—a way for multinational corporations to enjoy the appearance of being socially responsible without really changing how they do business. A typical criticism is that "industry will pay lip service to codes, but may not change its behavior where profits are at issue."[1] Nevertheless, as has been demonstrated in previous chapters, the profit motive does not necessarily pull corporations away from good labor standards; it can also draw them toward improvements in the treatment of workers.

In many industries that produce labor-intensive products such as garments, footwear, and toys, the leading firms derive their market position from "branding" their products—through, for example, expensive advertising campaigns and endorsements by prominent athletes or celebrities. For such firms, the adoption of a socially responsible image can strengthen the branding strategy by reinforcing product differentiation, and enhance the parent company's ability to collect oligopoly rents.

Avoiding downside risk is an even more powerful motivator for multinational firms. Public disclosure of corporate practices that contradict claims of social responsibility can threaten the parent firms' marketing strategy, its ability to achieve supranormal profits, its accumulated market valuation, and its access to capital (that is, its access to capital markets in general, since the brand-name rents that determine the firm's credit rating are involved, not just the firm's access to the capital that passes through a screening test for social responsibility—which, in the United States, for example, amounts to some $2 trillion).

Furthermore, the discovery of poor corporate behavior in one area, such as the treatment of workers, can undermine the goodwill the parent firm has accumulated in other areas, such as gender relations, race relations, community development, and environmental responsibility. In short, as Naomi Klein has observed, "brand image, the source of so much corporate wealth, is also, it turns out, the corporate Achilles' heel."[2] Given multinational corporations' vulnerability to bad publicity, actions that might be considered voluntary are increasingly demanded in the modern marketplace. "Voluntary" compliance becomes not-so-voluntary.

How are brand image considerations likely to affect multinational corporate strategy with respect to core labor standards? Since unit labor costs are a small fraction of final retail prices (less than 1 percent, for branded garments and footwear, as noted in chapter 4) the trade-off for high-profile international companies—between championing satisfactory treatment of workers and shaving expenses at the production stage—might be expected to weigh heavily in favor of the former. At the same time, however, given the potential damage to the corporate image that could be brought about by a single case (or a small number of cases) of worker abuse emerging from one of the hundreds of self-owned plants or one of the thousands of contract suppliers over whom an international company exercises imperfect control, the instincts of multinational corporations are likely to be to resist as much uncontrolled scrutiny of their internal operations as possible.

In this setting, in which a corporation's desire to avoid adverse publicity and the public's desire for accountability are at odds, corporate codes of conduct have shown themselves to be strong levers for changing corporate behavior. A study of "the social responsibility of transnational corporations," undertaken by John Kline for the United Nations Commission on Trade and Development (UNCTAD), sketches out a three- and sometimes four-phase process of interaction between image-building, on the part of firms, and the demand for accountability, on the part of critics and watchdogs in civil society.[3] In the initial stage firms seek to use a reputation for social responsibility to differentiate their companies and their products in the eyes of consumers and investors. Some do so with verve and commitment on the part of their senior executives, others with less willingness to commit resources or to change corporate behavior. In either case, however, corporate objectives become exposed to public scrutiny and external assessment.

Although some firms hope to pursue what the UNCTAD study calls a "trust me" strategy, this is an inherently unstable approach: the dynamics of accountability push firms toward a "tell me" phase, in which the companies find that they have to demonstrate how the principles they profess are translated into practical guidance on operational issues. In this phase, codes of conduct have to be implemented through internal guidelines for managers and employees and in instructions for external suppliers, indicating what is expected of them as they try to deal with competitive pressures to cut costs. These guidelines and instructions provide standards against which the behavior of managers, employees, and suppliers can be judged—and rewarded or punished. The parent firm might, for example, threaten to terminate contracts if suppliers fail to meet certain labor standards, or might set up procedures to facilitate whistle-blowing within supply chains.

This "tell me" phase leads, in turn, to a "show me" phase, in which companies find themselves having to demonstrate to shareholders—and, thereby, to outsiders—that they actually adhere to their principles and standards. During the "show me" phase, firms establish internal compliance offices, institute new record-keeping practices, provide training for managers and suppliers, and fashion incentive structures. Under some circumstances, the "show me" phase may finally lead to a "join me" phase, in which firms and various stakeholders—including representatives from civil society—work together to jointly devise standards and monitoring mechanisms. Thus, the promulgation of corporate codes of conduct—whether from motives that are initially sincere or cynical—can take on a life of its own, gradually loosening the company's grip over the monitoring of its own behavior.

The UNCTAD study identified the Mattel Corporation (one of the largest toy companies in the world, with Barbie, Fisher-Price, Hot Wheels, and Matchbox among its brands) as one of the companies that has moved furthest through the process of accountability. In 1997 Mattel established a code of conduct called Global Manufacturing Principles. Despite a complex production system that includes plants and suppliers in China, India, Indonesia, Malaysia, Mexico, and Thailand, the code delineated specific standards for wages and hours, safety and health, freedom of association, and business practices; restricted the use of child labor or forced labor; and prohibited discrimination on the basis of ethnic origin, individual characteristics, or religious-personal beliefs. The code's provisions would, at a minimum, meet the legal standards in force in the country in which a plant was located; where standards specific to the country were not available or were lower than Mattel's own standards, local plants would have to meet Mattel's standards. As a long-term objective, Mattel proposed that its plants try to meet or exceed best industry practices in the specific region or locality.

In moving to what the UNCTAD study called the "join me" stage, Mattel set a precedent by creating an independent monitoring council—

headed by three outside experts in corporate codes of conduct and labor and children's issues, and chaired by S. Prakish Sethi—to design and administer an audit system that would make the council's findings public.[4] According to the council's plan, the initial audit would cover all Mattel-owned plants and all plants where Mattel controlled 100 percent of the output. A subsequent audit would include a sample of Mattel's major suppliers (where Mattel accounted for at least 70 percent of the output), and a further audit would cover a sample of plants where Mattel controlled between 40 and 70 percent of the output. Each category of plant would be audited at least once every three years; the monitoring council was also given the right to authorize additional audits at its own discretion.

The first audit, which covered three plants in China, two in Indonesia, four in Malaysia, one in Thailand, and one in Mexico, was published in 1999 and included a list of shortcomings and proposed corrective actions. In the same year Mattel cut ties with sixteen Chinese subcontractors that had failed to meet minimum standards for factory conditions or the treatment of workers, and put forty-five factories on notice that they would have to improve if they wanted to keep their contracts.[5]

The ILO and the OECD have accumulated some evidence of other companies moving through the phases outlined by Kline. In 1998 the ILO reported that responsibility for corporate codes of conduct—once the preserve of shareholder-relations departments—had become more widely assigned to higher-level managers with direct functional responsibility for sourcing and supplier relationships.[6] The issue of how to implement codes of conduct had risen to become an agenda item in corporate boardrooms. Between 1998 and 2000 the OECD found that many of the 246 corporate codes in its inventory had been revised, updated, and made more specific.[7] Of those, 76 percent included a corporate responsibility to provide reasonable working conditions, and over 50 percent specified a commitment to "fair employment and labor rights." Within the apparel industry, 38 percent of the codes stated that contracts with suppliers would be terminated if they failed to meet the labor standards delineated in the code; many codes from other sectors included the same provision. Fifteen percent of the codes were issued by partnerships of stakeholders (corporations, NGOs, unions, and intergovernmental organizations).

Nevertheless, ensuring that firms comply with their own codes has not always been easy. And corporate leaders have found that the effort to reconcile published codes, internal standards, and self-image is often an educational experience. One example involved Alcoa and its chief executive officer, Paul O'Neill (who subsequently became U.S. secretary of the treasury). The American Friends Service Committee and the Congregation of Benedictine Sisters were concerned about the treatment of workers at the Alcoa plant in Ciudad Acuna, in Mexico.[8] In 1996, using the Benedictine Sisters' ownership of Alcoa stock to enter the annual shareholders' meeting, Sister Mika brought in Juan Tovar Santos, a worker at the plant, to provide testimony. Santos told of a gas leak that had led to the hospitalization of a hundred workers, and described Alcoa managers as being so stingy that they stationed a janitor at the door to the bathroom to limit employees to three pieces of toilet paper.

O'Neill flatly denied the existence of any safety problems and defended Alcoa's working conditions to the assembled shareholders. "Our plants in Mexico are so clean they can eat off the floor," he told the audience. Later, however, O'Neill's own internal investigation revealed that conditions were much worse than he had described, and exposed the fact that the local manager—who was subsequently dismissed—had undertaken a cover-up of the gas leak.

The new manager improved safety standards and working conditions at the plant (including revising the toilet paper policy), and gradually raised wages, albeit not without controversy about whether the company was doing enough. In 2001 the average wage for a forty-eight hour week was $83, according to Alcoa, or $70, according to The Border Workers' Committee, a group that has represented laborers in Acuna; in either case, Alcoa's wages were among the highest in the industrial park.[9] With perfect attendance, grocery coupons, and other benefits, Juan Tovar Santos's earnings reached $90 per week.

Among multinational companies based in various nations, the record on corporate codes of conduct has been mixed, as has the intensity of the pressure from civil society groups to hold senior management accountable for compliance with published codes. In the United States, most Fortune 500 companies have adopted codes of conduct, or some kind of internal guidelines, that include provisions for the treatment of workers.[10] The Ethical Trading Initiative (ETI) estimates that as many as 85 percent of all large U.S. companies, as of 2000, operated with some kind of social-responsibility guidelines.[11] A survey of 1,000 Canadian companies, selected on the basis of size, found that in 85 percent of the firms, management had issued written statements of values and principles.[12] In the United Kingdom, more than 60 percent of the largest 500 companies had established codes of conduct, up from 18 percent a decade ago.[13] Among international companies, Honda, Sony, and Siemens, as well as others, operate with codes of conduct.

But the practice of operating with codes of conduct is far from universal, and not at all homogeneous across countries. In 1999 the OECD inventory of 246 codes included 37 companies in the textile and apparel industries: U.S. firms made up 68 percent of the total; Swedish firms, 8 percent; U.K. firms, 5 percent; German firms, 5 percent; and Swiss firms, 3 percent. France and Japan were "conspicuously absent," in the words of the OECD investigators, despite the organization's attempts to obtain codes from French and Japanese apparel companies.[14] Eight of the nine branded apparel firms contacted in France indicated that they were unaware of apparel-industry codes and had "no plans to work on one." Japanese apparel companies reported that they simply had not felt public pressure to respond to concerns about labor standards in the industry.[15] Thus, while the trend toward the adoption of corporate codes of conduct—and toward holding senior management account-able—is positive, more can clearly be done on both fronts. And, even among the firms that have moved farthest through these phases—such as Nike and Levi Strauss—progress toward allowing genuinely independent monitoring of working conditions has been rather tortuous, as will be discussed in the next section.

Certification Mechanisms

After individual corporate codes of conduct, the second ingredient in a voluntary system to monitor and enforce core labor standards is a certification mechanism—a means of verifying that producers and subcontractors actually operate in compliance with such standards. Certification organizations have been growing in number, but the extent to which they actually meet the test of providing independent, objective, and accurate monitoring remains the subject of some dispute.[16]

One of the first certification organizations was the Rugmark Foundation, which was established in 1994 by a coalition of Indian human-rights and industry groups, and backed by the United Nations Children's Fund (UNICEF). Member retailers and manufacturers bind themselves to the foundation's code of conduct, whose main purpose is to replace child labor with adult labor and to provide educational opportunities for former child workers. Signatories pay licensing fees to the foundation, in exchange for which they are allowed to affix the Rugmark Foundation label to their carpets—as long as the companies pass inspections administered by monitors hired by the foundation. The monitors are thus the agents of the foundation, not of the retailers or manufacturers. Each label bears a coded registration number indicating the exporter, the manufacturer, and the specific loom used for the product. The inspection results, however, are kept confidential.

FIFA, the Fédération Internationale de Football Association, was initially formed to ensure that soccer balls met certain quality standards (regulation size, weight, and durability) before their manufacturers would be permitted to place the FIFA logo on the products. In 1996 FIFA reached an agreement with the International Textile, Garment and Leather Workers' Federation and the International Federation of Commercial, Clerical, Professional and Technical Employees to adhere to a code of conduct, based on the core ILO conventions, that would be incorporated into FIFA's established regulatory apparatus. To be permitted to use the FIFA logo, manufacturers would certify that they, their contractors, and subcontractors met the standards outlined in the code. The International Confederation of Free Trade Unions was given the task of monitoring the supply chains.

In the United Kingdom, the Ethical Trading Initiative was created, in 1998, through an alliance of companies, NGOs, trade unions, and the government. Funded by membership fees from companies and NGOs, plus a grant from the U.K. Department for International Development, ETI adopted a code—based on ILO conventions—to which all participants must commit themselves. Members are required to provide an annual report, and membership renewal is denied to members that fail to demonstrate compliance to the code. ETI has undertaken pilot projects to determine how best to monitor and enforce its base code in specific sectors, including clothing (in China), wine (in South Africa), horticulture (in Zimbabwe and Zambia), and bananas (in Costa Rica).

In the United States, the Council on Economic Priorities, a long-established institution devoted to research on corporate social responsibility, launched the Social Accountability 8000 (SA8000) program in 1997.[17] With a board of directors drawn from the business, labor, and NGO communities, the council, which was renamed Social Accountability International (SAI) in 2000, established a set of SA8000 operational requirements, based on ILO and United Nations (UN) conventions, that lent themselves to clear measurement. SAI then began to accredit auditors who could inspect the plants of SA8000 signatories.

Companies are allowed to display the SA8000 logo once their facilities have been audited; required periodic follow-up inspections include briefings for the auditors by local unions and human-rights organizations about issues at individual plants. An innovative aspect of the SA8000 approach is that each company certified must provide a confidential system allowing workers to lodge direct complaints with SAI headquarters about noncompliance with the SA8000 standards. Code violations are kept confidential, but outside parties may challenge the certification of a signatory firm or the accreditation of a particular monitor.[18] This challenge procedure has proved to be important—and necessary. Various organizations, including the National Labor Committee (NLC), have interviewed workers who asserted that local management had threatened them and coached them to lie about hours and working conditions.[19] In 2000 a plant in China under SAI audit supervision was decertified after the NLC reported a number of violations of the SA8000 code, which SAI investigators subsequently confirmed.[20]

As experimentation with certification has progressed, via Rugmark, FIFA, ETI, SAI, and other organizations, it has become increasingly clear that to gain credibility—and, hence, legitimacy—the system must provide transparency in supplier-producer-retailer chains, create confidence in the effectiveness and autonomy of inspectors, ensure public disclosure of violations, disseminate descriptions of remediation programs, allow findings to be subjected to public scrutiny, and provide mechanisms for outsiders to challenge the findings. Movement in the direction of meeting these prerequisites, however, has not been smooth.

With respect to transparency, some major U.S. companies in the garment, footwear, and other industries initially claimed that the names and locations of their plants and suppliers constituted trade secrets, and refused to provide such information. When the Fair Labor Association (FLA), a certification organization for the U.S. apparel and footwear industries, decided in 1998 to protect the confidentiality of plant and supplier locations, that decision was one of the factors that led some critics to break with the FLA and form an alternative organization, the Worker Rights Consortium; one of the purposes of the consortium was to draw away from the FLA universities that were concerned that their logos might appear on goods that had been produced under substandard working conditions. In partial recognition of the fact that a certification organization could hardly expect to achieve credibility without identifying supplier chains, the FLA's University Advisory Committee adopted a resolution in 2000 that required all members of that committee to publicly disclose the locations of factories producing goods with the member university's logo.[21] But FLA members continued to resist any broader disclosure of the location of their plants, and continued to claim that the locations were confidential business information.

With respect to the effectiveness and autonomy of the inspection system, many firms have chosen to use monitors from the business and auditing community, such as PricewaterhouseCoopers and Ernst and Young, to conduct regularly scheduled audits of sample plants. Critics did not take long to point out, however, that a system that relies solely on monitors who are financially dependent on the companies being monitored cannot be considered autonomous; that in order to keep investors and subcontractors from concealing problems, regularly scheduled visits must be supplemented by surprise "challenge inspections"; and that some form of backup checking is necessary to ensure that the inspectors are doing a competent job.

When Professor Dara O'Rourke, of the Massachusetts Institute of Technology, accompanied PricewaterhouseCoopers inspectors to factories in China and Korea, O'Rourke discovered that the inspectors had overlooked the use of a carcinogenic chemical, did not recognize some overtime violations, and failed to note that the labor union at a Shanghai garment factory was controlled by management.[22] In response, PricewaterhouseCoopers admitted that the inspectors were not trained to recognize that the spot remover posed hazards to the workers who used it, and that the auditing team may have missed some wage and overtime violations because they examined only a sampling of timecards.[23] PricewaterhouseCoopers pointed out that its inspectors did, however, find and report many overtime and safety violations, and disputed the contention that the auditors had a "pro-management" bias. Regardless of the details of this particular case, the episode underscores the fact that, to achieve legitimacy, monitoring systems will have to permit external scrutiny and generally pass inspection when backup checks take place. At the same time, however, any certification process will have to rely, to some extent, on spot-checks and samples; as many civil society groups acknowledge, no system can be expected to ensure perfect compliance every day of the year.

With the aim of gaining broader public support, the FLA decided, after some hesitation, to make available to the public the reports that were based on the external monitoring of its member firms, including information about noncompliance and remediation. The FLA set the quota for independent external audits at 30 percent of a member's factories each year, with both announced and unannounced inspections. The FLA also provided a channel for individual workers at the factories of its members to lodge a complaint, in confidence, directly with the association.

In 1999, to promote autonomous investigations of working conditions that would be credible to all sides, The World Bank, Nike, The Gap, and several NGOs that support workers' rights formed the Global Alliance for Workers and Communities.[24] Funding from the corporate members was placed in a blind trust designed so that the donors could not revoke their support if the investigations by the Global Alliance reflected negatively on the companies. The Global Alliance's initial study, conducted by universities in Vietnam and Thailand, surveyed 3,800 workers in twelve Nike factories in those countries, and recommended several initiatives to improve the quality of life for workers. Although the Global Alliance was not designed to be a certification agency per se, civic groups criticized its first report for failing to concentrate sufficiently on alleged violations and abuses. The Global Alliance's second study, paid for by a $7.8 million donation from Nike to the blind trust, found instances of physical and sexual abuse at nine of Nike's contract plants in Indonesia.[25]

In response, Nike announced a remediation plan that included a new system of social monitoring, which would rely on local organizations with expertise in women's issues; grievance procedures enabling workers to pass along information safely and confidentially; and separate verification, by a monitor certified by the FLA, of the steps taken on other specific compliance matters. The Global Alliance, in turn, was assigned the task of conducting follow-up investigations within twelve months.

There has thus been considerable (albeit contentious) movement toward the creation of a credible, voluntary system for certifying plants that comply with core labor standards and for identifying plants that do not. The Internet has offered unprecedented assistance in this process. Nike, for example, as an outgrowth of its experience in The Global Alliance, has launched what the company calls the Transparency 101 initiative, which allows any outside observer to track Global Alliance investigations and Nike remediation proposals, as well other certification results and ongoing worker disputes around the globe, via the company's own website.[26] Nike's online program might serve as a template for further progress in strengthening voluntary compliance. The goal would be to encourage companies to move toward adopting industry best practices with respect to independent monitoring and certification; to this end, the Internet could be used to provide near-real-time surveillance of investigation results and remediation efforts.

Compliance Labeling

Some certification groups, like Rugmark, have adopted compliance labeling to help consumers identify goods produced according to acceptable labor standards. The FLA has indicated plans to create a service mark that certified companies may use in their advertising or affix to their products.

Labeling is market-friendly: it allows consumers to reward or punish enterprises by restricting their purchases to goods from firms that comply with core labor standards. Firms that demonstrate compliance gain an increased market share, increased profits, and increased output, while firms that fail to demonstrate compliance experience a drop in market share, profits, and output. The prospects for success in the use of labeling are strengthened by the fact that consumers in various developed countries, including the United States, have indicated that they are willing both to pay more for goods produced under sweatshop-free conditions, and to avoid goods that are not so identified.[27] Labeling is also branding-friendly: it complements manufacturers' efforts to set apart the goods bearing their logo, reinforces their incentive to police their own supply chains, and enables them to differentiate themselves from producers that are more lax about compliance with fair labor standards.

But a labeling system can also provide a handsome return to counterfeiters; it is cheap and easy enough to put false labels on goods produced under substandard conditions. Counterfeit labeling can be overcome, however, if producers, in their own self-interest, begin to devote some fraction of the resources and imagination that they allocate to defending other aspects of their branding (like trademarks and intellectual property rights) to the prevention of counterfeit labeling. In efforts to protect against counterfeit labeling, the attentiveness of firms and the vigilance of NGOs and human-rights organizations would naturally overlap.

The creation of more generic labeling systems that covered multiple industries and multiple kinds of products—or even a single "sweatshop-free" logo—could simultaneously strengthen consumers' sensitivity to labor issues and make it easier for them to select appropriate products. But a more generic system might have an even stronger impact. If major retailers in, say, the garment, footwear, toy, jewelry, and hardware businesses—including the large discount outlets—chose to offer only sweatshop-free products, it would become genuinely inconvenient for even unconcerned consumers to buy goods produced in substandard or uninspected plants. And smaller producers and manufacturers without their own branded lines of products would find that, to stay in business, they would need to meet the requirements of the generic sweatshop-free label—and would thus be ushered into membership in certification organizations.

Are Voluntary Mechanisms Second Best?

The evidence introduced in this chapter suggests that codes of conduct, certification mechanisms, and compliance labeling can be woven together to strengthen the observance of core labor standards. The trend has been toward increased transparency in producer-supplier-retailer relationships, greater effectiveness and autonomy on the part of inspectors, broader disclosure of violations, more prompt follow-up and remediation, and increased opportunities for outsiders to challenge results. There is no reason that this trend cannot be made to continue.

But will a steadily more effective voluntary system always seem like a poor substitute for an authoritative, WTO-based trade-sanctions regime? The answer, quite arguably, may be no. In fact, the common-sense standards embodied in voluntary mechanisms are likely to prove far more usable—for exposing and bringing pressure to bear on violators—than any standards that could be negotiated and enforced within the WTO. Contrary to the concern that codes of conduct, certification mechanisms, and labeling initiatives would rely on vague or hortatory standards, the commitments adopted by leading firms and retailers (and, by extension, their suppliers) are becoming quite specific. As noted in chapter 4, it is unlikely that the international community could negotiate similarly precise standards as the basis for identifying violations and undertaking enforcement within the WTO. In short, "name-and-shame" techniques that rely on common-sense standards, and that place the burden of proof on the firm to show that its plants or suppliers are living up to the firm's own guidelines, or up to the guidelines that the firm has endorsed as a member of a compliance organization, are likely to produce more prompt and far-reaching results than a process that depends on dispute-settlement panels and appellate tribunals to find defendants guilty of legal violations and subject them to statutory punishments.

To give some examples:

—Freedom of association and collective bargaining:

We respect workers' rights to form and join organizations of their choice and to bargain collectively. We expect our suppliers to respect the right to free association and the right to organize and bargain collectively without unlawful interference. Business partners should ensure that workers who make such decisions or participate in such organizations are not the object of discrimination or punitive disciplinary actions and that the representatives of such organizations have access to their members under conditions established either by local laws or mutual agreement between the employer and the worker organizations ("Levi Strauss Terms of Engagement," 2001).[28]

—Discrimination:

Discrimination of any kind is not tolerated by Mattel, Inc. It is our belief that individuals should be employed on the basis of their ability to do a job—not on the basis of individual characteristics or beliefs. We refuse to conduct business with any manufacturer or supplier who discriminates either in hiring or in employment practices ("Mattel Global Manufacturing Principles," 2001).[29]

—Forced labor:

There shall not be any use of forced labor, whether in the form of prison labor, indentured labor, bonded labor or otherwise ("Fair Labor Association Agreement, Amended Version, Workplace Code of Conduct," 2001).[30]

—Health and safety:

The company, bearing in mind the prevailing knowledge of the industry and of any specific hazards, shall provide a safe and healthy working environment and shall take adequate steps to prevent accidents and injury to health arising out of, associated with or occurring in the course of work, by minimizing, so far as is reasonably practicable, the causes of hazards inherent in the working environment; . . . The company shall ensure that all personnel receive regular and recorded health and safety training, and that such training is repeated for new and reassigned personnel ("SA8000 Standards," 2001).[31]

—Child labor:

Use of child labor is not permissible. Workers can be no less than 15 years of age and not younger than the compulsory age to be in school. We will not utilize partners who use child labor in any of their facilities. We support the development of legitimate work-place apprenticeship programs for the educational benefit of younger people ("Levi Strauss Terms of Engagement," 2001).[32]

—Harassment or abuse:

Every employee shall be treated with respect and dignity. No employee shall be subject to any physical, sexual, psychological or verbal harassment or abuse ("Fair Labor Association Agreement, Amended Version, Workplace Code of Conduct," 2001).[33]

—International norms:

The company shall also respect the principles of the following international instruments: ILO Conventions 29 and 105 (Forced & Bonded Labor); ILO Convention 87 (Freedom of Association); ILO Convention 98 (Right to Collective Bargaining); ILO Conventions 100 and 111 (Equal remuneration for male and female workers for work of equal value; Discrimination); ILO Convention 135 (Workers' Representatives Convention); ILO Convention 138; ILO Convention 155 and Recommendation 164 (Occupational Safety & Health); ILO Convention 159 (Vocational Rehabilitation & Employment/Disabled Persons); ILO Convention 177 (Home Work); Universal Declaration of Human Rights; The United Nations Convention on the Rights of the Child ("SA8000 Standards," 2001).[34]

—Inspections:

The manufacturer maintains on file all documentation needed to demonstrate compliance with this Code of Conduct; agrees to make these documents available for Nike or its designated auditor to inspect upon request; and agrees to submit to labor practices audits or inspections with or without prior notice ("Nike Code of Conduct," 2001).[35]

—Penalties:

All members are required to report on their progress annually. This will be used to assess each member's contribution to the Ethical Trading Initiative process. Membership is on an annual basis, and will not be renewed for those members who have not demonstrated commitment to the Ethical Trading Initiative process ("Ethical Trading Initiative Base Code," 2001).[36]

—Transparency:

Nike remains an enthusiastic participant in the Global Alliance. We look forward to beginning this work in China, and continuing the work begun in Thailand, Vietnam and Indonesia. We encourage other companies with global supply chains to join efforts like this that combine the resources and talents of private and nonprofit organizations to effect positive impacts in the global economy. We also hope that other companies will not shy away from transparency. Ultimately we learn from open processes like this a great deal about workplace conditions and worker attitudes, and having that information makes it all the more likely that we can change those lives and our businesses for the better ("Nike Remediation Plan," 2001).[37]

The simplicity and straightforwardness of commitments such as these would make it relatively easy to identify the kinds of labor practices that would provoke a public response across borders. To avoid the distortions identified in chapter 4 in the discussion of living-wage proposals, and to eliminate the incentive for suppliers to substitute capital-intensive for labor-intensive production processes, the cost of higher labor standards would have to be borne by the more oligopolistic investors and retailers—and perhaps shared with consumers—rather than imposed on the more competitive array of suppliers in the developing world.

While offering no pretense of meeting the precise legal requirements that would be necessary to prove an actionable violation under a WTO-based system, the commitment of individual companies and compliance organizations to common-sense standards of fair and decent behavior may, in fact, lead to the identification of a larger number of undisputed violations; to broader pressure for remediation; and to faster resolution, under constantly changing conditions, than a hypothetical WTO-based sanctions regime could ever hope to achieve.

Strengthening the Role of the ILO

Progress in expanding and strengthening voluntary mechanisms to monitor and enforce core labor standards could be complemented by efforts to reinforce the activities of the International Labor Organization. The ILO provides a set of parallel channels through which violations of core labor standards could be identified, investigated, publicized, and corrected. In addition to helping to resolve conflicts in its member states over contentious labor issues, such as those that frequently arise in EPZs, the ILO has provided labor regulators and managers—often in the poorest nations and subnational regions of the developing world—with valuable practical training in modern methods of human-resource management. In addition to its increasingly important role as monitor, conciliator, and educator, the ILO has the potential to become involved in the enforcement of core labor standards. But would movement in this direction risk a loss of support, among ILO members, for the other work that the organization has undertaken, with increasing success, in recent years?

The ILO is unique among official international organizations in that its membership includes representatives of workers and employers as well as governmental delegates. Founded in 1919, it is one of the oldest international institutions—and, until fairly recently, one of the most underutilized. In the mid-1990s, however, appreciation of the ILO's capacity to help strengthen labor institutions around the world began to grow in unprecedented fashion. The portfolio of activities associated with the ILO might, with some oversimplification, be divided into the traditional program of supervision, and the new "promotional" follow-up to the 1998 Declaration on Fundamental Principles and Rights at Work.

THE TRADITIONAL PROGRAM OF SUPERVISION. The ILO's traditional program of supervision encompasses a "regular" system, based on periodic reports on, and reviews of, working conditions in member countries; and a "special" system, based on complaints about labor practices in individual member countries.[38] Within the regular system of supervision, member states are obligated to report on steps they have taken to achieve the objectives of the conventions they have ratified. Workers' and employers' groups have the opportunity to offer comments on these reports. A committee of twenty independent members (the Committee of Experts on the Application of Conventions and Recommendations, or CEACR) reviews the reports and comments, provides general observations about developments during the previous year, and makes "individual observations" about problems in particular countries. It may also solicit additional information from member states. Before each annual International Labor Conference, a tripartite body consisting of governmental, business, and labor members reviews the CEACR report and prepares its own observations—including "individual observations," which address especially serious or urgent instances of noncompliance or persistent failure to implement particular conventions.

The regular system of supervision provides an occasion to identify, request information about, and publicize problems, and to pass collective judgment on the efforts of individual states to rectify violations. It also provides an opportunity for nonconfrontational dialogue between the office of the ILO director-general and the country in which violations have been found, which may result in the provision of technical assistance or other help aimed at improving the treatment of workers. Accentuating the positive, the CEACR was able, in 1999, to "highlight progress" in thirty-nine cases in thirty-three countries, over half of which related to core labor standards: seventeen to freedom of association, one to discrimination, three to equal remuneration, four to forced labor, and one to child labor.[39]

The special system of supervision provides three principal channels for lodging specific complaints about working conditions: procedures under article 24, procedures under article 26, and complaints registered with the Committee on Freedom of Association. There are also provisions for ad hoc measures to deal with special labor problems—apartheid, for example, was addressed through special procedures.

Under article 24 of the ILO constitution, any workers' or employers' organization (not just those serving as ILO delegates) can bring a complaint, referred to as a representation, charging a member state with inadequate implementation of any convention that the member has ratified; in the case of inadequate respect for freedom of association, a complaint may be brought regardless of whether the member has ratified the relevant conventions. If they are not otherwise resolved, the charges made via an article 24 representation may be submitted to a tripartite committee appointed by the ILO executive for further examination and recommendation. Article 24 procedures have been used in no more than a handful of representations each year.

Under article 26 of the ILO constitution, only an official delegate to the ILO can submit a representation against a member state; moreover, one government can bring a complaint against another only if the first government has ratified the convention pertaining to the complaint. This regulation limits the ability of the U.S. government to use article 26, since the United States has ratified only thirteen conventions in all, and only two of the core conventions (105, on the abolition of forced labor, and 182, on the elimination of the worst forms of child labor). However, as business or labor delegates to the ILO, the U.S. Council for International Business and the American Federation of Labor–Congress of Industrial

Organizations (AFL-CIO) could still lodge a complaint, regardless of whether the United States has ratified the relevant convention.[40]

Once a representation has been made under article 26, the ILO executive then asks the member state accused of the violation for permission to send a "direct contact mission," representing the director-general, to explore the problem on site. If this visit does not lead to a resolution of the problem, a commission of inquiry can be appointed to investigate the charges and prepare a report recommending how the member might bring itself into compliance. If the accused country objects to the steps proposed in the report, it can appeal the commission's findings to the International Court of Justice. If the commission's findings are upheld, the country will be asked for a plan to implement the commission's recommendations. If this request does not bring about satisfactory progress, then the ILO executive—moving, under article 33, from assisting with conciliation to exacting compliance—can recommend to the membership "such action as it may deem wise and expedient to secure compliance."[41] Complaints made under article 26 are thus the most powerful actions within the ILO mandate.

Over the entire life of the organization, only twenty-four complaints have been submitted under article 26, and the transition from an article 26 proceeding to an article 33 recommendation has occurred only once. In 1998, in response to an article 26 complaint about the use of forced labor in Myanmar, a commission of inquiry confirmed the existence of "widespread and systematic" abuses, particularly by the military, and issued recommendations aimed at stopping such practices. In June of 2000 the ILO delegates approved a resolution under article 33 recommending that members of the ILO, the UN, and other international organizations review their relations with Myanmar to ensure that they were not serving to perpetuate or extend the abuses. The resolution stopped short of explicitly recommending the use of trade sanctions, and postponed the date on which the resolution would take effect to see if improvement occurred. In November 2000 the ILO's governing body concluded that actions to end forced labor were inadequate and voted to implement the resolution.

In contrast to actions under articles 24 and 26, complaints to the Committee on Freedom of Association have been lodged and investigated with some frequency. Such complaints may be filed by workers' or employers' associations in the country concerned; by international organizations of workers and employers, when one of their members is involved; and by international organizations of workers and employers with consultative status at the ILO. Furthermore, complaints to the Committee on Freedom of Association can be pursued regardless of whether a country has ratified conventions 87 and 98: the rationale is that membership in the ILO implicitly imposes an obligation to respect freedom of association. The use of this channel for filing complaints has expanded considerably: whereas two decades ago the number of cases averaged approximately three per year, between 1995 and 2000 the Committee on Freedom of Association examined more than 260 cases in some fifty-five countries. The types of complaints most commonly examined by the committee are allegations of "denial of civil liberties," "acts of antiunion discrimination," hindrance of "collective bargaining," "interference," "restrictive legislation," restrictions on "establishment of organizations," restrictions on "right to strike," and restrictions having to do with "by-laws, elections and activities."[42]

As noted in chapter 3, the Committee on Freedom of Representation has been useful in resolving labor disputes arising in EPZs. The ILO sent two technical missions to Costa Rica, for example, in 1991 and 1993, to help shape domestic legislation barring solidarist associations from engaging in collective bargaining or assuming other functions of trade unions.[43]

External bodies, such as the International Textile, Garment and Leather Workers' Federation, the International Metalworkers' Federation, and the International Confederation of Free Trade Unions, have been active in lodging Committee on Freedom of Association complaints. So have local bodies: the Trade Union Congress of the Philippines, for example, brought a complaint against the Philippine government concerning freedom of association at the Mitsumi plant, in the Danao City zone.[44]

Once again, with the exception of article 26 complaints that lead to article 33 actions, as in the case of Myanmar, the ILO relies on a combination of investigation, publicity, dialogue, and technical assistance to produce improvements in the treatment of workers.

THE FOLLOW-UP TO THE DECLARATION OF FUNDAMENTAL PRINCIPLES AND RIGHTS AT WORK. Following the 1998 ILO Declaration on Fundamental Principles and Rights at Work, the ILO launched an ambitious effort—distinct from the traditional supervisory systems—requiring members to "take stock" of where they were in relation to the four core labor standards. The promotional initiative, which the ILO undertook

with a view to formulating its strategy for technical help and cooperation, added to members' reporting responsibilities: the initiative required
each member to submit a new annual report outlining actions being
taken to promote workers' rights. And, as part of the initiative, the ILO
invited employers' and workers' groups within member states, as well as
international employers' and workers' organizations outside the member states, to review the text of each annual report and provide comments. This compilation of annual reports, with accompanying comments, could then serve as the basis for determining priorities in the
provision of assistance. The prospect of obtaining assistance has helped
solidify support for the work of the ILO: fifteen countries that had
abstained from the vote on the 1998 declaration submitted one or more
reports after the promotional program was instituted.[45]

A group of independent "expert advisers," appointed by the ILO's
governing body, was empowered to examine all the submissions and
accompanying commentaries, and to compose an introduction to the
compilation of annual reports. The first such introduction, in March
2000, included praise from the expert advisers for the frankness of some
governments in acknowledging areas of weakness and in suggesting cre-
ative approaches to overcoming difficulties.[46] Less satisfactory was the
fact that only about 55 percent of the countries obligated to submit
reports did so, although the list of those who did not included many of
the poorest and most strife-ridden members of the developing world
(such as Afghanistan, Bosnia, Haiti, Iraq, Malawi, Rwanda, Sudan, and
Yugoslavia). Most dismaying, however, was the fact that relatively few
employers' or workers' organizations, within or outside the member
states, offered comments on what the governments had reported—leaving a sizable gap, which could well be filled in the future, in assessment,
criticism, rejoinder, dialogue, and proposals for remediation.[47] This first
group of annual reports from individual countries, and the introductory
volume provided by the expert advisers, underscored the frailty of
domestic agencies' efforts, especially at the subnational and municipal
levels, to monitor and adjudicate labor disputes. The exercise illustrated
the pressing need for outside support to teach, demonstrate, and provide
assistance in strengthening labor-related institutions.

In addition to requiring the compilation of annual reports and creation of the expert advisers' introduction, the follow-up to the 1998
declaration instructed the ILO director-general to prepare an annual
global report on one of the four categories of fundamental rights, beginning with freedom of association and the effective recognition of the

right to collective bargaining. The first of these global reports, issued in May 2000, listed the countries in which various restrictions on freedom of association and the right to collective bargaining had been identified, as well as those in which progress had been recorded.[48] At the subsequent International Labor Conference, the global report was criticized for citing countries by name, but Juan Somavia, director-general of the ILO, defended the practice, arguing that "it is difficult to see how the [International Labor] Office can do credible reporting unless countries are identified and facts are stated." The global report concluded with a list of priorities for cooperation and promotion, including the reform of labor regulations and technical training in worker-management relations and modern human-resource policies. Under the rubric of what was referred to as The Global Compact, the report also called for the ILO to undertake more vigorous outreach efforts to international enterprises, in order to win endorsement for the fundamental principles and rights at work, and to organizations in civil society, in order to build partnerships and pursue complementary interests.

PROSPECTS FOR THE ILO. The ILO has thus positioned itself, in recent years, to play a broader and more active role than ever before in advancing the global observance of core labor standards. The ILO's regular system of supervision, its special procedures for receiving and processing complaints, and its newer follow-up initiative have increased its capacity to identify and publicize abuses. Its technical assistance programs have provided training and advice that have demonstrably helped to improve working conditions on the municipal, provincial, and national levels. All these activities can be expanded, streamlined (the reporting requirements may already be redundant and excessively burdensome), and better funded.

There remains considerable potential, moreover, to take advantage of the synergy between the operations of the ILO and voluntary efforts to monitor, investigate, and remedy violations of core labor standards. The work of certification and compliance organizations, and of local labor groups and NGOs, could be meshed much more thoroughly with Committee on Freedom of Association complaints and the complaint procedures under article 24; there is also the opportunity for workers' and employers' organizations to provide detailed comments to the follow-up annual reports.

The prospects for a strong ILO role in enforcement, however—either on its own or in conjunction with the WTO—are much more constrained. The experience with Myanmar showed the difficulty of garnering support among ILO members for article 26–article 33 actions, which are likely to continue to be reserved for extreme cases involving only the most egregious violations of core labor standards. Nor are proposals to harness the ILO to a WTO-based system, which would punish labor violations via sanctions or fines, likely to be any more popular among the majority of ILO members. Because the great expansion in the ILO's efforts to improve labor standards has come about through dialogue, conciliation, and assistance to its member states, there may be rather severe trade-offs between efforts to turn the ILO into more of an enforcement agency and its growing effectiveness in more cooperative areas.

7 Using Foreign Investment to Shape Host-Country Development

In the developing world, low-skilled labor is abundant and capital is scarce. As older economics textbooks often stressed, foreign investors are an important source of capital. Thus, foreign direct investment can augment local savings and put low-skilled labor to work. Indeed, it may appear from the discussions in the preceding chapters that job creation—particularly for lower-skilled and least-skilled workers—is the single most valuable contribution of foreign direct investment.

But this characterization of the contribution of foreign direct investment understates, by a large margin, the potential that foreign firms can bring to the process of development. Modern growth theory (especially endogenous growth theory) paints a different and much richer picture of the value of foreign direct investment, and of the ways in which it can enhance the growth and welfare of host countries.

What foreign investors have to offer are integrated packages that include hard-to-replicate technologies, business techniques, management skills, human-relations policies, and marketing capabilities; these are often referred to, somewhat awkwardly, as intangible assets.[1] As they introduce these assets into the local economy, foreign investors may position the host country at the frontier of best practices in international industries. Moreover, as the competitive frontier moves outward over time, foreign investors may, under the right conditions, continue to upgrade the capabilities of their subsidiaries, in a dynamic process, to ensure that they remain at the cutting edge. Further, foreign investors may find that it is in their own best interest to develop local supplier networks and to supervise and help improve the performance of those networks. The foreign firms may thus generate backward linkages, spillovers, and positive externalities for host-country workers, managers, and firms that exceed what is reflected in the parent firms' profits. Foreign direct investment and the globalization of industry, consequently, not only allow a host economy to do what it already does more efficiently, but make it possible for the host country to transform the set of activities that can be performed within the country's borders.

This process, in which foreign direct investment is used to reroute the development track of the host country, is not entirely different from the phenomenon of foreign investment in garments, footwear, and toys examined in earlier chapters. The process can be seen in low-skill, low-wage industries as well as in higher-skill, higher-wage industries. Indeed, one of the pioneers of endogenous growth theory, Paul Romer, gained a revelatory insight by looking at the role of foreign investment in the garment industry in Mauritius. Romer observed that foreign textile investors helped transform the host economy not simply because they brought in capital (much of the capital they used was raised locally), or because they brought in new technology (most of their technology was embedded in weaving and sewing equipment that could have been purchased openly in international markets), but because they brought in a package—production techniques, contacts with external retailers and style centers, and experience in maneuvering in the complex terrain of textile quotas in international markets—that transformed the host economy.[2] As chapter 2 showed, the Mauritian economy shifted from slow-growth agricultural activities and high unemployment to high-growth garment-export operations, a tight labor market, and rising wages.

The potential to alter the host country's development trajectory is even more pronounced when foreign direct investment occurs in more sophisticated industries. In fact, foreign direct investment and the globalization of higher-skill industries raise fundamental questions about traditional conceptions of comparative advantage. Twenty-five years ago, for example, the factor endowment of Costa Rica would have seemed to limit the production options of the local economy to bananas and coffee. Within a decade of the introduction of foreign direct investment, however, the production options of this small Central American country had grown to include garments and footwear as well. Today, the globalization of industry and continued foreign direct investment have expanded Costa Rica's production options to include bananas and coffee and garments and footwear and semiconductors and medical products and electronic devices and data processing and business services. The formidable power of foreign direct investment to alter the prospects of a host economy will be even more apparent in later sections of this chapter, which consider the impact of international companies in the automotive and in the computer and electronics sectors.

The progression from lowest-skill to increasingly higher-skill foreign investor operations is important not simply because of the improvement in the treatment of workers that it brings about, but because it allows host countries to tap into much larger amounts of foreign direct investment. As chapter 1 of this volume pointed out, the flow of foreign direct investment into higher-wage, higher-skill sectors in developing countries—such as those that produce transportation equipment, automotive parts, industrial machinery, plastics, chemicals, medical devices, computers, electronics, and electrical machinery—is more than twenty times greater than the flow into sectors that produce goods such as textiles, footwear, leather products, toys, and soccer balls.

But foreign direct investment has remained concentrated in a relatively small (albeit expanding) group of developing countries. And many host countries that have managed to attract foreign firms into industrial sectors have failed to achieve the same level of results observed elsewhere. Of even greater concern is evidence, introduced later in this chapter, showing that many foreign investment projects have damaged the development prospects of the host country.[3]

The question posed at the beginning of this volume must therefore be enlarged: what can host countries do to maximize the benefits and avoid the dangers of foreign direct investment, not only in lowest-skill, labor-intensive operations but in increasingly higher-skill activities as well?

In the past, conventional wisdom has held that imposing domestic-content and joint-venture and other technology-sharing requirements might be an effective means of harnessing foreign direct investment more closely to the development goals of the host country—a view that still resonates with considerable force in many developing countries. Under the "new paradigm" explored in this chapter, however, a much more effective means of capturing the benefits of foreign direct investment is to ensure that foreign subsidiaries are integrated as tightly as possible into the regional or global sourcing networks of their parent firms. Using evidence from the automotive and computer and electronics industries, where the globalization of higher-skill investor operations has been most far-reaching, this chapter compares the operations of foreign subsidiaries—and the backward linkages and spillovers to the host economy—under these two alternative approaches, revealing that the conventional approach is not only less successful but is in many cases actually harmful to the growth and welfare of the host country.

The chapter then turns to a difficult, and surprisingly underresearched, question: what steps should host countries take to strengthen and expand dynamic backward linkages from the operations of foreign investors? To explore this issue, the chapter first considers the vendor-development programs of Singapore and Malaysia, then examines "revisionist" interpretations of the economic growth in Korea and Taiwan; these interpretations suggest that, to a much greater extent than is traditionally acknowledged, indigenous firms in Korea and Taiwan began, and developed, as subcontractors to foreign multinationals. The chapter concludes with an assessment, based on endogenous growth theory, of the potential impact of following—and not following—the new paradigm. The analysis suggests that, in the contemporary era of the globalization of industry, the benefits of trade and investment liberalization are substantially greater than conventional estimates indicate—and so, too, are the costs of trade and investment restrictions.

The Impact of Domestic-Content and Technology-Sharing Requirements on Foreign Investors

During the early decades of the globalization of manufacturing production, there was great debate—based on little or no data—about what policies host countries should adopt toward multinational corporations. Evidence that has accumulated since the mid-1980s, however, has made it possible to identify those policies that enhance the benefits of foreign direct investment—and those that do not.[4]

Foreign direct investment in manufacturing operations in the developing world has traditionally taken two distinct forms: in the first, the foreign investor sets up operations oriented toward providing goods and services for the host country's domestic market; in the second, the foreign investor sets up operations oriented toward producing goods and services that fit into the parent firm's regional or global sourcing network and reinforce the parent firm's competitive position in international markets. Occasionally, the two overlapped, but hindsight has revealed that the two forms are quite distinct, and that the relationship between the parent firm and the local subsidiary differs significantly depending on the form of investment.

When a multinational investor depended on the subsidiary facility to meet the challenge of rival companies around the world—including markets in developed countries—the parent firm showed a strong preference for "unambiguous control" over all aspects of the subsidiary's operations.[5] Whether the plant was located in an EPZ or not, the foreign investor insisted, as a condition of entry, that the subsidiary be wholly owned (or at least majority-owned); that the host country impose no technology-sharing or domestic-content requirements; and that inputs be duty-free. Developing countries assumed that this freedom from host-country mandates and requirements would yield "screwdriver operations" that would be minimally integrated into the local economy and share minimal amounts of technology with local companies. Indeed, the parent-subsidiary relationship seem designed to ensure that the phrase *technology transfer* would be an oxymoron.

The literature on international business strategy initially referred to such plants as captive facilities; but what was first coined as an objective description soon took on pejorative connotations in the language of host-countries' policy analysis.[6] To ensure that foreign direct investment would contribute more to domestic development than a few export earnings and some assembly jobs, host countries judged that they had to impose joint-venture, domestic-content, and technology-sharing mandates on foreign investors. In the case of manufacturing operations oriented primarily toward the host-country domestic market (as opposed to that of subsidiaries that were tightly knit into international sourcing networks), multinational investors were largely willing to tolerate domestic-content requirements and to accept, or even seek out, local partners to assist in penetrating the market.[7] However, to ensure that producing for the local market would be profitable even under regulations that required high domestic content, the foreign firms usually demanded trade protection, a concession that fit easily into the import-substitution strategy that predominated among many developing countries in the early decades of globalization. The hope of host-country development strategists was that the protection would prove temporary, and that the sheltered subsidiaries would gain know-how that would transform them from infant industries into operations with full competitive standing.

The sections that follows consider the impact of domestic-content and joint-venture and other technology-sharing requirements on the foreign subsidiaries themselves—and on the backward linkages from the foreign subsidiaries to local suppliers—in the automotive and computer and electronics industries, those in which globalization has been most extensive.

DOMESTIC-CONTENT AND TECHNOLOGY-SHARING REQUIREMENTS AND THE AUTOMOTIVE INDUSTRY. In the automotive industry, domestic-content requirements led to a proliferation of boutique assembly plants that often produced no more than 15,000 units a year; to achieve economies of scale, output on the order of 150,000 to 225,000 units a year would have been necessary. According to a survey of seventeen countries undertaken in the mid-1980s, tariffs had to average 100 percent in order to keep such small plants profitable,[8] and consumers in host countries paid from 20 to 60 percent more for models whose features typically trailed by several years those available in external markets.

The picture has not improved over time. In the 1990s the efficiency of small, protected, modern assembly plants seldom exceeded one-tenth that of full-sized facilities. Granted, these small-scale operations generated jobs for host-country workers—but at a cost of as much as $300,000 for each job created.[9] Since trade protection allows foreign investors to shift the burden of inefficient production onto host-country consumers, and to add a significant markup, the arrangement has not been unappealing to the foreign investors. Just as Chrysler used its small, protected operations in Mexico to help keep itself afloat in the United States in the 1970s and 1980s, so General Motors (GM) enjoyed trade rents from the assembly of Opels in Hungary in the late 1990s, on the order of $50 million to $75 million a year.[10] As for the hope among host-country authorities that workers and managers at the local plants would acquire knowledge that could transform protected infant industries into full-scale competitive operations, the technologies and business techniques deployed in the baby boutique plants have turned out to preclude such a transition. The parent auto firms created semi-knocked-down (SKD) and completely-knocked-down (CKD) kits that could be sent for assembly in protected local markets. In contrast to the highly automated, precision-controlled processes used in full-scale production lines, automobiles created from these car-in-a-box kits are held together with temporary jigs, and welded by hand—procedures that cannot be used as components of a larger-scale operation.[11] Indeed, since workers install engines, transmissions, electrical systems, seats, and other interior parts by hand, kit assembly itself might properly be characterized as a screwdriver operation. High domestic-content requirements thus lock host country operations into production technologies and business practices well behind contemporary standards in the industry.

The decision of a foreign investor to create a full, state-of-the-art assembly plant requires the construction of a completely new operation, not a buildup from kit assembly. And, when foreign investors evaluate such an investment decision, instead of receiving positive feedback from a favorable demonstration effect at a small plant, they are likely to receive negative feedback when they see that production peaks at eight vehicles an hour, versus ninety vehicles an hour elsewhere.[12]

Joint-venture requirements further discourage the use of the most advanced production technology. Despite markets that are large enough to support medium-sized assembly plants—and, eventually, full-sized assembly plants—foreign automotive investors in China have used manufacturing processes that are, on average, ten years behind industry best practices. According to Chrysler, the refusal of foreign automotive investors to introduce the newest production methods springs from a concern that their joint-venture partners will appropriate trade secrets.[13] Nor is this fear completely unfounded: in 1997, when Audi's license expired, the Chinese partner in the Audi–First Automobile Works joint venture "expropriated" the production technology. As noted earlier, foreign investors willingly choose local partners to help penetrate host-country markets; however, if the focus of the business shifts substantially to export operations, foreign firms are likely to withdraw from such partnerships.

Despite the hope among host-country authorities that high requirements for domestic content would generate substantial and vibrant backward linkages to local suppliers, such expectations turned out to be handicapped from the start. Because high-value-added components—such as transmissions, catalytic converters, axles, and fuel-injection and exhaust systems—required larger production runs than kit assemblers could achieve, local suppliers were either hindered from entering into production of such components, or from using the most advanced processes and quality-control techniques if they did. Even less sophisticated components, such as electrical harnesses, windows, coils, springs, and stamped or molded plastic parts, have some economies of scale—again, limiting the ability of local firms to accommodate the mini-orders of kit assemblers. The aim of Vietnam's "localization program," undertaken in the mid-1990s, was to generate domestic-content levels of 30 percent, but backward linkages to local firms did not extend beyond finishing and painting parts, tasks that relied on technology equivalent to that found in a modern body shop.[14]

DOMESTIC-CONTENT AND TECHNOLOGY-SHARING REQUIREMENTS AND THE COMPUTER AND ELECTRONICS INDUSTRY. In the computer and electronics industry, the use of domestic-content and joint-venture and other technology-sharing requirements led to even greater disparities between the hopes of host-country authorities and the realities of development effects. In Latin America, for example, the effort to build up an indigenous computer sector by requiring foreign investors to take on a national partner and to use locally produced components led to prices that were 150 to 300 percent higher than those on the international market, for models whose capabilities were three or more years behind.[15] Evidence from the 1980s indicates that in Brazil and Mexico, this result not only imposed a burden on individual consumers but penalized advanced industrial sectors such as aerospace, industrial equipment, and petroleum exploration. According to their own testimony, domestic firms were more severely damaged by the lag in capability, which deprived them of access to the most sophisticated computer-assisted design and manufacturing techniques, than by the disadvantage in price.

Like their counterparts in the automotive sector, foreign investors in the computer and electronics sector used older technology, in highly concentrated markets, under protected regimes, to reap a second round of oligopoly rents, without worrying that their local partners would ascend to the status of rivals.[16] In the mid-1980s, for example, Apple's mini–joint venture in the protected Mexican market enjoyed a market share of 58 percent and sold the Apple LC-II at a price that was 74 percent higher than the U.S. price. Hewlett-Packard's joint venture maintained a market share of 18 percent for the HP 150-II, at a price that was 61 percent higher than the U.S. price. In 1985 both companies lobbied actively against the liberalization of Mexico's informatics policy, lest a more open regime undermine the comfortable positions they occupied in the sheltered local market.

In the computer and electronics industry the spread of backward linkages was even more disappointing than in the automotive industry. To meet domestic-content requirements in Mexico, for example, foreign investors contracted out for cables, resistors, keyboards, cabinets, and other passive components for production runs of a few thousand units a year. For such small orders, local companies used older materials, such as fiberglass and aluminum, for cabinets and cases, rather than the newer, lighter composite materials; they also utilized less sophisticated assembly techniques, such as hand-soldering, rather than high-volume, high-precision, automated operations.[17]

In Mexico, local suppliers of foreign computer firms were unable to adopt the sophisticated quality-control and large-batch testing procedures used by host-country suppliers, under the careful guidance of exported-oriented foreign investors, in the more open economies of Hong Kong, Malaysia, and Singapore. Despite the domestic-content requirements in place during the era of import substitution, the later liberalization of trade and investment saw an increase in the integration of the computer industry in Mexico and a decrease in the level of imports as a percentage of production.[18]

Toward a New Paradigm

The detrimental effects of trying to use domestic-content and joint-venture requirements to enlarge foreign investors' contribution to host-country development were not limited to the automotive and computer and electronics sectors. Small, inefficient plants using designated amounts of high-cost local inputs provided a negative demonstration of the "infant-industry formula" across other industrial sectors as well. As a result of joint-venture requirements, foreign investors transferred technologies and business practices that were three years older, or more, than those transferred to wholly owned subsidiaries.[19] And where host countries prevented foreign investors from operating wholly owned subsidiaries, no amount of effort to strengthen the protection of intellectual property rights could compensate for the foreign investors' reluctance to use their most advanced techniques.[20] Nor have parent firms provided as much practical assistance for partially owned affiliates—for example, sending host-country employees to headquarters for training, or sending experts from headquarters to conduct training in the host country—as they have for wholly owned subsidiaries.[21]

Domestic-content and joint-venture mandates have not only failed to lay the foundation for the success of infant industries but appear to do absolute damage to the host-country's development prospects. On the basis of more than ten years of data collected from 183 projects in some thirty developing countries, cost-benefit analysis showed that a majority of foreign investor operations generated an increase in the income of the host country (of between 55 and 75 percent, depending on shadow-price estimates).[22] At the same time, however, the analysis revealed that a large minority of operations (25 to 45 percent) actually lessened the income of the host country; that is, the developing country would have been better off if it had not hosted these foreign investment projects at all. The effect of foreign investment on the host country's economic welfare depended principally on the level of protection associated with the foreign firms' operations (including the protection afforded by domestic content requirements): projects with little or no protection tended to enhance the welfare of the host country, and those with high protection tended to damage it. Export-oriented projects, which were typically wholly or majority-owned by the foreign parent and free of domestic-content requirements, had a uniformly positive effect on the host country.[23]

Developing countries discovered early on that foreign investors seldom set up export-oriented manufacturing facilities—in low-skill or higher-skill activities, within or outside of EPZs—as other than wholly owned (or at least majority-owned) plants free of domestic-content requirements. As the use of the term *screwdriver operations* implied, the conventional wisdom—even among some authorities in the most successful Asian tigers, as well as elsewhere in the developing world—was that such facilities would generate negligible backward linkages or spillovers, and therefore had little to offer in the way of dynamic contributions to the economic welfare of the host country. For reasons that have become quite clear, at least in hindsight, the reality has turned out quite differently.

When firms build subsidiary plants to produce goods that are crucial to their competitive position in international markets, it is in their self-interest to ensure that those plants perform at the highest level possible in terms of quality, reliability, timeliness, and price. The plants are designed to capture all potential economies of scale, and to sustain a position at the cutting edge of industry best practices. The relationship between the parent firm and the subsidiary is much closer, and more potent, than the term *outsourcing*—which seems to imply that the parent firm is merely shopping around for the cheapest inputs—suggests. "Parental supervision" of the subsidiary is intimate and ongoing, and both technologies and business practices are frequently upgraded—a process that the telecommunications revolution of recent years has rendered even more rapid. The dynamic nature of the alliance between the parent firm and its subsidiaries is in sharp contrast to the distant and hesitant arrangements that emerge when host countries impose domestic-content and joint-venture requirements.

Furthermore, the close connections between the parent and the sub-sidiary can extend backwards to local suppliers—a finding that may at first seem surprising, in light of the multinational corporations' desire to maintain "unambiguous control" over technology and business prac-tices and to avoid being saddled with technology-sharing requirements. The phenomenon becomes more understandable, however, in light of Richard Caves's distinction between the horizontal and vertical transfer of technology and management techniques.[24] On the horizontal axis, international companies closely guard against the dispersion of technol-ogy or business practices, so as not to create competitors. On the verti-cal axis, however, foreign investors' desire to strengthen their position in international markets may lead them to build up a cadre of timely, reli-able, and low-cost suppliers. Thus, self-interest becomes a powerful tool for generating backward linkages from the foreign investor to suppliers (both foreign-owned and indigenously owned) in the host economy, and is typically coupled with larger-scale subsidiary operations than are found in highly protected, domestically oriented plants. Although the automotive and computer and electronics sectors again provide the most thorough data on the development of international sourcing networks, supplemental evidence from other industries shows that these two sec-tors are not exceptional.

THE NEW PARADIGM AND THE AUTO INDUSTRY. In what may have been the first deliberate attempt at international sourcing in the automotive industry, GM decided, in the late 1970s, that to meet the competition from the lower-priced Japanese cars that were flooding the American market, it would build full-scale, wholly owned plants in Mexico and Brazil to produce engines that would be interchangeable with those of the Pontiac automobiles made at U.S. plants.[25] Within eighteen months of GM's decision, Chrysler, Ford, Nissan, and Volkswagen followed suit, establishing plants in Mexico and Brazil.[26] Within the first six years, automotive exports from Mexico grew by a factor of ten, to $1.5 billion a year, and from Brazil by a factor of three, to $3 billion a year.

The decision to stake the parent company's competitive position in its home market on the performance of engines and other components manufactured offshore brought a new intensity to the relationship between the parent and subsidiary firms. Training took on a heightened importance: in addition to receiving instruction in the technical skills needed to run the machinery used in full-scale engine production, workers and managers participated in quality circles and were taught to undertake production audits and to implement zero-defects procedures.

By the mid-1980s Mexican auto workers numbered more than 100,000, and the hourly wages in their collective labor contracts ranged from $0.62 to $1.44 (not including benefits); the average hourly wage of their counterparts in the automotive industry in the United States at that time was $12. The Mexican auto workers' wages were the second-highest in the country, trailing only those of employees in the state-owned petroleum sector.[27] Relations between the foreign auto firms and Mexican unions were not always smooth, however. The unions sought to limit foreign companies' freedom to determine job classifications, and engaged in strikes to prevent the use of quality circles and other similar practices. The unions also fought to centralize collective bargaining and to restrict not only the companies' power to order layoffs but also their authority to conduct their own hiring.[28] With the Mexican economic crisis of 1982, however, the foreign auto firms managed to roll back what they regarded as excessively rigid limitations on job classifications, hirings, and layoffs, and to gain acceptance for quality circles, team-coordinated production, and other new human-relations practices.

At the end of the 1980s, one of GM's plants in Mexico achieved the lowest number of quality-related rejects in the company's worldwide production system, and GM headquarters began to assign responsibility for various engineering design functions to its Delphi Automotive Systems division, in Ciudad Juarez.[29] According to independent tracking agencies, the export-oriented assembly plant that Ford had built in Hermosillo, to challenge the Japanese competition in the U.S. market, achieved higher quality ratings than other producers in the United States or Japan.[30]

In Brazil, U.S., European, and Japanese auto and auto-parts investors designed local plants to produce perfect substitutes for engines and other parts sourced from anywhere in the world. GM, in particular, began to use the country as a training ground for senior managers hoping for promotion in Detroit. "We can take what we've learned in the manufacturing and technology in Brazil and apply that in the United States, and that's every bit my intention," asserted Mark T. Hogan, the latest in a series of former presidents of Brazilian operations who were brought back, during the 1990s, to run major GM divisions in the United States.[31]

In Asia, the pivotal event that led to offshore sourcing in the automotive sector was the competition Thailand managed to generate, in 1985, among one European and three Japanese investor groups: offering to lower domestic-content requirements on all Thai production for any investor who would establish a full-scale export plant to build diesel engines for one-ton trucks, Thailand then allowed all four entrants to "win" the competition, leading to an eightfold increase in automotive exports—to more than $2 billion annually—within the first five years.[32] Eager to maintain their reputation for reliability in the truck market, the Japanese investors brought to the Thai plants the same rigorous intolerance for defects that they were famous for at home.

GM's Szentgotthard facility, a full-scale plant established in Hungary to build 1.4- and 1.6-liter engines for GM's Opel, which is sold throughout the European Union, offers perhaps the most detailed illustration of "parental concern" about the performance of a subsidiary that is to be incorporated into the parent firm's sourcing network. In contrast to the autos produced for domestic consumption at the small, inefficient Hungarian assembly plant described earlier, the output of GM's export-oriented engine plant at Szentgotthard had to be indistinguishable in performance and reliability from engines produced at similar facilities in Germany and the United Kingdom.[33] GM launched the plant as a test facility in 1992, with "half-module" dimensions, producing 200,000 units a year. The design of the engine machining and cylinder-head production processes made it possible to implement changes rapidly, within extremely narrow tolerances, without rebuilding the line. Thus, each of the three shifts of Hungarian workers and managers had to be equipped to answer call checks and troubleshoot as well as to maintain line operations.

Of the Hungarians initially selected to work at the plant, 65 percent had degrees from technical or vocational schools, and 30 percent had college or university degrees. Employees in the 890 production-line jobs were put through a twelve-week, on-the-job training sequence in which they were taught to work in teams while they acquired functional skills. Those who passed received wages and social contributions totaling $540 a month, or approximately $3.00 an hour—a wage rate that was almost twice the national average, but that was nonetheless no more than one-tenth the cost of a counterpart GM worker at a plant in Germany. Host-country candidates for managerial positions, after a test period at the Szentgotthard site, were sent to other GM plants in Europe for approximately six months of operational training. At the initiation of operations, seven of the nine most senior managers came from posts in Europe or the United States, and two from Hungary. By 1995 the proportions were reversed: six were Hungarians who had completed the EU-based on-the-job training, and three were from outside Hungary.

GM opted to expand the Hungarian plant to full scale (460,000 units a year) only after internal audits showed, in 1995, that the Hungarian output met specifications identical to those already established in sister plants in Europe. Although GM had entered Hungary as a joint-venture partner with the state-owned Raba auto-parts manufacturer, the company shed its local partner before proceeding with the expansion of the engine facility.[34]

In the case of plants whose output is incorporated into Volkswagen (VW) automobiles sold in international markets, the link between VW headquarters and subsidiaries in developing countries is similarly close. Volkswagen produces four categories of components—engines, axles, chassis, and gear boxes—at full-scale, wholly owned plants in Argentina, Brazil, Mexico, and Eastern Europe. To ensure that each component in each category is indistinguishable from corresponding components produced at any other plant, the workers, managers, and production facilities at each plant are set up to incorporate new engineering changes into the production schedule within sixteen hours.[35]

Although, as noted in chapter 3, some automotive parts are produced in export processing zones, the spread of the global sourcing networks of the major auto firms has proceeded quite independently of the EPZ phenomenon in the principal Latin American, Asian, and Eastern European host economies. Regardless of where they locate their plants, however, the parent companies have insisted on duty-free inputs, freedom from domestic-content and technology-sharing requirements, and full ownership of their local affiliates. In 1996, when GM chose Thailand as the site for its first export-oriented assembly plant in Southeast Asia, the host country's willingness to let the subsidiary operate without domestic-content or joint-venture restrictions was cited by the company as a key criterion in site selection; this freedom was highly valuable, in GM's view, because it would permit the rapid integration of the most advanced engineering and management procedures.[36]

The parent investors' assiduous efforts to ensure the quality and reliability of the sourcing network have extended beyond the investors' own subsidiaries to local suppliers. In Mexico, for example, foreign auto investors supplied technical assistance, insisted on weekly coordination meetings and production audits, and set up regular training meetings to teach local firms about zero-defect, just-in-time, and other cost-saving procedures.[37] According to the Mexican suppliers, these measures—

along with an infusion of "team spirit"—lowered costs and raised quality. Within five years after the establishment of export-oriented foreign plants, 115 local auto-parts firms had sales greater than $1 million each, and 40 had sales greater than $10 million. More than half of the auto parts and accessories (excluding engines) manufactured in Mexico were produced by indigenous firms, and of the thirty largest auto-parts exporters, sixteen were entirely Mexican owned. This creation of backward linkages in the auto industry—and in the computer and electronics industry, which will be examined next—was in marked contrast to the *maquiladora* experience, in which use of Mexican inputs was minimal until foreign investors became able to locate their plants throughout the economy, and NAFTA trade liberalization came into play.

In Thailand, to instill the same devotion to quality and punctuality that was the hallmark of the production system in the home market, Japanese investors set up "cooperation clubs" for assemblers and local suppliers.[38] In addition to hosting "social gatherings" to create "deeper relationships" between Thai producers and Japanese purchasers, these clubs sponsored factory visits; technical guidance; workshops on quality improvement and cost reduction; and training trips to Japan. In the first decade after the beginning of offshore sourcing, eighty-three wholly owned Thai producers were certified as Original Equipment Manufacturer (OEM) suppliers to the Japanese multinationals.[39] More than half reported receiving technical assistance from Japanese investors in their quest for OEM qualification. Some 200 to 250 additional Thai firms achieved Replacement Equipment Manufacturer (REM) status.

THE NEW PARADIGM AND THE COMPUTER AND ELECTRONICS INDUSTRY. In the computer and electronics sector, the decision on the part of U.S. and European firms to move their labor-intensive operations offshore— first to Asia, and later to Latin America, to meet competition from low-cost Japanese and Korean exports—is a well-known story, reviewed in part in the discussion of EPZs in chapter 3. Less well known is the fact that the development of international sourcing networks was not merely a matter of searching out the lowest-cost assembly sites in the lowest-wage countries; instead, it can more accurately be described as an increasingly intense effort, on the part of the parent firms, to build a production base that was integrated closely into their global competitive strategies, and that could be upgraded even more rapidly than that of the automotive industry. Beginning with hand-assembly of printed circuit boards (PCBs) in Hong Kong and Singapore, and later in Malaysia and Thailand, the subsidiaries of General Electric, Motorola, National Semiconductor, and Philips climbed steadily up a technological ladder that eventually required the installation of high-precision, computer-controlled systems for the large-scale assembly and testing of semiconductor and telecommunications components. During this transition, a study from the factory floor of four subsidiaries of one U.S. firm in Malaysia documented a steady flow of modifications in machinery and changes in testing procedures, both of which were accompanied by the rapid retraining of workers to supplement their skill sets.[40] The foreign plants were wholly owned, large enough to capture full economies of scale, and free of domestic-content or technology-sharing requirements. As an executive from Texas Instruments observed, "We came for the cheap labor and the tax advantages, but we are staying because of the expertise we have built up here. As far as assembly and testing are concerned we have more expertise here than we have in the U.S. We sometimes have to send our Malaysian engineers to the States to solve their problems."[41]

In their search for superior assembly processes many of the multinational computer and electronics firms began assigning their Southeast Asian subsidiaries with responsibility for design and development as well as manufacturing.[42] Hewlett-Packard turned over tooling development and process design for portable printers, desktop computers, and servers, and Motorola did the same for circuit boards, disk drives, and peripherals. Aiming to lower costs and to reduce the time between the design and delivery of new printer models, Matsushita Electric reassigned die-making to the region,[43] as did Seiko Epson, for new television models.

In Latin America, the insistence of many governments on reserving portions of their computer and electronics sector for national companies—and on requiring joint-venture, domestic-content, and technology-sharing arrangements in the remainder—effectively blocked multinational firms from integrating regional plants into their global production strategies. As discussed earlier, under the informatics regime in place until 1985, Apple and Hewlett-Packard plants, each with a mandatory Mexican partner, assembled kits from abroad, in mini–production runs far below the scale required for maximum efficiency, using techniques (hand-soldering) and inputs (fiberglass rather than lightweight composites) well behind what was demanded in international markets. When President de la Madrid decided to approve IBM's proposal to build a wholly owned plant, free of domestic-content or joint-venture requirements, for integration into the parent firm's hemispheric network for the production of computers and electronic typewriters, the new operation turned out to be ten times larger than any other facility in the Mexican market.[44] Not only did the IBM plant use automated, high-precision assembly techniques and quality-control procedures—continuously updated in response to innovation cycles in the United States—but Mexican suppliers were able, for the first time, to make profitable use of sophisticated production techniques and materials.

Despite the absence of explicit requirements for domestic content, the level of integration in the Mexican computer sector actually increased: imports as a percentage of production declined, and IBM's use of local suppliers grew steadily.[45] Hewlett-Packard then reversed direction and copied IBM, building a new, wholly owned export operation in Mexico. Exports of computers and electronic typewriters climbed by a factor of ten in less than five years: 60 percent of the increase originated with IBM and 20 percent with Hewlett-Packard.

Observing this positive demonstration effect, major, system-integrating electronics companies—including Ericsson and Motorola—chose to build export-oriented assembly plants in Mexico; they were followed by contract manufacturers such as Flextronics, SCI, and Selectron. In 1991 Ericsson designated Mexico as the company's only site for software engineering in the Western Hemisphere (outside of the United States); Motorola followed suit in 1999, equipping its software center in Puebla with engineers originally trained in Ericsson's facility.[46] The presence of export-oriented foreign investment in Mexico produced clearly identifiable externalities for the host economy, moreover, by stimulating increases in unrelated exports from Mexican firms, purely as a function of the Mexican firms' proximity to the foreign plants.[47]

In Asia the development of backward linkages in the computer and electronics sector began tentatively, but soon far overshadowed what had already occurred in the automotive industry. In the early stages—in the late 1970s, in Singapore and Hong Kong—the pattern of foreign investment might accurately be characterized as a search for inexpensive inputs. But the buyer-seller relationship soon evolved into one in which local suppliers undertook carefully monitored contract manufacturing of PCBs and other subassemblies, power supplies, mechanical parts, and some chips. By 1981 one U.S. semiconductor investor in Singapore was purchasing components from some 200 local suppliers.[48] Six of the investor's largest ten suppliers (by value of purchases) were affiliates of other Japanese, American, or European multinationals; the other four were Singaporean companies. The investor provided the local firms with technical plans and detailed specifications for parts and assisted with the installation of quality-control procedures; the multinational's own engineers from the United States provided troubleshooting assistance.

A second consumer electronics manufacturer, from Europe, made four of its largest contract-manufacturing arrangements with other foreign affiliates, and four with Singaporean firms.[49] The European multinational helped the Singaporean suppliers automate their production facilities—even, at times, buying the necessary machinery and renting it to the suppliers, then taking payment in the form of future deliveries. As part of the package, the firm also helped to retrain the suppliers' work force.

To enable the Singaporean suppliers to achieve economies of scale, both the American and the European investors walked the Singaporean suppliers through the process of penetrating international markets. The Singaporean suppliers began by supplying sister plants of the parent firms, then began selling to independent external buyers. Three indigenous firms (Flextronics, NatSteel Electronics, and Venture) that began by supplying PCBs to the local affiliates of foreign firms grew to be among the top ten contract manufacturers of electronics in the world.[50]

In Malaysia the development of backward linkages was slower—and more tortuous. Malaysia's strategy was a prime example of the use of EPZs to attract foreign investors in the computer and electronics sector. As noted in chapter 3, however, EPZs are of limited use in creating a large and vigorous base of local suppliers unless the indigenous firms, both within and outside the zones, have the same advantages provided foreign investors: freedom from duties; business-friendly treatment; adequate infrastructure; and access to pools of skilled labor. In contrast to the approach used in Malaysia, authorities in both Singapore and Hong Kong essentially turned each country, in its entirety, into a single, integrated EPZ.

Over time, however, foreign computer and electronics investors in Malaysia began to generate backward linkages similar to those that had been established in other countries. One study of seven semiconductor and telecommunications multinationals (five American, one Japanese, and one Canadian) showed that the foreign affiliates steadily expanded their subcontracting relationships with indigenous machine-tool firms: they began by ordering parts that involved simple stamping and machining, then provided prototypes for machinery used in the assembly and testing of electronics components, then began to work with the suppliers to jointly develop advanced new devices to mount wafers and accomplish other complicated tasks in the production of semiconductors.[51] Of the nine machine-tool firms, seven had been created by entrepreneurs previously employed at the foreign plants; 10 percent of the workers in the supplier companies had also been employed at the foreign plants.

As the backward linkages grew, the foreign firms began to contract out for design as well as production services, assigning their own engineers to work jointly with those of the host-country firms. During the 1980s the interaction between the foreign investors and the local suppliers became less unequal and more interactive, with managers and engineers from the foreign firms instructing less, and collaborating more, with their counterparts at the indigenous firms.

As was the case in Singapore, all the Malaysian suppliers reported that they had entered export markets through channels provided by the foreign investors—assistance that enabled the suppliers to become high-volume producers. Seven of the nine Malaysian machine-tool companies shipped their goods to the parent firms' sister plants in Korea, Southeast Asia, and the United States. Within the first ten years of operation, two of the nine had also won orders from independent buyers, outcompeting machine-tool makers in Germany, Japan, and Taiwan in the process. As they began to concentrate on more advanced operations, the Malaysian firms developed second- and third-tier Malaysian suppliers, to whom they delegated less complicated tasks.

A separate study of backward integration, conducted in 1995, found that for nine wholly owned Japanese investors, local procurement had climbed to 37 percent of total output: Japanese firms in Malaysia accounted for 60 percent of the suppliers (by number) and 83 percent of the value of procurement; other foreign firms constituted 17 percent of the suppliers (by number) and 10 percent of the value of procurement; and local Malaysian firms constituted 24 percent of the suppliers (by number) and 10 percent of the value of procurement. As in the case of the local machine-tool industry, the Japanese investors provided the Malaysian suppliers with "deliberate transfers of technology," in the form of product design specifications, process technologies, assistance in the use of assembly equipment, and troubleshooting for technical problems.[52] There is evidence that similar patterns of evolution occurred among Malaysian firms involved in circuit design and other microelectronics assembly processes.

Perhaps no sector reveals more clearly than the hard disk drive industry the need for close integration between the parent and its subsidiaries.[53] Disk drives are plates, containing highly compacted data, which spin at a rate of many thousands of revolutions a minute. Disk heads, held by a suspension above or below the disk, find information at an ultra-precise location on the disk and transmit it to the computer's processors. In 1984, two years after it had developed the first hard disk drive for use in desktop computers in Silicon Valley, Seagate Technology began to assemble disk drive components in Singapore. Within five years, eleven other U.S. assembly firms followed, making Singapore the world's largest producer of hard disk drives: by 1990, 55 percent of all units shipped in international markets were produced in Singapore.

With the launch of each new generation of disk drives, the foreign investors would bring managers, engineers, and as many as two dozen operators from the offshore site to try out a pilot version of the proposed production line in the United States. Ten or more home-country engineers would follow the production team back to the offshore site to set up the new line, and to help troubleshoot until rejection rates stabilized and production objectives had been met.

By paying $1.00 an hour to assemble in Singapore, versus $5.00 to $6.00 an hour to assemble in Silicon Valley, disk drive producers found that they could reduce the share of labor from 25 percent to 5 percent, while maintaining sufficient productivity to cut unit costs. Offsetting this advantage, however, were higher transportation costs, quality-control problems, and trans-Pacific communication difficulties. Instead of pulling back, however, Seagate and other firms began to shift larger segments of the value chain to Singapore and to integrate home and offshore operations even more closely. At the same time, they encouraged their own U.S. suppliers to set up operations near their offshore plants.

In addition to reducing transportation costs, the strategy of colocating larger and larger portions of the production chain allows faster feedback and facilitates joint problem solving. For example, plant-level studies show that after a new product has been codesigned with suppliers, assemblers may discover that some mismatch—which does not become apparent until a large volume of the product has been produced—is causing a high rejection rate. Coordinating with a supplier in the United States might take a week—more time than is affordable for an offshore assembler with two weeks of unusable product already in the pipeline. Engineers from colocated suppliers, in contrast, could be at the plant within an hour and fashion a solution for trial within a day.

To participate effectively in offshore supply relationships with the major assemblers, component producers demanded the same essential operating conditions that the assemblers had—namely, freedom to set up wholly owned ventures, to bring inputs into the host country duty-free, and to operate without domestic-content requirements. Working with host-country development agencies, the disk drive assemblers and foreign component makers devoted considerable effort to identifying local firms to provide subassemblies, other inputs, and services that might provide a competitive edge in international markets—a process that will receive more detailed examination shortly.

Rising wage rates and more demanding quality-control specifications contributed to the increasing automation of production in Singapore, and in the second half of the 1980s, both assemblers and component producers began to shift more labor-intensive segments of the industry to Malaysia and Thailand. Disk drive–related exports from Thailand, which had been $2.6 million in 1985, had reached $1.3 billion by 1990. Seagate became the largest private employer in Malaysia, Singapore, and Thailand. By 1995 70 percent of the world's supply of disk drives came from Southeast Asia. Eighty-six percent of all firms that made disk heads or head assemblies had operations there, and component producers had begun to add plants in China, Indonesia, and the Philippines. The principal alternative locations in the developing world were Brazil, Mexico, and Puerto Rico.

The advantages of colocating assemblers and component producers were not limited to foreign firms and their foreign suppliers. Working with host-country development agencies, the disk drive assemblers and foreign component makers, such as Conner Peripherals, Maxtor, Seagate, and Tandon, set up vendor-development programs to secure PCBs, precision-tooled products, and motor assemblies from local firms, adding to the indigenous contract-manufacturing base associated with computers, semiconductors, and other electronics that was discussed earlier in this chapter. Some foreign firms sent engineers to check in on their principal suppliers daily, and some indigenous suppliers delivered specially machined parts and components to the foreign assemblers two and three times a day.

Overall, foreign investment in the disk drive industry provides a particularly vivid example of processes observed in other segments of the computer and electronics sector, and in the automotive industry as well.

—A dynamic relationship develops between parent firms and their subsidiaries when the parent firm depends on the subsidiaries to maintain a competitive position in international markets.

—Somewhat counterintuitively, backward linkages may be larger and more robust when foreign suppliers and assemblers are free to carry out operations as they wish, than when the host country imposes domestic-content and joint-venture requirements.

—The mere presence of foreign suppliers and assemblers provides an opportunity for the creation and expansion of indigenous firms.

Singapore and Malaysia were particularly successful in the last endeavor. The next section examines the measures those two countries used to foster the development of local suppliers.

EXPANDING BACKWARD LINKAGES TO INDIGENOUS SUPPLIERS. Chapter 2 listed the basic ingredients needed for local supplier firms to flourish. The first ingredient is a stable macroeconomic environment for locally owned businesses to operate in. No less than foreign firms, national companies need low inflation and realistic exchange rates. The second ingredient is for host-country authorities to reduce or eliminate the impediments to the operations of local firms, just as they do for foreigners: that is, to allow access to duty-free imports and to reliable infrastructure services; to minimize bureaucratic red tape, corruption, and discrimination; and to ensure the transparency and efficiency of institutions such as courts and regulatory agencies. The third ingredient is for host-country authorities to enlarge the supply of both capital and skilled labor (workers, technicians, engineers, and managers) available to local firms.

The goal is to create a vibrant national business community that, instead of being dependent on special favors and on protection from competition, is accustomed to meeting the standards of quality and price demanded by open markets and willing to take whatever risks are required for business expansion. Beyond fostering the creation of such a community, however, what particular steps should host governments take to support local suppliers and nurture local supplier relationships? The answer to this question raises further questions that have not been well-studied in the literature on backward linkages.

—How can host authorities provide special assistance to certain firms, workers, or communities while avoiding the cronyism that has so often accompanied the provision of public subsidies in the developing world?

—What market failures should host-country strategists address, and what positive externalities should they try to capture? And how can they avoid creating yet more local actors intent on wrenching scarce resources away from other, equally deserving claimants?

—Should host authorities create special means of providing capital to small local suppliers, or to local suppliers of any size, at the inevitable expense of the broader universe of host-economy firms?

—Should host authorities create special educational programs to target the skills needed by companies that aspire to become suppliers to foreign exporters, or should educational resources be directed toward the forms of training that are most needed by workers in the economy at large?

David McKendrick, Richard Doner, and Stephan Haggard suggest that the experiences of Singapore and Malaysia show how host-country authorities can, with reasonable success, nurture indigenous supplier firms and link them up with foreign investors while avoiding the potential pitfalls associated with such efforts.[54] Singapore is their preferred model.

As noted in chapter 3, the Economic Development Board of Singapore was among the first investment-promotion agencies in the developing world to acquire industry-specific expertise, which the board then deployed aggressively to seek out and attract foreign investors. Building on the largest technical and engineering base and the best infrastructure facilities in Southeast Asia, the country's 1991 strategic plan identified information technology and precision engineering as the two sectors in which Singapore would try to build clusters of foreign investors and local suppliers. While other less developed countries were still waiting for multinational firms to show up at their door, were still greeting them with ambivalence, and were still imposing domestic-content and joint-venture and other technology-sharing requirements on them, Singapore pioneered the approach identified in chapter 3 as "marketing the country."

The Singapore EDB was endowed with sufficient authority to gain approvals rapidly and to ensure that host-country promises were carried out. Working with the EDB, the Local Industry Upgrading Program (LIUP) had responsibility for linking potential local suppliers to foreign investors. Using EDB funds, the LIUP paid the salary of an LIUP manager on the staff of each participating multinational investor. To justify the salary subsidy, the LIUP manager had to show that the foreign investor was trying to identify local companies that had the potential to become globally competitive as suppliers, and was including managers and engineers from such local companies in its own quality- or process-training programs.

As part of vendor development, the foreign affiliate often recommended that local firms buy specific machinery to improve their performance in a particular operation. On the basis of such recommendations, the Small Industry Finance Scheme, along with the LIUP, helped local firms purchase the designated equipment. To acquire the skills needed to meet the performance criteria of the foreign affiliate, each local supplier had access to the Skills Development Fund, which was financed by a compulsory payroll tax. Both indigenous and foreign firms could recoup their tax contributions by sending their employees to government-approved training programs, and the foreign investors helped to determine what kinds of training programs would gain approval. As wage rates rose in Singapore, the EDB upgraded the training programs for local suppliers and created incentive packages to encourage foreign investors to incorporate higher-end, more automated operations.

In addition to the Singapore EDB, McKendrick, Doner, and Haggard investigated Malaysia's Penang Development Corporation (PDC). Although Malaysia had a much lower proportion of scientists and engineers than Singapore, in terms of absolute numbers Malaysia had more than twice as many people enrolled in computer, math, engineering, and social science classes. Malaysia's infrastructure, however, was decidedly less well developed than that of Singapore. And the central control that Kuala Lumpur exercised over policy instruments, including subsidies and tax concessions, complicated the coordination of policies aimed at developing foreign investment and local suppliers. As noted earlier, Malaysia relied on EPZs, of which the Penang export processing zone was the most prominent, to attract foreign direct investment, whereas Singapore had essentially created a nationwide EPZ.

To rectify these deficiencies, the PDC used whatever autonomy it could gain from a supportive state government, strengthening infrastructure services and troubleshooting delays in the provision of central-government benefits to foreign investors. To strengthen links between local firms and foreign investors, the PDC began to construct industrial areas adjacent to the EPZ for use by local firms, and compiled directories of supporting industries that were tailored to the specific needs of foreign investors.

In 1989 the state government established the Penang Skills Development Center, a private entity that was awarded publicly funded buildings to use for its training activities. As in the case of Singapore, because the development center's courses had government accreditation, both local and foreign firms could tap into the Human Development Fund (financed by a 1 percent levy on corporate payrolls) to pay to send employees to the center. Through the first half of the 1990s courses focused on basic assembly-line work, including time and information management, statistics, and team building; in the second half of the decade the curriculum emphasis shifted to specific gaps in skills that had been identified by the companies themselves (part of the purpose of the training was to short-circuit a pattern that had developed, in which companies tried to steal each other's best employees). The foreign firms often provided instructors. In 1992 the Penang Industrial Council created a center devoted to the needs of small and medium-sized local firms, organizing training in finance, technology enhancement, quality management, and occupational safety to help overcome the problems smaller firms faced in trying to become vendors to foreign investors.

In describing the vendor-development programs in Singapore and Malaysia, McKendrick, Doner, and Haggard do not address some of the public policy trade-offs—that is, between providing subsidies and preferential services for smaller versus larger firms, or between sponsoring general versus specialized training. But their analysis does suggest that there may be some promise in an approach that does not pressure foreign firms to use choose favored suppliers or to buy specified amounts of domestic input, but that instead uses foreign investors as a screening mechanism—to identify potential suppliers who can then, with state assistance, follow the foreign investors' recommendations. In Singapore and Malaysia, the vendor-development programs appeared to be sufficiently transparent and competitive to avoid the ever-present risk of favoritism. To justify spending public funds on potential suppliers to foreign investors (as opposed to spending those funds on programs that might benefit all local businesses equally), McKendrick, Doner, and Haggard argue that the foreign-local export clusters generated various externalities for the host economy: the movement of workers and managers among firms; the nearly instantaneous matching of machinery purchases and imitation of successful production and quality-control procedures by proximate rival companies; the accumulated knowledge that suppliers with multiple clients could apply to new orders; and the coaching that foreign investors provided to assist local producers in expanding their exports. The researchers also argue that the host countries gained both the economies of scale and the specialization in niche tasks that come with the agglomeration of interrelated activities. Finally, public support for training helped address the "public goods" problem—that is, the reluctance of private firms to invest extensively in training workers and managers in the face of job-hopping and poaching during periods of high demand for workers and managers.

CONTRACT MANUFACTURING AND OEM RELATIONSHIPS AS A PART OF DEVELOPMENT STRATEGY. Increased scrutiny of the way in which multinational corporations provide a channel through which technology and management know-how can reach local suppliers has led to something of a reinterpretation of the sources of the Asian tigers' development success. The conventional view of the export-led growth of the Asian tigers contrasts Hong Kong and Singapore's open approach to trade and foreign investment with Korea's more closed approach (leaving Taiwan somewhere in between). In this rendition, Hong Kong and Singapore fostered relations with multinational companies and used them as a central vehicle in their development strategies; Korea and Taiwan did not. A more recent view, championed by Michael Hobday, holds that that this apparent dichotomy has diverted attention from what might be an important underlying similarity.[55] In fact, all four countries built their modern export sectors by relying on contract manufacturing and OEM (Original Equipment Manufacturing) relationships between domestic firms and foreign multinationals. The OEM production pattern was most pronounced in the computer and electronics industry but was evident in other sectors (including cameras and bicycles) as well. All four countries used versions of the same model, in which international companies provided local firms with design plans, process technology, and quality-control procedures, and ensured that the local firms were equipped to meet demanding specifications for goods sold in international markets under the parent firm's brand name.

In the case of Korea, the celebrated *chaebol* that grew to worldwide prominence in electronics actually began operations via subcontracting arrangements with wholly owned subsidiaries of multinational corporations located within the Korean economy; the subsidiaries produced more than 70 percent of all electronics exports at the end of the 1960s, and still accounted for 40 percent of all electronics exports a decade later. As the share of exports from the Korean *chaebol* firms expanded, the largest channel for entry into international markets came via OEM relationships. At the end of the 1980s, 60 to 70 percent of all electronics exports left Korea under OEM contracts with foreign multinationals. Even for the largest *chaebol*—Samsung, Lucky Goldstar, and Hyundai—the figure was 60 percent.[56] Thus, although Korean authorities did eventually restrict the presence of foreign direct investors in the course of promoting the indigenous *chaebol*, they continued to use the OEM channel to penetrate international markets. The paucity of second- and third-tier indigenous supplier industries in Korea may be traced, in large part, to the requirement that foreign investors relinquish a direct presence in the country and deal only with the designated *chaebol*.[57]

Similarly, in Taiwan, production of computer and electronic products for export began in plants owned by DEC, IBM, Philips, Hitachi, Texas Instruments, and other multinationals. As late as 1989, the combined share of exports from such firms still totaled approximately 35 percent.[58] A large number of small Taiwanese suppliers, meanwhile, moved up the ladder from selling the foreign assemblers components for consumer electronics (such as calculators, electronic clocks, and videocassette recorders) to undertaking contract manufacturing of computer products (such as monitors, motherboards, and power supplies). The more skillful—ACER, Mitac, Tatung, and Wyse, for example—evolved from selling assemblies and subassemblies under OEM arrangements with the foreign multinationals to producing personal computers of their own design that were marketed under the buyer's label.

There is thus more of a common path in the diverse experiences of Hong Kong, Singapore, Korea, and Taiwan than is customarily recognized.[59] The pressure of meeting changing specifications and providing more advanced capabilities in the context of international markets led indigenous firms in all four countries, under the guidance of multinational companies, to move from Original Equipment Manufacturing (OEM) to Original Design Manufacturing (ODM)—and, in the most successful cases, to Own Brand Manufacturing (OBM) in competition with the leaders in the industry. This process combined teaching and coaching on the part of foreign purchasers with imitation, catch-up, and incremental innovation on the part of the indigenous producers. The potential for local firms to follow this path all the way to the end is likely to depend on the level of technological sophistication and the pace of change in each individual industry.

In a study of computer and electronics producers in Hong Kong, Indonesia, Malaysia, the Philippines, Singapore, South Korea, Taiwan, and Thailand, Robert Lipsey has found two categories of outcome, depending on the type of industry.[60] In the electrical machinery classification (consisting largely of consumer electronics and parts) for these eight countries, subsidiaries of U.S. and Japanese investors produced more than half of all exports in 1977, but by the mid-1990s had been overtaken by indigenous producers and accounted for only 22 percent of exports. In the nonelectrical machinery classification (consisting mainly of computers, accessories, and parts), where the pace of innovation was higher, subsidiaries of U.S. and Japanese investors accounted for more than 20 percent of exports at the end of the 1980s and remained roughly at that level throughout the 1990s, although the absolute levels of exports from local producers expanded steadily.

Foreign Direct Investment and Development: New Assessments

This chapter has shifted the focus from a scenario in which foreign investors provide jobs to the lowest-paid workers in the lowest-skill jobs to one in which foreign investors position their subsidiaries and suppliers—and their managers and workers—along the cutting edge of industry best practices. In the second scenario, the contribution to development comes not only from the creation of higher-paid jobs but from the continuous upgrading of plant operations and workers' skills to meet competitive conditions in international markets, and from the creation of dynamic linkages to other firms and workers in the domestic market. How large are the gains to host countries when foreign investors play this role—and how large are the losses when they cannot?

Early efforts to assess foreign investors' potential contribution to a host economy sprang from attempts to explain the unusually large economic gains that were observed when host countries loosened restrictions on the importation of capital goods.[61] One way to view the imported machinery was simply as an addition to the country's physical capital. But this view far underestimated the actual impact, because advanced capital goods embodied new technologies and production processes, developed elsewhere, that the host economy could incorporate without having to pay all the accumulated research and development costs. Thus, the globalization of production does not simply mean that host economies in the developing world can more effectively perform the tasks consigned to them by comparative advantage, but that they can enter entirely new realms of activity.

As noted earlier in this chapter, endogenous growth theory, as represented in the writings of Paul Romer and others, has taken this line of analysis a major step further: in the context of this theory, the importation of new machinery represents only a pale reflection of the force that an entire foreign investment package—complete with technology, management techniques, quality-control procedures, and human-relations practices—could contribute to transforming the prospects for the host economy. This difference of perspective significantly enlarges both the estimated benefits of trade and investment liberalization and the estimated cost of trade and investment restrictions. In a world undergoing the globalization of production, such restraints prevent new kinds of endeavors from being tried out and mastered at all.

In the conventional growth framework, the calculated value of trade restriction or liberalization is relatively modest (the welfare loss or gain is the square of the tariff-rate equivalent of the restriction); in the endogenous growth framework, however, the calculated value of trade restriction or liberalization may be some twenty times greater.[62] But the evidence introduced in this chapter suggests that even this more expansive calculation does not fully account for the dynamic benefits of the liberalization of trade and investment.

As illustrated earlier in this chapter, the integration between the parent multinational and its subsidiaries does not lead merely to a one-time injection of even the most advanced off-the-shelf technology and business practices; it leads, instead, to a continuous upgrading of technology and business practices on a near-real-time basis, in a cycle that extends backwards from the subsidiaries to embrace local suppliers as well. Thus, the value of the close linkage between the multinational headquarters of auto companies and their subsidiaries in Mexico, or between the multinational headquarters of computer and electronics firms and their subsidiaries in Malaysia, is sure to be even greater than so far envisioned in endogenous growth theory. Similarly, the cost of the very limited connections between, say, the multinational headquarters of auto firms and the boutique, car-in-a-box assemblers operating within a host regime that demands a local joint-venture partner and high domestic content, or between the multinational headquarters of a computer and electronics firm and its affiliates in a host country where joint-venture mandates and lax enforcement of intellectual property rights prevail, is certain to be even greater than the most pessimistic current assessments suggest.

As clear as the differences between these types of ventures are, faulty research design can nevertheless blur the contrast. For example, studies that mix data recording the performance of joint ventures with data recording the performance of wholly owned subsidiaries, or that mix data recording the performance of affiliates that are—and are not—subject to mandatory domestic-content requirements, have yielded a muddled assessment of the impact of foreign direct investment on development.[63]

The evidence introduced in this chapter highlights yet another dimension in efforts to assign value to the potential effects of trade and investment policies. The consideration of the automotive and computer and electronics industries illustrated the importance, in organizing an international production network, of capturing all possible economies of scale. Contemporary economic assessments confirm that in industries with increasing returns to scale, rationalizing production across borders can yield quite large gains. James Markusen, for example, has found that when a country protects intermediate goods and services (machinery, components, and engineering or managerial services) used to produce a final product that has increasing returns to scale, the country is likely to underproduce the final product for the domestic market and to underexport the final product abroad.[64] On the basis of this insight, Markusen, along with Florencio Lopez-de-Silanes and Thomas Rutherford, estimated the benefits, when increasing returns to scale are present in the industry, of allowing multinational corporations to rationalize production across borders.[65] In the case of the North American auto industry, they estimated that the host country (Mexico) would experience an increase in output of more than 100 percent for each firm, an increase in auto production of almost 150 percent, and an overall increase in host-country economic welfare of 1 percent. In one iteration, the researchers compared complete and simultaneous trade and investment liberalization with partial liberalization (under which markets continue to be segmented). In the case of the auto industry the two outcomes differed by a factor of twelve, with almost all the extra benefits from complete and simultaneous trade and investment liberalization accruing to Mexico. In fact, under the trade and investment liberalization of the NAFTA, Mexican passenger-vehicle exports to the United States rose from less than $1 billion in 1994 to $4.5 billion in 2000, while Mexican automotive-component exports to the United States rose from $1 billion to $2.5 billion during the same period.[66]

As large as the impact of the rationalization of production across borders appears to be, such estimates are almost surely too small. The models used to generate these results hold constant the technology used in production, but there is a dramatic difference between the technology used, say, in the high-volume, highly automated, precision-controlled assembly of autos, and in the small-batch, hand-assembly of knocked-down car kits. Moreover, such differences in technology extend to the kinds of support activities that domestic firms are able to provide to foreign subsidiaries.[67] Thus, the potential benefits of trade and investment policies that encourage the use of cutting-edge production technologies—and the potential losses that would accrue from policies that encourage the continued use of older technologies—are certain to diverge even more than the econometric calculations indicate. Overall, the evidence in this chapter indicates that the benefits of trade and investment liberalization, and the costs of trade and investment restrictions, are likely to be much larger than even the most sophisticated contemporary estimates indicate.

8 The Impact of Outward Investment on the Home Economy of the Investor

The evidence and analysis in the preceding chapters have demonstrated that foreign direct investment can create jobs—not only lowest-skill, but higher-skill as well—in host countries in the developing world. But are these jobs created at the expense of jobs—especially good jobs—in the investor's home country? Similarly, earlier chapters have highlighted the benefits to host-country development when sophisticated technologies and industry best practices are transferred from foreign investors' headquarters to offshore sites. Does this transfer of technology and business practices weaken, or undermine, the economic health and dynamism of the home country? Might outward investment generate, in the phrase made famous by Ross Perot, a "giant sucking sound," hollowing out the home economy by transferring jobs and know-how abroad? Would the home economy be better off if national, state, or local authorities took steps to inhibit outward investment by home-country firms?

Outward Investment: Exporting Jobs instead of Products?

Concern about the giant sucking sound originates with the view that when home-country firms engage in outward investment, "they export jobs rather than products." To counter this line of argument, multinational companies often point to their own exceptionally vigorous performance in the home economy. In the United States over the past two decades, U.S. multinationals have contributed the majority of all domestic investment in physical capital in the manufacturing sector (between 54 and 57 percent), and have undertaken the majority of all domestic research and development (between 51 and 62 percent).[1] To provide the wherewithal for this level of domestic investment and research and development, they have repatriated roughly 73 percent of the profits earned abroad. To support their production within the home economy, they have purchased more than 90 percent of their intermediate inputs from U.S., rather than foreign, sources. Finally, multinationals point out that they constitute the home country's largest group of exporters: in fact, one prominent organization of multinationals has claimed that American companies with overseas investments export a larger percentage of all the goods they produce at home than do "all other U. S. manufacturers." This superior export performance on the part of U.S. multinationals—which is far above average, better than the rest of the companies in the home economy—contradicts the contention that outward investment shifts jobs abroad: "Rather, the exact opposite is true. Investment abroad by multinational companies provides the platform for growth in exports and creates jobs in the United States."[2]

But this defense requires careful scrutiny. International companies that do most of the outward investment from the home economy differ, in many respects, from "the rest of the companies in the home economy": they are typically larger, engage in more research and development, and spend more on advertising. It would be odd indeed if Dupont, General Electric, or IBM did not export more than companies that were smaller, did less research and development, and advertised less. Perhaps what generates high export levels is not outward investment but the size of the firm, its level of research and development, or the intensity of its advertising.

A rigorous approach to the giant sucking sound debate requires comparisons between "apples and apples"—that is, not simply between firms that do and do not engage in outward investment, but between *otherwise similar* firms that do and do not engage in outward investment. A statistical analysis that holds company characteristics constant, an approach pioneered by Thomas Horst in the case of outward investment, allows such comparisons to be made.[3] As can be seen in table 8-1, Horst divided his sample of U.S. firms according to various characteristics that might be expected to influence the level of exports, then compared the export levels of those that essentially remained at home (column 1) with those

Table 8-1. *Exports as a Percentage of Domestic Shipments in Industries with Various Characteristics*

	1. Little or no foreign investment	*2. Low to middle range of foreign investment*	*3. Upper-middle range of foreign investment*	*4. Highest level of foreign investment*
High-tech	2.3	7.8	9.7	7.6
Low-tech	1.3	3.0	2.5	3.5
High use of advertising	1.0	2.8	2.4	4.6
Low use of advertising	1.4	4.8	7.5	7.7
High unionization	1.9	5.5	4.4	3.8
Low unionization	1.3	3.2	7.0	7.8

Source: Adapted from C. Fred Bergsten, Thomas Horst, and Theodore H. Moran, *American Multinationals and American Interests* (Brookings, 1978), table 3-3, pp. 81—82.

that had begun to set up overseas operations (column 2), those that had vigorously expanded overseas operations (column 3), and those that had most completely globalized their operations (column 4).

This carefully structured analysis reveals that outward investment pulls exports out from the home-country firm that carries out the investment: the contrast between the percentage of domestic shipments that were exported for firms in column 1 (the stay-at-home firms) and the percentage of domestic shipments for firms in columns 2 through 4 shows that increasing levels of foreign direct investment lead to a sharp climb upward in exports. As subsequent research (discussed later) has confirmed, this "pull" effect can be accounted for by the fact that home-country firms have established distribution networks abroad, are shipping intermediate products for assembly abroad, and are shipping larger amounts of final products abroad.

The type of analysis performed by Horst also affords a clear view of the counterfactual—of what would have happened if the home-country firm had not invested abroad. The second, third, and fourth columns contrast the export performance of firms that did invest overseas with firms of the same kind that stayed at home (first column). This comparison of "likes with likes," under identical conditions, is the closest that social science can come to determining what the outcome would have been if something that *did* take place had not occurred. Thus, the figures in column 1 indicate what the home country would have been left with if the companies under consideration had not engaged in outward investment. The stay-at-home scenario does not allow workers to export more from home-country plants: investing abroad does. Perhaps surprisingly, the stay-at-home scenario does not even benefit union workers—quite the reverse. Just as it generates more export-related jobs for home-country workers in general, outward investment creates more export-related jobs for union workers. Moreover, outward investment adds to the export intensity of home-country firms in industries with relatively high, as well as relatively low, levels of unionization.

These unconventional discoveries may be easier to understand in the context of the discussion, in the preceding chapter, of the computer and electronics industry. Seagate's decision to outsource the production of disk drives to China, Malaysia, Singapore, and Thailand provided a rapidly growing foundation for the creation of Seagate jobs in California, Idaho, and Texas. Had Seagate stayed at home, in Silicon Valley, it would have been relegated to the ranks of small-time suppliers of engineering services and would never have become a system-integrating manufacturer—if it had managed to survive at all. Similarly, IBM's decision to build a full-scale assembly plant in Mexico supported an increase in exports, throughout the Western Hemisphere, of components and final products that had originated in the United States—growth that continued even as the Mexican industry itself became more integrated. Similarly, the high wages and benefits of Ericsson's work force in Sweden depended upon the electronic funds-transfer software created in the subsidiary in Saltillo.

These examples support the general finding that outward investment increases export levels from the home economy. But, at least in the United States, unions do not figure prominently in the computer and electronics sector. What are the effects of outward investment in industries that are more highly unionized in the home country? The history of the automotive sector, recounted in the previous chapter, offers some insights. By abandoning their stay-at-home strategy and developing a regional network for producing engines and auto parts in Mexico and Brazil, the U.S. auto firms were able to reverse their decline in the home market. Heated criticism from the United Auto Workers Union notwithstanding, the parent firms' outsourcing strategies ultimately helped secure the relatively high-wage, high-benefit jobs of unionized autoworkers in the United States. In the same way, the tight integration between Volkswagen's home-country operations and its offshore plants producing engines, axles, chassis, and gear boxes in Argentina, Brazil, Mexico, and Eastern Europe underpins the high wages and high benefits of autoworkers in Germany.

Robert E. Lipsey and Herle Yahr Weiss followed Horst in undertaking what has become a long series of rigorously structured investigations that show a positive link between outward investment and the expansion of exports from firms both within and outside the United States.[4] Examining data for multinational investors in fourteen manufacturing industries in the United States and thirteen other developed countries, Lipsey and Weiss found a statistically significant relationship between the level of production by affiliates of home-country firms located in an overseas economy and exports from the home country to the economy in which the affiliates were located. The complementarity between outward investment and exports was strong not only for intermediate products shipped for further assembly but for finished products as well.

Lipsey and Weiss discovered, moreover, not only that foreign investor operations attracted exports from the home country, but that the presence of foreign firms in the host economy also tended to preempt exports from other developed countries that did not have affiliates of their own multinationals producing there. That is, they found a negative relationship between the presence of U.S.-owned affiliates and the level of exports from other developed countries, and a similarly negative relationship between the presence of non-U.S. affiliates and the level of exports from the United States. This finding suggests that home-country authorities and home-country workers both have an interest, for competitive reasons, in seeing home-country companies well-positioned with respect to production in external economies.

The positive impact of outward investment might be limited, however, if home-country affiliates in an external market exported to third countries, displacing exports from the home country to those third countries. When Lipsey and Weiss searched for this possible effect, however, they found that whatever displacement occurred was overshadowed by increased exports from the home country itself: that is, in each industry, firms with larger overseas operations also exported more in the aggregate.

Studies of outward investment by multinationals based in Sweden, where the issue of "exporting jobs" has also generated controversy, have revealed a similar positive correlation between foreign production and exports. Magnus Blomstrom, Robert Lipsey, and K. Kulchycky found a positive relationship between increases in output at the affiliates of Swedish firms and increases in exports across seven industrial categories—a relationship that remained unchanged as the foreign production expanded.[5] The same is true of outward investment by Japanese multinationals and exports from Japan.[6]

To see whether levels of exports and levels of foreign direct investment might be simultaneously determined by common factors such as market size, income level, or geographic distance, Edward Graham tested the relationship for U.S. and Japanese multinationals while holding these factors constant. He, too, found an independent positive relationship between the output of U.S. and Japanese affiliates and the home countries' export levels.[7]

The Impact of Outward Investment on the Home Economy

Since firms that engage in outward investment have higher exports than similar firms that do not, outward-investing firms have a larger proportion of export-related jobs than do their counterparts without offshore affiliates. What are the consequences for workers and wages in the home economy?

Howard Lewis and David Richardson report that in U.S. manufacturing plants that export some of their output, the wages of blue-collar workers are 13 percent higher than those of workers in nonexporting plants (23 percent higher in large plants and 9 percent higher in small plants); among white-collar workers, the difference is an average of 18 percent more;[8] benefits are 40 percent higher for both groups. When Lewis and Richardson controlled for region, wages remained 10 percent higher and benefits 11 percent higher. When they controlled for skill level, more than half of the difference in wages and benefits remained.

Mark Doms and J. Bradford Jensen, and Zadia Feliciano and Robert E. Lipsey, have found that the positive impact on home-country workers in firms that invest abroad is larger and more general than can be accounted for by the higher export levels of the home-country plants. They show that at plants of American companies with global operations, average annual earnings are higher than comparable earnings at either larger or smaller plants without global operations. After controlling for region, sector, skill level, and age, they found that wages for production workers were some 7 percent higher at large plants of companies with global operations, and 15 percent higher at small plants of companies with global operations. Wage premiums for nonproduction workers were 5 percent at large plants and 10 percent at small plants. Thus, far from draining the good jobs out of the home economy, outward investment increases the proportion of good jobs in the home economy. And the evidence suggests that blue-collar workers actually gain relatively more, on average, from working at plants with global operations than do nonproduction workers.

Doms and Jensen show that to sustain higher levels of wages and benefits, U.S. firms that invest abroad use frontier production processes more frequently, have higher levels of productivity, and enjoy more rapid growth in overall productivity than U.S. firms that do not.[9] Once again, however, the aggregate comparisons have to be adjusted for size of firm, type of industry, and location in the home country. When these characteristics are held constant, the findings are as follows: for large firms with offshore operations, the use of a standard compilation of advanced manufacturing technologies is 31 percent higher, productivity is 11 percent higher, and the rate of growth in overall productivity is 2.5 to 4 percent faster than in otherwise comparable large firms without offshore operations. For small firms with offshore operations, the use of a standard compilation of advanced manufacturing technologies is 50 percent higher, productivity is 33 percent higher, and the rate of growth for overall productivity is 7 to 11 percent higher than in otherwise comparable small firms without offshore operations. On the basis of these findings, Lewis and Richardson conclude that outward investment enhances the performance of all firms, even small firms in unexpected industries and in less promising geographic locations.[10]

Moreover, according to Lewis and Richardson, American communities that have a larger proportion of companies that engage in international investment find themselves better off as well. To a large extent, the positive impact of the presence of multinationals can be attributed directly to the fact that the workers and managers in the firms are higher paid than those in other firms. The presence of Kodak, for example, has helped Rochester rank thirtieth, and Denver rank sixty-seventh, among the top export cities in the United States, with three-quarters of what the company ships going to an offshore Kodak factory for further work or packaging.[11] Further, Mary E. Lovely and Stuart S. Rosenthal have found evidence that the spatial concentration of firms that, like Kodak, have global operations, may also generate spillovers that enhance the productivity, wages, and profits of other companies in the same area.[12]

The evidence in this chapter brings the analysis full circle: in both developed and developing countries, the globalization of industry, through the spread of foreign direct investment, generates win-win outcomes for workers in home and host economies alike.

Winners and Losers: Policy Implications for Home Countries

But while the aggregate news may be favorable, there are certainly winners and losers among home-country workers as some operations expand and others contract or are abandoned altogether. Moreover, even within the same industry or the same company, the costs and the benefits tend to be concentrated in specific plants, rather than spread evenly across all plants. This pattern accentuates the difficulties, and the fears, associated with plant closings, none of which are directly offset by the promise of more jobs or plant expansions elsewhere.

According to Lori Kletzer, once manufacturing workers become displaced, for whatever reason, they are exposed to an average earnings loss of 16 percent, but this average masks large variations.[13] About one-third of the workers initially laid off report the same or even increased earnings in a new job, but one-quarter report earnings losses of 30 percent or more. The workers with large earnings losses tend to be older and less skilled, and are often women.

What measures should be taken, in the United States and other home countries, to deal with the displacements that accompany outward investment? The analysis presented in this chapter indicates that efforts to slow or stop the process of outward investment would not leave home-country workers or the home-country economy better off. On the contrary, such measures would reduce the proportion of good jobs in the home economy and lower the wages and benefits available to production workers, union and nonunion alike. Instead of offering false solutions—such as legislation, tax treatment, or other regulations that would hinder or prevent outward investment altogether—home countries need to take steps that address the real problems.[14] Such measures would include reforms of unemployment insurance and adjustment assistance that would make these programs more effective, more easily accessible, and more generous; continuation of health insurance, at subsidized rates, for workers who are between jobs, to compensate for their sudden loss of earnings; portable pension benefits; a new kind of wage insurance for displaced workers; expanded educational loan programs that would cover skill training offered through part-time and night courses; and use-them-or-lose-them tax incentives to encourage firms to provide workers with continuous on-the-job training. These and similar measures would enable the many who benefit from the globalization of industry to assist the few who do not, while reducing pressures to prevent the entire process of globalization from moving forward.

9   *A Summing Up*

The preceding eight chapters explored the ways in which developing countries could take advantage of the globalization of industry, via foreign direct investment, to provide the greatest benefits to workers and average citizens. They described how developing countries could protect workers in low-skill, labor-intensive operations from mistreatment and abuse. They considered how the international community might most effectively protect the welfare of workers in foreign-owned and foreign-controlled plants. They explored the ways in which foreign direct investment could improve the lives of workers and average citizens, other than by creating jobs at the lowest skill levels. They probed the conditions under which foreign direct investment in progressively higher-skill activities might transform the development trajectory open to a host country—or, conversely, damage the host-country's development prospects. Reversing the angle of analysis, the previous chapter explored the impact of the globalization of industry, via foreign direct investment, on the well-being of workers and average citizens in the home country of the investor. This concluding chapter steps back from the details of the preceding chapters to draw together the findings in twelve overlapping areas.

1. Placing the Globalization of Industry, via Foreign Direct Investment, and the Welfare of Workers in Developing Countries in Perspective

Developing countries that wish to take advantage of the spread of foreign direct investment in labor-intensive industries—and, at the same time, to protect workers from potential abuse or mistreatment—face complex and difficult policy challenges. Appropriately structured multilateral support may be of assistance with these challenges. The contribution that the globalization of industry, via foreign direct investment, can make to the lives of workers and average citizens to the overall welfare of developing countries extends, however, far beyond the creation of jobs for the lowest-skilled, lowest-paid workers.

Leaving aside investment in natural resources and infrastructure, the annual flow of foreign direct investment to relatively more sophisticated industrial sectors—such as transportation equipment, electrical machinery, chemicals, computers and electronics, and other industrial products—is more than twenty times larger than the flow to less sophisticated, lower-skill sectors. Wages and benefits in the more sophisticated sectors are two to five times greater, or more, and working conditions are demonstrably superior. The value of foreign direct investment does not come primarily from the creation of employment (even if indirect employment is included) but from a transformation in the range of productive activities available to the host country.

The possibility of using foreign direct investment to reconfigure the development profile of the host economy is addressed in point 11 and explored thoroughly in chapter 7. But this broader perspective is important from the beginning because it shapes the policy choices that host governments must make, and that the international community must support, in order to ensure access to the larger array of benefits from the globalization of industry even as all parties attempt to cope with the specific risks of sweatshop conditions in labor-intensive sectors.

2. Assessing the Dangers and Opportunities of Foreign Investment in Lowest-Skill Operations

Foreign direct investment in labor-intensive sectors such as garments and footwear carries a much more complex set of attributes, good and bad, than is commonly supposed. On the one hand, workers in plants owned by foreign exporters or their subcontractors may be exposed to a variety of ills. They may be paid appallingly low wages, denied even the wages and benefits to which they are entitled, penalized for failure to meet quotas, obliged to work double shifts and other compulsory over-time, and be subject to corporal punishment and sexual harassment. Their working conditions may be uncomfortable and unsafe, and their living conditions may lack rudimentary elements of sanitation and secu-rity. Such conditions are described in more unsparing detail in chapter 2, and the circumstances under which they are most likely to occur are explored there and in chapter 3.

In other plants in the same sectors, however, workers may be paid more than the minimum wage and gain rising levels of benefits; may have access to medical and child care facilities; and may receive subsi-dized housing, meals, and transportation. They may participate in a sys-tem that combines regular, on-the-job training with learning-by-doing and job rotation; and they may be offered opportunities for skill certifi-cation, supervisory responsibilities, and promotion. Their employers, in conjunction with public and civil society groups, may offer after-work classes in language, business, and other skills. The mechanisms that are likely to generate these more favorable conditions are the subject of point 3 and find fuller treatment in chapters 2 and 3.

Single investors in garment, footwear, and other low-skill operations can create jobs numbering in the tens of thousands, providing entry-level employment for fifteen to twenty times more workers than single investors in higher-skill activities. In some countries and cultures these entry-level jobs provide repressed segments of the population, including women and minorities, with access into the formal economy not other-wise available. In the terminology of Nobel laureate Amartya Sen, employment enhances not only the welfare but the "agency" of the workers, augmenting their status and increasing their bargaining power in relation to their spouses or the members of their nuclear family. The positive social externalities for the host country may include lower fertil-ity rates and a reduction in the intergenerational transmission of poverty.

The challenge for developing countries is to design policies that simultaneously capture the benefits of foreign direct investment in low-wage sectors and protect workers from mistreatment or abuse. The examples of export processing zones in Mauritius, Madagascar, the Philippines, the Dominican Republic, and Costa Rica, in chapters 2 and 3, provide some guidelines about what measures host governments might adopt (or avoid) to accomplish these goals.

3. Harnessing the Most Powerful Mechanism to Improve the Treatment of Workers

Workers are most likely to be mistreated or abused where there are only a small number of alternative employers, where labor markets are fragmented, and in operations that pay scant attention to quality control or to imaginative solutions to the challenges of production. As the number of investors increases, as workers gain more knowledge of employment opportunities elsewhere, and as plants that produce more sophisticated goods—and require more attention to quality control from a stable and productive work force—are mixed in with those that produce less sophisticated goods, the treatment of workers improves. Moreover, the evidence in chapters 2 and 3 shows that firms engaged in higher-skill operations are not the only ones that take measures to attract and retain good workers: with the introduction of more sophisticated activities, a broader transformation of worker-management relations occurs that embraces lower-skill sectors; smaller, older firms; and older EPZs.

The multiplication of the number of firms, and the increasing sophistication of foreign investors' operations, combine to create the most powerful mechanism available for bringing about broad improvement in the treatment of workers in developing countries. In other words, the most potent remedy for the mistreatment of workers that can occur during the globalization of industry comes from more and greater globalization of industry.

As EPZs in the Philippines, the Dominican Republic, and Costa Rica moved out of lowest-skill operations and into higher-skill activities, the ILO provided all three countries with training and assistance in labor-management relations, dispute settlement, conflict resolution, and the enforcement of labor statutes. But even with broad overall improvements in the treatment of workers, some firms continued to treat their employees poorly, and new kinds of worker-management controversies inevitably arose. How might the international community participate most effectively in helping to mediate controversies and punish abuses? More fundamentally, what forms of labor abuse might the international community collectively agree to prohibit? And within each category of labor abuse, what would the international community define as an actionable violation, or as an insufficient effort at enforcement, that deserves multilateral punishment? A consideration of these questions will help determine which instruments and procedures might be most effective in applying multilateral pressure on behalf of workers in developing countries.

4. Identifying Core Labor Standards for the Treatment of Workers around the World

The four ILO core labor standards that have broadest international recognition and support appear quite simple and straightforward: the elimination of discrimination in employment and occupation; the elimination of all forms of forced or compulsory labor; the effective abolition of child labor; and freedom of association and the effective recognition of the right to collective bargaining. But as chapter 4 explores in some detail, determining what obligations these core principles impose on ILO members—either explicitly, among countries that have ratified the associated conventions, or implicitly, via membership in the ILO—is an effort fraught with controversy.

In the areas where foreign direct investment in low-wage, low-skill operations has aroused the most contention—freedom of association, collective bargaining, and union organizing—firms in EPZs have long been a source of complaints to the ILO. These complaints focus on a range of actions on the part of management, including antiunion discrimination, "interference" in the representation of workers, inadequate recognition of the right to strike, hiring of permanent replacement workers during strikes, allowing permanent replacement workers to participate in elections to decertify a given union, and threatening to close down plants that accept union representation. But these are also the very areas in which complaints to the ILO about practices in developed countries—not least, the United States—have been highest as well. As is often pointed out, the United States has not ratified many of the basic ILO conventions. But the obstacle to stronger multilateral enforcement of core labor standards is not simply U.S. failure to ratify various conventions; rather, it is controversy about the substance and enforcement of federal, state, and provincial labor statutes in the United States and in other developed countries.

The contention that, through the WTO, the international community could authoritatively address the disputes that arise in EPZs in developing countries—without sweeping changes in U.S. labor regulations and enforcement procedures—does not stand up to careful scrutiny. Moreover, obtaining agreement across the entire WTO membership as to what constitutes actionable violations of core labor standards is not likely be an easy or a rapid undertaking, if it is possible at all.

The idea that each country should "just enforce its own labor laws"—an approach that is embodied in the labor side-letter to the NAFTA and in the U.S.-Jordan Free Trade Agreement—offers little promise of providing a shortcut. As noted in chapter 4, painstaking negotiations would still be required to create guidelines that WTO dispute-settlement panels and appellate bodies could use to determine innocence or guilt. Nor do the NAFTA or the U.S.-Jordan Free Trade Agreement offer guidance about how such negotiations might be undertaken. The NAFTA side-agreement on labor does not oblige the parties to include any specified content or to require any minimum level of enforcement of domestic labor legislation. Moreover, out of respect for the sovereignty of its signatories, the NAFTA specifically excludes from any extranational review whatsoever all complaints about freedom of association, right to bargain collectively, right to organize, and right to strike. Although the U.S.-Jordan Free Trade Agreement requires each signatory to "recognize and protect" the ILO core labor standards, it does not specify what this obligation entails.

Obtaining agreement, across nations, about what constitutes a violation of the core labor standards and what constitutes adequate enforcement would be a task of enormous magnitude and complexity; the difficulty involved in such an undertaking shapes any assessment of the trade-offs between two alternatives: one the one hand, attempting to transform the WTO into an authoritative benevolent dictator charged with enforcing core labor standards; and on the other, relying on less authoritative voluntary measures.

5. Using the WTO to Enforce Core Labor Standards

Assuming agreement could be reached on the definition of actionable violations and appropriate enforcement, and that the other risks to the international trading system associated with introducing labor issues into the work of the WTO could be avoided—both rather formidable assumptions—how might it be possible to design a WTO-based enforcement system that would protect the interests of workers in developing countries while avoiding capture by protectionist interests in importing countries?

The evidence referred to in point 2, and discussed in chapters 2 and 3, demonstrates the central importance of limiting punishment to individual plants or companies rather than expanding it to include entire EPZs, or all EPZs, or to embrace the entire host economy. Granted, even the most narrowly constructed WTO-based enforcement system would have drawbacks: penalties (trade sanctions or fines) imposed on individual plants or firms might punish the victims by forcing the workers who were being mistreated to be laid off, or even to lose their jobs permanently if their plant closed. But a far worse outcome would emerge from a broader enforcement system, which would inevitably involve collective punishment of firms that enforced core labor standards along with those that did not. Similarly, firms engaged in higher-skill operations would be punished along with firms that engaged in lowest-skill operations; OECD firms would be punished along with non-OECD firms; and multinational producers would be punished along with indigenous subcontractors. Since, taken together, overall growth in the number of investors and the mixing of firms that export higher-skilled products with firms that export lower-skilled products constitute the single most powerful force for the improvement of worker-management relations, a broad enforcement system would have enormous counterproductive potential for progress in the treatment of workers in developing countries. Thus, efforts to correct abuses in the lowest-skill sector of foreign investor operations risk undermining the very processes that have the greatest hope of improving both the treatment of workers and the overall development trajectory of the host country.

Moreover, a broadly implemented enforcement system would offer a lucrative target for capture by a broad array of interests in importing countries—by the firms and workers producing transportation equipment, by the firms and workers producing electrical and electronic products, and by the firms and workers producing industrial machinery, for example, as well as by the firms and workers producing textiles and footwear. Finally, such an enforcement mechanism would undermine the principal instrument international producers and retailers have to ensure that their suppliers conform to good labor practices: namely, the assurance of uninterrupted purchases for those who comply.

A WTO-based enforcement system that limited retaliation to exclusion orders against the output of individual plants or firms that were found to be in violation, or to fines that would be passed on to such plants or firms, might avoid these adverse outcomes. But, as noted in point 4 and in chapter 5, an examination of the labor side-agreement to the NAFTA and of the Canada-Chile Free Trade Agreement suggests that even a narrowly conceived WTO-based enforcement system is likely to be plagued by national sensitivities about what constitutes adequate treatment of workers and adequate enforcement of labor statutes. In light of the drawbacks associated with using the WTO to enforce core labor standards, what are the prospects for voluntary alternatives?

6. Using Voluntary Mechanisms to Monitor and Enforce Labor Standards

Are mechanisms that rely on cooperation, persuasion, and publicity— rather than on legally enforced trade sanctions or fines—destined to be less effective than a hypothetical, WTO-based system? As noted in chapter 6, a so-called voluntary regime for dealing with sweatshop conditions—a regime that includes corporate codes of conduct, certification organizations, and compliance labeling—has become an increasingly effective means of applying pressure on firms to improve the treatment of workers. The common-sense standards of decent treatment for workers embodied in these informal commitments of producers and retailers, moreover, have turned out to be much more specific than any that are likely to be agreed to as the basis for WTO-based adjudication. Progress in strengthening these voluntary measures, and weaving them into a tighter and more comprehensive system to identify violations and monitor remediation, might prove to be more rapid than movement toward the creation of an authoritative WTO alternative—and the outcome is likely to be quite a bit more effectual.

As shareholders and other outside observers insist on knowing how the principles embodied in the codes are being applied in practice, codes of conduct can introduce pressures for accountability into the decision-making processes of multinational investors, whatever the original intentions of the corporate leadership. Certification organizations can enhance the credibility of individual corporate efforts to demonstrate social responsibility, and help differentiate the more committed from the less committed firms. But voluntary mechanisms still fall far short of constituting a transparent, autonomous, and reliable system for recording and investigating complaints or producing compliance. The tortuous evolution of the voluntary practices of some prominent corporations and certification organizations, recounted in chapter 6, shows that formidable challenges remain. To gain legitimacy, a voluntary monitoring system requires internal and external procedures for complaints and whistle-blowing, public identification of supply chains, provisions for allowing unscheduled inspections and protecting the autonomy of inspectors, and procedures permitting outside scrutiny of remediation efforts.

Attempts to create monitoring systems that meet these criteria have been slow and contentious, but the trend line has been positive. The wider adoption of best practices already visible in some portions of the garment, footwear, toy, and sports equipment industries—backed by near-real-time surveillance of labor disputes via the Internet—could significantly improve the treatment of workers.

Contrary to the expectations of critics, the codes of conduct developed by corporations and certification organizations include remarkably detailed standards, covering not only the ILO's four core principles but health and safety practices and compensation levels as well. With the burden of proof on corporations to show that their production chains comply with common-sense definitions of decent treatment for workers, the identification and correction of labor abuses in the supposedly "second-best" voluntary system might prove to be quite a bit more prompt and effective than prosecution through a WTO-based system of adjudication could soon—if ever—become. Voluntary measures might be used, with some effect, to spur producers of labor-intensive products to provide better treatment and higher wages for the workers in their supply chains.

7. Obliging Producers to Pay a Living Wage versus Pressuring Multinationals to Provide Decent Treatment of Workers

As noted in chapter 5, a global minimum wage would cause poorer countries to lose the comparative advantage that comes with being able to provide less expensive labor: under a global minimum wage, producers of low-skill, labor-intensive goods would be drawn away from the poorest and lowest-skill countries and toward those where the wage could attract higher-skilled workers—away from Bangladesh and toward the Philippines, away from El Salvador and toward the Dominican Republic. Under a living-wage system, the minimum wage paid by foreign investors and their subcontractors would vary with the standard of living in each host country, thus averting the principal danger of a global minimum wage.

But the analysis in chapter 5 shows that the living-wage approach is unavoidably accompanied by distortions and discrimination. Since, for example, employers would be required to pay workers enough to support an average family, countries where the average family size was larger would suffer in relation to countries where the average family size was smaller. Based on its experience in Indonesia and other countries, the Center for Reflection, Education, and Action has recommended that the living wage be calculated to support one adult and one minor child. The National Labor Committee, drawing on its knowledge of family size in El Salvador, has advised that the living wage be set to support a family of 4.3 people. All other things being equal, an international company guided by considerations of wage costs would build a plant in Indonesia and avoid El Salvador.

The living-wage approach produces similar distortions and discriminatory effects among regions. A group of researchers from Columbia University have pointed out that in rural El Salvador, where many of the garment and footwear workers originate, the average family has 5.2 people. An employer who has to choose between otherwise identical workers, some of whom are to be paid enough to support 4.3 family members and others of whom are to be paid enough to support 5.2 family members, would likely avoid the rural areas—the very regions where, from the host-country's perspective, the establishment of a plant would have the most beneficial result.

A living-wage system would also discriminate among workers. Survey evidence presented in chapters 2 and 3 suggests that the work force producing garments and footwear includes large numbers of widowed and divorced women with families, women supporting nuclear families back in their original villages, and women who are largely on their own and entering the formal economy for the first time. A living wage high enough to support the workers in the first category would discriminate against the second two; a living wage low enough to support the third category would discriminate against the first two. Under a living-wage system, an employer with one opening for an entry-level employee might well find workers in the first two categories concealing their familial obligations to compete for the available slot. Finally, the relatively higher costs that living-wage requirements would impose on foreign investors would shift the composition of activities within the economies of developing countries away from foreign-owned and foreign-controlled operations and back toward traditional industries and subsistence agriculture.

The drawbacks of a mandated living wage do not mean, however, that international companies—both producers and retailers—cannot be pressured by civil society "from the top," so to speak, to pay decent wages and provide decent treatment to their workers around the world. Evidence introduced in chapter 5 shows that unit labor costs for garments and footwear amount to no more than 1 to 3 percent of the final retail price (in the case of highly branded products, unit labor costs are only a few tenths of 1 percent). As part of their marketing strategy, oligopolistic producers and retailers might well be able to absorb a larger bill for wages and benefits and adequate working conditions. Such firms are eager to differentiate themselves by presenting a socially responsible image, and are therefore likely to respond to pressure from a voluntary system that places the burden of proof on them to show that they treat their workers in a way that can be publicly justified.

Consumers, for their part, report that they would be willing to pay a higher price for sweatshop-free goods, and are thus in a position to join international investors and retailers in compensating producers for the higher costs—if any—associated with decent wages and working conditions; again, such an approach would avoid the distortions that would arise with the imposition of either a global minimum wage or a living wage. As for the definition of *decent,* chapter 6 shows that the labor standards to which many international companies have committed themselves, and their suppliers, are often quite specific.

Within the array of authoritative and voluntary international mechanisms to prevent labor abuse examined in chapters 5 and 6, how might the ILO best help to improve the treatment of workers?

8. Strengthening the Role of the ILO

During the past decade the ILO has taken on broader responsibilities for monitoring the observance of labor standards; investigating complaints; and providing training in modern human-relations practices, dispute resolution, and enforcement procedures. In one case—in which Myanmar was accused of allowing forced labor to be used in the production of exports—the ILO has also taken a step toward multilateral enforcement of core principles.

As noted in chapter 6, the membership has most strongly supported a more expansive and assertive role for the ILO when the organization has focused on conciliation and assistance rather than on punishment. Chapter 6 also noted that the ILO has a number of procedures already in place for the examination of disputes and the identification and publication of violations; these procedures could be substantially augmented—using mechanisms already in place—by greater input from labor, management, and civil society groups that are afforded, under ILO rules, various forms of direct access to the organization. However, proposals to push the ILO in the direction of authorizing and imposing penalties—either alone, or in conjunction with the WTO—run the risk of undermining the support that has sustained the ILO's recent progress.

9. Using the WTO to Combat Unfair Advantages

Apart from any potential role for the WTO in monitoring and enforcing core labor standards, might there be a separate rationale for charging the WTO with responsibility for ensuring that substandard labor practices are not used to gain unfair advantages in attracting investment or boosting exports? More fundamentally, do such practices in fact create unfair advantages?

To consider these questions, chapter 5 draws on earlier evidence, presented in chapter 3, that as firms engage in higher-skill operations in sectors such as transportation, computers and electronics, plastics, and chemical products—and therefore have to pay attention to the quality and reliability of their manufactures—the degree to which they can use poor working conditions and wage suppression to augment the competitiveness of their exports is quite limited. In the case of lowest-skill operations, unit labor costs range from 3 to less than 1 percent of the final retail price: thus, the gains from squeezing workers' wages by as much as one-third would yield no more than a few cents per item—hardly enough to "injure" firms and workers in the developed world. Aggregate studies confirm that substandard treatment of workers does not enhance the market penetration of exporters who engage in such practices. In fact, there are some indications that countries with low labor standards have difficulty moving their export sectors beyond the least complicated assembly operations. Nor do low labor standards attract foreign investors: the data consistently show that countries where core labor standards are poorly enforced receive less—rather than more— flows of foreign direct investment than would be predicted on the basis of other characteristics.

Thus, the evidence does not support the contention that low labor standards boost exports or help host countries to increase the level of foreign investment. The prospect that firms and workers in importing countries could prove, by any objective measure, that they were being unfairly injured by developing countries' failure to enforce core labor standards is rather improbable. The real danger, however, is that developed countries would capture the WTO's investigative processes, effectively ensuring that findings would be less than objective. Like other antidumping procedures, measures to prevent what is sometimes called social dumping could be distorted by faulty definitions of unfair practices and politically driven findings of injury.

For developing countries to run the risk of such an outcome, the endeavor would have to offer some correspondingly substantial incentive. One possibility might be to expand the definition of "unfair advantage" until *all* measures designed to attract international investment or alter global patterns of industrial production were brought under multilateral discipline. Although, for example, developing countries routinely provide tax breaks and other incentives to attract international investment—in particular, as part of the treatment afforded to EPZ firms— these measures are comparatively paltry, and are much less effectively wielded, than the incentives and subsidies deployed by developed countries to accomplish the same objectives.

Chapter 5 surveys econometric evidence that the locational decisions of international companies are becoming increasingly sensitive to the incentive packages offered by national and provincial or state governments, and that the overlap among rival sites in developed and developing countries is rising. Thus, if in addition to monitoring and enforcing labor standards, the WTO took responsibility for ensuring a level playing field for trade and investment around the world, developing countries might have some incentive for supporting a broader role for the WTO.

An even larger question, however, is whether host-country authorities might want to consider abandoning the use of special treatment in EPZs altogether.

10. Shifting the Focus of Development Strategy from EPZs to the Liberalization of Trade and Investment

The examples in this volume demonstrate that there is something of a dialectic in the way that an EPZ-based development strategy gradually gives way to a recognition of the need for broad liberalization of trade and investment.

The concept of creating export processing zones originates from a desire to provide foreign investors with a special enclave in which they enjoy not only access to duty-free inputs but freedom from the red tape, corruption, regulatory instability, and poor infrastructure that characterize the rest of the host economy. With the hope of generating jobs for the most desperate and least skilled workers, host authorities often place EPZs in the most isolated, poverty-stricken areas; but EPZs in such locations often fail to attract investors—and when they do, they are unlikely to provide a ladder up from the most dead-end jobs, or to yield any but the most minimal backward linkages to the host economy. The early difficulties, as well as the later successes, of EPZs in Mauritius, Madagascar, the Philippines, the Dominican Republic, and Costa Rica show the value of moving away from a strategy that is based on isolated zones in impoverished areas, and instead allowing foreign investors, subcontractors, and indigenous exporters to locate near commercial and industrial hubs that are surrounded by at least modestly skilled work forces; and ensuring that development efforts are backed by reliable infrastructure, dependable regulatory institutions, realistic exchange rates, and increasing trade liberalization. The experiences of these five countries suggest that prudent development policies can overcome the geographical or cultural exceptionalism that predicts dismal outcomes for countries in particular locales (such as the tropics) or in particular regions (such as Africa).

As the countries discussed in chapters 2 and 3 integrated foreign investors more tightly into the workings of their economies, they also altered their approach to attracting multinational investment, especially as they tried to diversify beyond the production and exportation of lowest-skill, labor-intensive products. Whereas host-country authorities had once waited passively for multinational corporations to appear, screening applicants and imposing onerous conditions when they did, the authorities began instead to deploy investment-promotion agencies that proactively marketed the country—seeking out potential international investors, preparing customized proposals to meet their needs, and providing them with a swift and centralized "one-stop shop." Among the examples cited in chapter 3, the Costa Rican Investment Promotion Agency, which followed the lead of the highly successful Economic Development Board of Singapore, provides a model of the more proactive approach. The examples of the Philippines and the Dominican Republic illustrate the dynamic role of private developers in seeking out multinational investors and helping them get settled in integrated industrial estates complete with housing, transportation, medical facilities, day care, and recreational services. For the privilege of locating in private zones, foreign firms paid rents and fees that were as much as three times as high as those that prevailed in the less management- and worker-friendly public zones.

In all five countries, a growing number of indigenous firms—often founded and staffed by former employees of foreign exporters—established operations alongside the foreign investors. But unless the host government provided the indigenous companies with the same business-friendly treatment enjoyed by foreign firms, the use of local inputs remained marginal. But whereas second-class treatment for local firms led only to second-class possibilities for building backward linkages to the host economy, trade, investment, and regulatory reforms gave local companies the chance to become vigorous suppliers to multinational investors. Moreover, as indicated by evidence from both Asia and Latin America, indigenous suppliers not infrequently achieved competitive status as independent producers serving international markets.

In developing countries, much of the globalization of industry, via foreign direct investment—in the automotive sector, for example—has taken place quite apart from a strategy that is based on locating plants in specific EPZs. Some countries, like Singapore and Hong Kong, essentially transformed themselves into single, integrated export processing zones. Backward linkages from Mexico's *maquiladora* program began to expand only after foreign investors were allowed to locate throughout the country, not simply along the border with the United States (and with the liberalization that accompanied the NAFTA, these backward linkages have grown appreciably). The evidence in chapter 5, summarized more extensively in point 11, shows that by far the greatest contribution of foreign firms to host-country development—including the expansion of backward linkages and the generation of spillovers to local companies and workers—takes place in the context of the overall liberalization of trade and investment.

The most successful host countries described in chapters 2, 3, and 7 followed a build-up rather than a trickle-down strategy for incorporating foreign direct investment into their plans for national development. In addition to demonstrating the value of proactive efforts to attract foreign investment, the experiences of these countries show the importance of creating strong educational and vocational programs for their workers; of providing fair and equal support to small and medium-sized as well as large indigenous companies (while avoiding special favoritism); of modernizing and privatizing infrastructure; and of undertaking general reforms of their commercial institutions—including those that monitor, adjudicate, and enforce national labor statutes—within a framework of macroeconomic stability and declining barriers to imports.

In developing countries, this shift from a narrow, EPZ-based strategy to a broader approach—one that incorporates trade and investment liberalization—lays the groundwork for host-country authorities to consider how foreign direct investment might be harnessed to transform the nation's entire development trajectory.

11. Using Foreign Direct Investment to Transform the Host Country's Development Trajectory

The way in which the globalization of industry, via foreign direct investment, touches the lives of workers and average citizens in developing countries is not primarily through job creation. Nor is it primarily through the provision of capital. The greatest contribution of foreign direct investment comes, instead, through integrated packages—technologies, business techniques, management skills, human-relations policies, and marketing capabilities—that place host-country plants on the frontier of industry best practices, and keep them there. This outcome is most likely when the subsidiaries are tightly integrated into the parent multinational's strategy to reinforce its competitive standing in international markets. The parent firm then has a self-interest in positioning the plants along the cutting edge, and in continuously upgrading local operations.

Developing countries that succeed in attracting sophisticated subsidiary operations that are essential to the parent firms' supply chains have almost always had to allow the multinationals to wholly own the plants and to source inputs from wherever they choose. Because of these requirements, host authorities have often feared that such plants would engage in no more than screwdriver operations that would be unlikely to generate any but the most minimal backward linkages to the local economy. Evidence presented in chapter 7, however, suggests that such fears may be exaggerated. In the case of the automotive and computer and electronics industries in Asia and Latin America, the sectors in which globalization has been most extensive, it has often been in the foreign investors' self-interest to find inexpensive local suppliers and to assist them in raising their efficiency and quality to world-class levels. The experiences of Singapore and Malaysia provide examples of successful vendor-development programs designed to strengthen the linkages between foreign investors and local companies. Latin America offers examples of similar dynamics, in which foreign firms provided support to improve the performance of domestic suppliers. Evidence from the automotive and computer and electronics sectors in both Asia and Latin America also shows various kinds of externalities for the local economy when host countries attract affiliates that are closely incorporated into the parent firms' international supplier network. Knowledge of production techniques and quality-control procedures, as well as expertise in marketing exports, moves from the multinational parents to affiliates, to local suppliers, and to the host economy more generally.

The most sophisticated techniques currently used to estimate the impact of trade and investment liberalization—endogenous growth theory and computable general equilibrium models, as used for industries in which there are increasing returns to scale—suggest that, in the case of foreign direct investment that is tightly linked to the parent firms' global sourcing strategy, the benefits of the foreign direct investment are twelve to twenty times greater than conventional calculations, based on trade liberalization alone, would indicate. But the evidence examined in chapter 7 indicates that even these optimistic predictions almost surely understate the positive benefits by a large margin, since they overlook the ongoing improvement in the capabilities of subsidiaries and suppliers that is sponsored by the parent investors.

This new paradigm, according to which foreign affiliates that are integral to their parent firms' global competitive strategy offer the greatest potential benefits to the host countries in which they are located— has had less than universal acceptance in the developing world. In some developing countries, a legacy of suspicion (toward parent firms and their wholly owned subsidiaries) still shows itself in a reluctance to allow multinational investors to operate without domestic-content or joint-venture requirements. The evidence presented in chapter 7 shows, however, that instead of encouraging backward linkages and creating vibrant and competitive local industries, domestic-content and joint-venture requirements yield inefficient, high-cost operations that utilize technologies well behind the cutting edge in international markets. Moreover, plants subject to such requirements seldom acquire the economies of scale or dynamic learning that would be required to propel them from infant industry to full competitive status. In fact, a large proportion of such plants are a drain on host-country income—meaning that the country would have been better off if the foreign investment had never occurred at all.

When the subsidiary plants of foreign investors are of small size and rely on older technologies, backward linkages to local suppliers and spillovers to the larger economy suffer as well. In both the automotive and computer and electronics sectors, domestic companies that supplied such plants were unable to take advantage of economies of scale or of sophisticated quality-control techniques.

Endogenous growth theory and computable general equilibrium models predict that the costs of restrictions on the operations of foreign investors—especially in the case of industries with increasing returns to scale—will exceed even the most adverse estimates of traditional trade theory.

What are the results if the perspective is reversed—if the focus shifts from the impact of inward investment on developing economies to the impact of outward investment on developed economies? Is the globalization of industry, via foreign direct investment, a zero-sum phenomenon that benefits workers and firms in the developing countries at the expense of workers and firms in the home country of the investors?

12. The Globalization of Industry, Foreign Direct Investment, and the Well-Being of Workers in the Home Country

The long-standing concern that outward investment could siphon off productive activity—and hence, jobs—from the home country has been most memorably encapsulated in Ross Perot's reference to a "giant sucking sound." A series of studies conducted over many years has found, however, that in developed countries, firms that engage in outward investment have higher export levels than otherwise similar firms that do not invest abroad. Moreover, as is shown in chapter 8, this positive relationship holds not only for components shipped for assembly overseas but for final products sold in the host economy. In fact, the pull of exports from the home country to the host country is high enough to offset any displacement of exports from the host country to third markets. The same study findings also reveal what would happen if outward investment from the home country were inhibited or prevented altogether: exports would drop—and both union and nonunion jobs would drop with them.

The findings presented in chapter 8 are consistent with the observations made about specific industries in chapter 7. The advent of global sourcing on the part of multinational corporations in the automotive and computer and electronics sectors reversed the decline of the parent firms and reinforced their competitive positions in the home market and around the world. The creation of supply chains, via foreign direct investment in developing countries, fortified the high wages and productive jobs available to workers in developed countries. Companies with less successful strategies for the globalization of production faltered and shrank, both at home and abroad.

Outward investment improves the composition of jobs in the home market by raising the number of export-related jobs, which pay between 5 and 18 percent more than non-export-related jobs. The presence of "globally engaged" firms may also generate productivity spillovers and other externalities in the communities in which they are located. The globalization of industry, via foreign direct investment, thus turns out to be, like trade, a win-win phenomenon for workers and the overall economy in home and host countries alike. Like trade, however, the globalization of industry also produces dislocations for less competitive firms, workers, and plants in the home economy. As outlined in chapter 8, employees need to be cushioned from the effects of displacement; in the long term, strong and effective measures along these lines will be much more effective, both for displaced workers and for the larger economy, than ineffective and counterproductive efforts to slow down or try to halt the process of globalization itself.

Notes

Chapter Two

1. For a good introduction, see Pamela Varley, ed., *The Sweatshop Quandary: Corporate Responsibility on the Global Frontier* (Washington: Investor Responsibility Research Center, 1998).

2. The description of the Bataan Export Processing Zone in chapter 2 provides evidence of employers denying employees a fifteen-minute break between two consecutive shifts.

3. The use of benzene at footwear plants in Indonesia and Korea, which was overlooked by monitors from PricewaterhouseCoopers but discovered by Professor Dara O'Rourke, of the Massachusetts Institute of Technology, is discussed in chapter 5.

4. "Made in Squalor: A Deadly Fire," *New York Times*, April 15, 2001.

5. International Labor Organization (ILO), *Labour and Social Issues Relating to Export Processing Zones* (Geneva: 1998), p. 28.

6. Bureau of International Labor Affairs, U.S. Department of Labor, *Wages, Benefits, Poverty Line, and Meeting Workers' Needs in the Apparel and Footwear Industries of Selected Countries* (February 2000).

7. Dorsati Madani, "A Review of the Role and Impact of EPZs," Working Paper (World Bank, August 1999). For sources on Mauritius, Madagascar, the Philippines, the Dominican Republic, and Costa Rica, see the discussions of those countries in this chapter and in chapter 2. For information on Bangladesh, see Debapriya Bhattacharya, "Export Processing Zones in Bangladesh: Economic Impact and Social Issues," Working Paper 80 (Geneva: ILO, 1998).

8. Michael Walzer, *Sphere of Justice: A Defense of Pluralism and Equality* (Basic Books, 1988), p. 102. For a discussion of the conditions under which

wage offers may be considered coercive, see C. B. Macpherson, "Elegant Tomb-stones: A Note on Friedman's Freedom," in Macpherson, *Democratic Theory* (Oxford University Press, 1973), p. 146.

9. Reported at www.nclenet.org (January 3, 2002).

10. Chulalongkorn University Social Research Unit, "Needs Assessment for Workers and Communities" (www.theglobalalliance.org [January 3, 2002]), ch. 2.

11. CESAIS Center for Economic and Social Applications, University of Ho Chi Minh-Vietnam (now Truong Doan), "Workers' Voices: A Study of the Assets and Needs of Factory Workers in Vietnam" (www.theglobalalliance.org [January 3, 2002]), ch. 2.

12. Rita Afsar, of the Bangladesh Institute for Development Studies, quoted in Barry Bearajm, "Made in Squalor," *New York Times,* April 15, 2001; Bhat-tacharya, "Export Zones in Bangladesh."

13. Tripartite Meeting of Export Processing Zones—Operating Countries, *Note on the Proceedings* (Geneva: ILO, 1998), p. 8.

14. Economist Intelligence Unit, *Country Profile 2000: Bangladesh* (London: 2000).

15. Mari Pangestu and Medelina K. Hendytio, "Survey Responses from Women Workers in Indonesia's Textile, Garment, and Footwear Industries," Policy Research Working Paper 1755 (World Bank, April 1997), p. 10, cited in Carl Aaron and Teresa Andaya, "The Link between Foreign Direct Investment and Human Poverty Alleviation and Social Development: A Framework," Working Paper (World Bank, December 1998), p. 22. See also Diane Wolf, *Factory Daughters* (University of California Press, 1992).

16. Lourdes Beneria and Martha Roldan, *The Crossroads of Class and Gender* (University of Chicago Press, 1987). Some husbands, however, simply took possession of their wives' paychecks. See Susan Tiano, *Patriarchy on the Line: Labor, Gender, and Ideology in the Mexican Maquila Industry* (Temple University Press, 1994).

17. Gillian H. C. Foo, "Work and Marriage: Attitudes of Women Factory Workers in Malaysia," Ph.D. dissertation, University of Michigan, Ann Arbor, 1987, cited in Linda Y. C. Lim and Pang Eng Fong, *Foreign Direct Investment and Industrialization in Malaysia, Singapore, Taiwan, and Thailand* (Organization for Economic Cooperation and Development, 1991), p. 117.

18. For the impact of outside earnings on female "agency," as distinct from female "welfare," see Amartya K. Sen, "Gender and Cooperative Conflicts," ch. 8 in *Persistent Inequalities: Women and World Development,* ed. Irene Tinker (Oxford University Press, 1990). More generally, see Sen, *On Ethics and Economics* (London: Basil Blackwell, 1987), ch. 2.

19. Aaron and Andaya, "Human Poverty Alleviation."

20. The discussion of the Dominican Republic, in chapter 2, notes that the availability of jobs in the apparel and footwear industries reduced the propor-

tion of poor women in the population by an average of one percentage point a year during the period of rapid expansion in EPZ employment.

21. Aaron and Andaya, "Human Poverty Alleviation."

22. Ana Teresa Romero, "Labour Standards and Export Processing Zones: Situation and Pressures for Change," *Development Policy Review,* vol. 13 (1995), pp. 247–76. For supporting evidence, see the discussions of the Philippines, the Dominican Republic, and Costa Rica in chapter 2.

23. The problems associated with the use of foreign direct investment for import substitution, in the hope of developing internationally competitive export-oriented operations within the host country, are treated in detail in chapter 6.

24. See Steven Radelet, "Manufactured Exports, Export Platforms, and Economic Growth," Consulting Assistance on Economic Reform II, Discussion Paper 43 (Harvard Institute for International Development, November 1999); Madani, "Role and Impact of EPZs."

25. Ravi Gulhati and Ray Nallari, *Successful Stabilization and Recovery in Mauritius,* Economic Development Institute Analytical Case Study 5, Development Policy Case Series (World Bank, 1990); Larry W. Bowman, *Mauritius: Democracy and Development in the Indian Ocean* (Boulder, Colo.: Westview Press, 1991).

26. A study by James Meade cited in Paul M. Romer, "Two Strategies for Economic Development: Using Ideas and Producing Ideas," in *Proceedings of the World Bank Annual Conference on Development Economics* (1992), p. 76.

27. Economic indicators released by the Ministry of Economic Planning and Development, as reported in Economist Intelligence Unit, *Country Profile 2000: Mauritius, Seychelles* (London: 2000), p. 24.

28. International Monetary Fund, *International Financial Statistics: Mauritius* (Washington: 2001).

29. Radelet, "Manufactured Exports," table 3.

30. Romer, "Two Strategies," p. 76.

31. ILO, *Labour and Social Issues,* p. 22.

32. Radelet, "Manufactured Exports," p. 47.

33. ILO, *Labour and Social Issues,* p. 22.

34. Yung Whee Rhee, Katharina Katterback, and Jeanette White, *Free Trade Zones in Export Strategies* (Industry Development Division, World Bank, December 1990), p. 39.

35. Ibid.

36. Mireille Razafindrakoto and Francois Roubaud, "Les Entreprises Franches à Madagascar: Economie d'enclave ou promesse d'une nouvelle prospérité? Nouvel esclavage ou opportunité pour le développement du pays?" *Economie de Madagascar,* no. 2 (1995), p. 226; Rhee, Katterback, and White, *Free Trade Zones,* p. 39.

37. Razafindrakoto and Roubaud, "Les Entreprises Franches."

38. Ibid., p. 223, table 2.

39. Economist Intelligence Unit, *Country Profile 2000: Madagascar* (London: 2000), reference table 12.

40. Razafindrakoto and Roubaud, "Les Entreprises Franches," pp. 233–34.

Chapter Three

1. This analysis draws on Keith E. Maskus, "Should Core Labor Standards Be Imposed through International Trade Policy?" Policy Research Working Paper 1817 (World Bank, August 1997). See also Glen C. Cain, "The Economic Analysis of Labor Market Discrimination: A Survey," in *Handbook of Labor Economics,* vol. 1, ed. O. Ashenfelter and R. Layard (Amsterdam: Elsevier Science Publishers BV, 1986).

2. Peter G. Warr, "Export Promotion via Industrial Enclaves: The Philippines' Bataan Export Processing Zone," *Journal of Development Studies* (January 1987), pp. 220–41.

3. Summarized in Elizabeth M. Remedio, "EPZs in the Philippines: A Review of Employment, Working Conditions, and Labour Relations," International Labor Organization (ILO) Working Paper 77 (Geneva: 1996), pp. 26–27.

4. Charles W. Lindsey, "Transfer of Technology to the ASEAN Region by U.S. Transnational Corporations," *ASEAN Economic Bulletin,* November 1986, pp. 237–38.

5. Remedio, "EPZs in the Philippines," p. 7 and table 1.

6. Warr, "Export Promotion." As part of his critique, Warr points out that foreign firms were given access to the local capital market, where interest rates were controlled, and received government guarantees for their borrowings. In the first six years of the Bataan EPZ, 91 percent of all private investment was financed in this way, an approach that diverted capital from the domestic market to foreign operations in the zone. To review the legacy of skepticism about using EPZs to generate economic growth in host countries, see Helena Johansson, "The Economics of EPZs Revisited," *Development Policy Review,* vol. 12 (1994), pp. 387–402.

7. Remedio, "EPZs in the Philippines," p. 20.

8. Mark Jacobson, "The Philippines: The Case of Economic Zones," in *Alleviating Poverty through Foreign Direct Investment: Country Case Studies* (World Bank, 1999), app. C, tables C-1, C-28. The figures are for 1998.

9. Elizabeth M. Remedio, "Foreign-Owned Firms and Skill Formation at the Mactan Export Processing Zone, Philippines: A Case-Study," in *Human Resources Management and Economic Development in Asia* (Tokyo: Japan Institute of Labor, 1994), summarized in Remedio, "EPZs in the Philippines." The issue of on-the-job-training in EPZ firms will reappear in the case study of the Dominican Republic, where the data show steep improvements in the productivity of workers who received training.

10. Remedio, "EPZs in the Philippines," p. 25.

11. This information is based on local interviews conducted by Remedio; see "EPZs in the Philippines," p. 22.

12. Ibid., p. 31.

13. Ibid., p. 20.

14. Ibid., p. 31, and appendix C, table C-31.

15. Marie E. Aganon, Rosalinda Pineda Ofreneo, Rosario S. Del Rosario, Ma. Socorro Paulin Ballesteros, and Rene E. Ofreneo, *Strategies to Empower Women Workers in the Philippine Economic Zones,* March 27, 1997, cited in Jacobson, "Case of Economic Zones," p. 31.

16. Remedio, "EPZs in the Philippines," p. 31; Jacobson, "Case of Economic Zones," app. A.

17. Ibid., app. C, tables C-28, C-31.

18. Jacobson, "Case of Economic Zones," app. C, table C-34.

19. Remedio, "EPZs in the Philippines," p. 23.

20. Figures released by the Philippine Economic Zone Authority, Cavite Zone Administration, July 1988; cited in Jacobson, "Case of Economic Zones," app. C, table C-34; converted to 2000 dollars.

21. Ibid., p. 31.

22. Reported in Ana Teresa Romero, "Labor Standards and EPZs: Situation and Pressures for Change," *Development Policy Review,* vol. 13 (1995), p. 266.

23. Louis T. Wells Jr., "Afterward," in *Marketing a Country: Promotion as a Tool for Attracting Foreign Investment*, rev. ed.; ed. Louis T. Wells Jr. and Alvin G. Wint (Washington: International Finance Corporation, Multilateral Investment Guarantee Agency, and World Bank, 2000).

24. Jacobson, "Case of Economic Zones," table 20, p. 36.

25. As will be seen later in the chapter, foreign plant managers in the Dominican Republic reported paying fees in private zones that were triple those of other zones, in order to ensure that their plants offered adequate housing, transportation, security, health-care, and day-care facilities. Their reasoning was that such facilities helped to ensure a stable and more productive work force and that they were more appropriate to their corporate image.

26. Jacobson, "Case of Economic Zones," app. A, table A-8; app. C, table C-31.

27. Ibid., app. C, table C-17.

28. Ibid., table C-23.

29. Because of rounding, figures do not total 100 percent.

30. Jacobson, "Case of Economic Zones," table C-1.

31. Remedio, "EPZs in the Philippines," pp. 29–30.

32. ILO, *Labour and Social Issues Relating to Export Processing Zones* (Geneva: 1998), pp. 23–24.

33. Ibid., p. 23.

34. Eugenia Fernandez, quoted in Remedio, "EPZs in the Philippines," p. 8.

35. Unlike the case of Mauritius, the improvements in the treatment of workers in the Philippines during the 1990s did not take place under conditions of full employment.

36. ILO, *Labour and Social Issues*, p. 24. The Center for Labor Relations Assistance is referred to as DTI-CLARA.

37. Ibid.

38. ILO, *Your Voice at Work: Global Report under the Follow-Up to the ILO Declaration on Fundamental Principles and Rights at Work* (Geneva: 2000), p. 33.

39. ILO, *Labour and Social Issues*, p. 24.

40. Yung Whee Rhee, Katharina Katterback, and Jeanette White, *Free Trade Zones in Export Strategies* (Industry Development Division, World Bank, December 1990), p. 30.

41. Ibid.

42. National Free Zone Council of the Dominican Republic, *Free Zone Statistical Report Year 2000* (Santo Domingo: 2001), charts 20, 29, 39.

43. Romero, "Labor Standards and EPZs," p. 263. ILO, *Labour and Social Issues*, p. 24.

44. ILO, *Your Voice at Work*, p. 34.

45. Rhee, Katterback, and White, *Free Trade Zones*. The sectors surveyed include manufacturers of apparel, footwear, electronics, electrical components, and electrical assemblies.

46. According to the team of World Bank investigators that carried out the study, these results indicate that there are "remarkable private returns to skill formation," and "refute the usual argument that there is very low skill acquisition" in EPZ firms. Ibid., pp. 18, 22.

47. Ibid., p. 22.

48. Dorsati Madani, "A Review of the Role and Impact of EPZs," Working Paper (World Bank, August 1999), p. 39.

49. National Free Zone Council of the Dominican Republic, *Free Zone Statistical Report*. The amount of investment dedicated to textiles, footwear, jewelry, and leather products continued to grow in absolute terms but declined as a proportion of overall activity in the zones, accounting for 56 percent of all zone investment, 65 percent of all zone firms, and 79 percent of all zone employment in 2000.

50. The National Free Zone Council of the Dominican Republic began its reports in 1993. According to the council, legally mandated fringe benefits add approximately 35 percent to basic wages. The American Chamber of Commerce in the Dominican Republic estimates that its members add 45 percent in fringe benefits to basic wages.

51. Madani, "Role and Impact of EPZs," p. 40.

52. Ana T. Romero, *EPZs: The Social and Labour Issues* (Geneva: Bureau for Multinational Enterprise Activities, ILO, 1996), p. 2.

53. The accomplishments of the Singapore EDB will receive more attention in chapter 6.

54. Wells and Wint, *Marketing a Country.*

55. Avinash K. Dixit and Robert S. Pindyck, *Investment under Uncertainty* (Princeton University Press, 1994).

56. Unlike a used-car dealer, a would-be host country can neither let a prospective investor have a test drive nor share the risk of future failure by offering a lengthy warranty. George Akerlof, "The Market for 'Lemons': Quality Uncertainty and the Market Mechanism," *Quarterly Journal of Economics*, vol. 84, no. 3 (August 1970), pp. 488–500.

57. For more information on the Singapore EDB, see chapter 6. CINDE has operated as a private nonprofit organization guided by an executive board whose members are all from the private sector. The Foreign Investment Advisory Service of the World Bank reports that CINDE has succeeded in building a strong relationship with the government while avoiding the risk that board members might use the agency for their own purposes (such as preventing rival investors from entering a particular sector, as has happened elsewhere). Foreign Investment Advisory Service, World Bank, "Strengthening Investment Promotion Agencies: The Role of the Private Sector" (draft, March 1999).

58. Debora Spar, *Attracting High Technology Investment: Intel's Costa Rican Plant,* Occasional Paper 11 (Foreign Investment Advisory Service, World Bank, 1998).

59. Ibid.

60. Intel wanted its prospective affiliate to be entirely staffed and managed by Costa Ricans as quickly as possible, and was impressed by the fact that Baxter had achieved that goal in a short period of time. Ibid., p. 15.

61. Costa Rican authorities took great pains to ensure that potential internal conflicts and jurisdictional overlaps among government agencies were smoothed out before face-to-face meetings with Intel. Ibid., p. 15.

62. Felipe Larrain, Luis Lupez-Calva, and Anres Rodriguez Clare, "Intel: A Case Study of Foreign Direct Investment in Central America" (draft, 2001), table 6-4, p. 11.

63. Ibid.

64. Eduardo Alonso, "Trade and Investment Promotion: The Case of CINDE in Costa Rica, 2000," presentation at the InterAmerican Development Bank, Washington, September 18, 2001; U.S. Department of State, *Country Commercial Guide 2000: Costa Rica* (GPO, 2001); Economist Intelligence Unit, *Country Report: Costa Rica* (London: March 2001), p. 5.

65. Larrain, Lupez-Calva, and Rodriguez Clare, "Intel: A Case Study."

66. ILO, *Your Voice at Work,* p. 51.

67. Ibid., pp. 34–35, 50–51; ILO, *Labour and Social Issues,* p. 24.

68. Ibid.

69. The behavior of foreign investors in the three countries examined here is consistent with that of individual firms trying to reduce the costs of high turnover and low morale among workers and supervisors, as explored by David Card and Alan Kreuger, *Myth and Measurement: The New Economics of the Minimum Wage* (Princeton University Press, 1995). What is novel in these examples is the discovery of a spillover effect among firms with different approaches to the treatment of workers, and an institution-building impact on the conduct of labor-management relations across entire labor markets.

70. The accomplishments of Mauritius, Madagascar, the Philippines, the Dominican Republic, and Costa Rica in harnessing foreign direct investment on behalf of internal economic development—while in no sense "miracle" successes—nonetheless provide hope that sensible economic policies can break the link between geography and poverty. Compare Jeffrey Sachs, "Tropical Underdevelopment," Working Paper 8119 (Cambridge, Mass.: National Bureau of Economic Research, 2001).

Chapter Four

1. International Labor Organization (ILO), *Your Voice at Work: Global Report under the Follow-Up to the ILO Declaration on Fundamental Principles and Rights at Work* (Geneva: 2000), p. 1. The declaration was adopted at the June 1998 International Labor Conference with no opposing votes. These principles are also endorsed by the ICFTU and the Trade Union Advisory Committee of the OECD.

2. *World Development Report 1995: Workers in an Integrating World* (Oxford University Press for the World Bank, 1995), p. 74.

3. Transcript from *Sixty Minutes,* October 20, 1996.

4. ILO, "Part 1: Introduction by the ILO Declaration Expert-Advisers to the Compilation of Annual Reports," in *Review of Annual Reports under the Follow-Up to the ILO Declaration on Fundamental Principles and Rights at Work* (Geneva: March 2000), pp. 21–23.

5. T. N. Srinivasan, "Trade and Human Rights," Discussion Paper (Yale Economic Growth Center, December 1996), p. 21.

6. W. Sengenberger and D. Campbell, eds., *International Labor Standards and Economic Interdependence* (Geneva: ILO, 1995); Richard Freeman and James Medoff, *What Do Unions Do?* (Basic Books, 1987).

7. The World Bank suggests that bargaining at the enterprise level has the highest likelihood of generating positive economic effects. *World Development Report 1995,* p. 83. See also Lars Calmfors and Hohn Driffil, "Centralization of Wage Bargaining and Macroeconomic Performance," and Richard B. Freeman,

"Labor Market Institutions and Economic Performance," both in *Economic Policy: A European Forum*, vol. 3 (April 1988).

8. The ILO lists the United States, along with Burkina Faso, Cape Verde, the Central African Republic, Djibouti, Madagascar, and Niger, as countries that permit the replacement of strikers. *Your Voice at Work*, p. 38.

9. The virtual impossibility of enforcing international health and safety standards will be discussed in chapter 4. It will be suggested in chapter 5, however, that such standards might well be incorporated into a voluntary regime, in which the burden of proof is on the employer to show that plants comply with widely accepted standards for the treatment of workers.

10. In New Jersey, a 1992 increase in the minimum wage did not reduce employment in the fast-food industry. Across states, 1990 and 1991 increases in the federal minimum wage did not reduce teenage employment overall. David Card and Alan Krueger, *Myth and Measurement: The New Economics of the Minimum Wage* (Princeton University Press, 1995).

11. For evidence that the relative level of the minimum wage declines as income rises, see *World Development Report 1995*, p. 75, figure 11.1.

12. Mandatory minimum compensation packages for firms in the formal economy could also have the effect of pushing operations back into the informal sector, where standards are lower and the visibility of worker treatment is minimal.

13. In the mid-1980s, Mauritius provided a kind of "natural experiment" regarding the effect of raising and lowering minimum wages for export processing occupations. In 1984, plants that qualified for export-zone status paid men a higher minimum wage than women. At the time, the demand for female workers exceeded the supply, and the supply of male workers exceeded the demand, resulting in unemployment among men. In December 1984, when the government eliminated the minimum wage for men, the recruitment of male employees rose sharply, and more than 95 percent of those recruited in January 1985 were paid less than the previous minimum. *World Development Report 1995*, p. 75.

14. *Report of the Living Wage Symposium* (Robert M. La Follette Institute of Public Affairs, University of Wisconsin–Madison, February 8, 2000), p. 19. This symposium provides an extensive analysis of the difficulties (and expense) of conducting (and keeping up-to-date) country-by-country household surveys that could be used to support living-wage calculations.

15. Ibid.

16. Ibid., p. 19.

17. Ibid.

18. Melissa Connor et al., "The Case for Corporate Responsibility: Paying a Living Wage to Maquila Workers in El Salvador" (www.nlcnet.org [January 9, 2002]).

19. While the majority of women working in EPZs often appear to be young and single, survey research shows that large proportions (22 percent in Hon-

duras, 45 percent in Guatemala, and almost 50 percent in the Dominican Republic) are divorced, widowed, or otherwise heads of households or the sole source of household income. Dorsati Madani, "A Review of the Role and Impact of Export Processing Zones," Working Paper (World Bank, August 1999), p. 38. See also Diane Lauren Wolf, *Factory Daughters: Gender, Household Dynamics, and Rural Industrialization in Java* (University of California Press, 1992).

20. *Living Wage Symposium,* p. 19.

21. In chapter 4, evidence that unit labor costs are a slight fraction of the selling price is introduced in the context of assessing whether weak labor standards among export firms might constitute an unfair advantage that would harm firms and workers in importing countries.

22. For a summary of survey evidence, see Kimberly Ann Elliott and Richard B. Freeman, *White Hats or Don Quixotes? Human Rights Vigilantes in the Global Economy* (Washington: Institute for International Economics, 2001). The data show that consumers exhibit a greater sensitivity to avoiding child labor and to providing safe working conditions than to ensuring the right to unionize.

23. Card and Krueger, *Myth and Measurement,* p. 373. For models of a labor market in which employers spend a great deal of time and energy recruiting and training new workers and new supervisory personnel (as opposed to the theoretically ideal situation, in which an employer simply announces job openings at the going market wage and instantly fills all positions), see chapter 11 of Card and Krueger ("Is There an Explanation? Alternative Models of the Labor Market and the Minimum Wage"), pp. 373–79.

24. ILO, *Your Voice at Work,* pp. 32–36.

25. ILO, "Part 2: Compilation of Annual Reports by the International Labour Office," in *Review of Annual Reports,* pp. 160–61. Employers' associations did not submit an observation or a response.

26. ILO, "Part 2: Compilation," pp. 136–37.

27. "Grassroots International Pressure Leads to Watershed Human Rights Victory in El Salvador" (www.nlcnet.org [January 9, 2002]).

28. ILO, *Your Voice at Work,* p. 37.

29. ILO, "Part 2: Compilation," pp. 162–63.

30. Ibid., p. 160. Employers' associations did not submit an observation or a response.

31. Pamela Varley, ed., *The Sweatshop Quandary: Corporate Responsibility on the Global Frontier* (Washington: Investor Responsibility Research Center), pp. 141–49.

32. ILO, "Part 2: Compilation," p. 161. Employers' associations did not submit an observation or a response.

33. ILO, "Part 2: Compilation," p. 161.

34. A comparison of practices in developing and developed countries other than the United States would reveal additional areas of divergence, such as the

right of workers to participate in the management and ownership of an enterprise, and to serve on the board of directors.

35. For the workings of dispute-settlement and appellate bodies in determining what constitutes actionable violations within the current structure of the WTO, see John H. Jackson, *The World Trade Organization: Constitution and Jurisprudence* (London: Royal Institute of International Affairs, 1998), ch. 4.

36. Kimberly Ann Elliott, "Fin(d)ing Our Way on Trade and Labor Standards?" International Economics Policy Briefs, PBO1-5 (Washington: Institute for International Economics, April 2001); Jacqueline McFadyen, "NAFTA Supplemental Agreements: Four-Year Review," Working Paper 98-4 (Washington: Institute for International Economics, 1998), app. A; Organization for Economic Cooperation and Development, "The North American Agreement on Labor Cooperation (NAALC)," in *International Trade and Core Labor Standards* (Paris: 2000).

37. William Daley, written submission to the U.S. Senate in response to the question, "Why hasn't the U.S. adopted a number of ILO conventions?" U.S. Department of Commerce, January 2000.

38. U.S. Trade Representative, press release, *U.S. and Jordan Sign Historic Free Trade Agreement* (October 24, 2000).

39. For a description of adjudication and appellate practices in the WTO, see Jackson, *World Trade Organization*, ch. 4.

Chapter Five

1. A WTO initiative along these lines would raise important issues for the world trading community quite apart from the enforcement of core labor standards per se. Allowing members to suspend trade obligations on the basis of differences in production processes opens the door to controversy about whether there are acceptable and unacceptable methods of producing goods, a distinction that the GATT and the WTO have attempted to avoid in the past.

2. Compare Alan B. Krueger, "International Labor Standards and Trade," in *Annual World Bank Conference on Development Economics 1996*, ed. Michael Bruno and Boris Pleskovic (World Bank, 1996).

3. "Internal U.S. TR Paper Discusses Fines as Enforcement Tool," *Inside U.S. Trade*, vol. 19, no. 17 (April 27, 2001).

4. Jacqueline McFadyen, "NAFTA Supplemental Agreements: Four-Year Review," Working Paper 98-4 (Washington: Institute for International Economics, 1998), app. A; Kimberly Ann Elliott, "Fin(d)ing Our Way on Trade and Labor Standards?" International Economics Policy Briefs, PBO1-5 (Washington: Institute for International Economics, April 2001).

5. Elliott, "Fin(d)ing Our Way," table 1.

6. U.S. Trade Representative, "Using Monetary Assessments to Enforce Panel Decisions under Bilateral Free-Trade Agreements" (draft, April 2001), p. 1-D.

7. The case was brought by the Support Committee for Maquiladora Workers, the National Association of Democratic Lawyers, the International Labor Rights Fund, and the Union of Metal, Steel, Iron, and Allied Workers. See Organization for Economic Cooperation and Development (OECD), "The North American Agreement on Labor Cooperation (NAALC)," and table 3 in *International Trade and Core Labor Standards* (Paris: 2000); McFadyen, "NAFTA Supplemental Agreements," app. A.

8. McFadyen, "NAFTA Supplemental Agreements," app. A.

9. Tripartite Meeting of Export Processing Zones—Operating Countries, *Note on the Proceedings* (Geneva: International Labor Organization, 1998), p. 8.

10. Muzaffer Ahman and M. Shahidul Islam, "Bangladesh Productivity in Selected Ready-Made Garments Units," in *Productivity Analysis and Projections in Selected Key Areas in Asian Countries,* ed. Imre Bernolak (Tokyo: Asian Productivity Organization, 1987); cited in Richard Rothstein, "Developing Reasonable Standards for Judging Whether Minimum Wage Levels in Developing Nations Are Acceptable," Working Paper (Washington: Economic Policy Institute, 1996), pp. 21–25.

11. In 1992, the U.S. Trade Representative's investigation to determine Bangladesh's eligibility for duty-free access recorded that the minimum wage for semiskilled garment workers was $19 per month—which implies that the $0.25 an hour used a few years earlier in the Asian Productivity Organization study was more than twice the official minimum wage ($0.25 per hour for a forty-hour week equals $40 a month).

12. National Labor Committee, "Anatomy of Exploitation" (www.nlcnet. org [January 7, 2002]).

13. National Labor Committee, "Made in China: Behind the Label" (www. nlcnet.org [January 7, 2002]).

14. "Price Make-Up of a U.S. $100 Sport Shoe Made in Indonesia" (www. cleanclothes.org [January 7, 2002]).

15. "What Exactly Is the Labor Cost of Nike Shoes?" (www.nikebiz.com/ labor [January 7, 2002]).

16. OECD, *Trade, Employment and Labour Standards: A Study of Core Workers' Rights and International Trade* (Paris: 1996), pt. 2.

17. Ibid.

18. Mita Aggarwal, "International Trade, Labor Standards, and Labor Market Conditions: An Evaluation of the Linkages," Working Paper 95-06-C (Office of Economics, U.S. International Trade Commission, June 1995).

19. Dani Rodrik, "Labor Standards in International Trade: Do They Matter and What Do We Do about Them?" in *Emerging Agenda for Global Trade: High Stakes for Developing Countries,* ed. Robert Lawrence, Dani Rodrik, and John Whalley (Washington: The Johns Hopkins University Press for the Overseas Development Council, 1996).

20. Ibid., p. 57.

21. Peter Morici with Evan Schulz, *Labor Standards in the Global Trading System* (Washington: Economic Strategy Institute, 2001).

22. Ibid., p. 53.

23. Aggarwal, "Evaluation of Linkages," pp. 13–17.

24. Rodrik, "Labor Standards in International Trade," p. 57.

25. Morici, *Labor Standards*, p. 57.

26. Kimberly Ann Elliott, "Getting Beyond No . . . ! Promoting Worker Rights *and* Trade," in *The WTO after Seattle*, ed. Jeffrey J. Schott (Washington: Institute for International Economics, 2000), p. 198.

27. Economist Intelligence Unit, *Bangladesh: Country Report* (April 2001), p. 19.

28. International Labor Organization, "African Regional Workshop on the Protection of Workers' Rights and Working Conditions in EPZs and the Promotion of the Tripartite Declaration of Principles Concerning Multinational Enterprises and Social Policy," Johannesburg, July 15–18, 1996, p. 11.

29. Anwar Shah, ed., *Fiscal Incentives for Investment and Innovation* (Oxford University Press for the World Bank, 1995).

30. Harvard Business School, *Adam Opel AG*, Case 9-392-100 (1993), pp. 101, 127.

31. James R. Hines, "Tax Policy and the Activities of Multinational Corporations," Working Paper 5589 (Cambridge, Mass.: National Bureau of Economic Research); Gary Hufbauer, "Directions for International Tax Reform," in *Borderline Case: International Tax Policy, Corporate Research and Development, and Investment*, ed. J. M. Poterba (Washington: National Academy Press for the National Research Council, 1997).

32. R. Altschuler, H. Grubert, and T. S. Newton, "Has U.S. Investment Abroad Become More Sensitive to Tax Rates?" in *International Taxation and Multinational Activity*, ed. James R. Hines Jr. (University of Chicago Press for the National Bureau of Economic Research, forthcoming).

33. John Mutti and Henry Grubert, "Empirical Asymmetries in Foreign Direct Investment and Taxation" (draft, Institute for International Economics, 2001).

34. Daniel Chudnovsky and Andres Lopez, "Policy Competition for Foreign Direct Investment: The Global and Regional Dimensions" (paper presented to the InterAmerican Development Bank, Washington, November 9, 2000); Chudnovsky and Lopez, "El boom de inversion extranjera directa en el Mercosur en los anos 1990: Caracteristicas, determinantes e impactos, Centro de Investigaciones para la Transformacion" (paper presented to the InterAmerican Development Bank, Buenos Aires, November 2000).

Chapter Six

1. "Commerce with Conscience?" (www.ichrdd.capublications [January 15, 2001]).

2. Naomi Klein, *No Logo: Taking Aim at the Brand Bullies* (New York: Picador, 1999), p. 343; Debora L. Spar, "The Spotlight and the Bottom Line: How Multinationals Export Human Rights," *Foreign Affairs*, vol. 77, no. 2 (March/April 1998).

3. United Nations Conference on Trade and Development, *The Social Responsibility of Transnational Corporations* (New York: 1999).

4. Dr. Prakash Sethi is professor of management at the Zicklin School of Business, Baruch College, and adviser to the executive office of the United Nations secretary-general. The other two members are Dr. Paul McCleary, president of ForCHILDREN, Inc., and Dr. Murray Weidenbaum, Mallinckrodt Distinguished University Professor and chairman, Center for the Study of American Business, Washington University.

5. Rebecca Christie, "Manufacturers Sign Up to Foreign Workers' Bill of Rights," *Financial Times,* January 3, 1999.

6. International Labor Organization (ILO), *Overview of Global Developments and Office Activities Concerning Codes of Conduct, Social Labeling and Other Private Sector Initiatives Addressing Labour Issues* (Geneva: November 1998).

7. Kathryn Gordon and Maiko Miyake, "Deciphering Codes of Corporate Conduct: A Review of Their Contents," Working Paper on International Investment 99/2 (Paris: Organization for Economic Cooperation and Development [OECD], March 2000), pp. 8, 9, 14, 26, 29.

8. Sam Dillon, "Profits Raise Pressures on U.S.-Owned Factories in Mexican Border Zone," *New York Times,* February 14, 2001.

9. Ibid.

10. OECD, *International Trade and Core Labor Standards* (Paris: 2000), p. 73.

11. See www.ethicaltrade.org (January 10, 2002).

12. Gordon and Miyake, "Codes of Corporate Conduct," p. 3.

13. OECD, *Core Labor Standards*, p. 73.

14. Gordon and Miyake, "Codes of Corporate Conduct," p. 24.

15. In Japan, however, the leading Japanese business group, the Keidanren, has been active in designing, revising, and promulgating a model known as the Charter for Good Corporate Behavior (see www.keidanren.org [January 12, 2002]).

16. Robert J. Liubicic, "Corporate Codes of Conduct and Product Labeling Schemes: The Limits and Possibilities of Promoting International Labor Rights through Private Initiatives," *Law and Policy in International Business,* vol. 30 (1998), pp. 129–30; ILO, *Overview.*

17. See www.cepaa.org (January 10, 2002).

18. "How to File a Complaint or an Appeal Related to the SA8000 Certification System" (www.cepaa.org/guideline [January 10, 2002]).

19. "Lizhan Footwear Factory, Dongguan City, Guangdong Province, China" (www.nlcnet.oreg/report00/newbalance [January 10, 2002]).

20. Dexter Roberts and Aaron Bernstein, "A Life of Fines and Beating," *Business Week,* October 2, 2000.

21. "Are the Companies That Are Licensed to Produce University Apparel under the FLA Required to Disclose the Locations of the Factories That Produce That Apparel?" (www.lchr.org/sweatshop [January 11, 2002]).

22. Dara O'Rourke, "Monitoring the Monitors: A Critique of Price-waterhouseCoopers (PwC) Labor Monitoring," White Paper (September 28, 2000).

23. Steven Greenhouse, "M.I.T. Report Says International Accounting Firm Overlooks Factory Abuses," *New York Times,* October 28, 2000.

24. See www.theglobalalliance.org (January 11, 2002).

25. "Report Says Nike Plant Workers Abused by Bosses in Indonesia," *New York Times,* February 22, 2001, available at www.theglobalalliance.org.

26. See www.nikebiz.com/labor (January 11, 2002).

27. See Kimberly Ann Elliott and Richard R. Freeman, *White Hats or Don Quixotes? Human Rights Vigilantes in the Global Economy* (Washington: Institute for International Economics, 2001).

28. See www.levistrauss.com (January 11, 2002).

29. See www.mattel.com (January 11, 2002).

30. See www.lchr.org/sweatshop/amendedFLA (January 11, 2002).

31. See www.cepaa.org/sa8000 (January 11, 2002).

32. See www.levistrauss.com (January 11, 2002).

33. See www.lchr.org/sweatshop/amendedFLA (January 11, 2002).

34. See www.cepaa.org/sa8000 (January 11, 2002).

35. See www.nikebiz.com/labor/code (January 11, 2002).

36. See www.ethicaltrade.org (January 11, 2002).

37. See www.nikebiz.com/labor (January 11, 2002).

38. This analysis draws on discussions with ILO officials. See also OECD, *Core Labor Standards;* and Kimberly Ann Elliott, "Getting Beyond No . . . ! Promoting Worker Rights and Trade," in *The WTO after Seattle,* ed. Jeffrey J. Schott (Washington: Institute for International Economics, 2000).

39. OECD, *Core Labor Standards,* p. 45.

40. Compare Elliott, "Getting Beyond No . . . !" on this point.

41. International Labor Organization (ILO), *Measures, Including Action under Article 33 of the Constitution . . . to Secure Compliance by the Governments of Myanmar,* GB.276/6, 267th session of the governing body, Geneva, November, 1999.

42. ILO, *Your Voice at Work: Global Report under the Follow-Up to the ILO Declaration on Fundamental Principles and Rights at Work* (Geneva: 2000), p. 26.

43. Ibid., pp. 50–51.

44. ILO, *Labour and Social Issues Relating to Export Processing Zones* (Geneva: 1998), p. 24.

45. OECD, *Core Labor Standards,* p. 49.

46. ILO, "Part 1: Introduction by the ILO Declaration Expert-Advisers to the Compilation of Annual Reports," in *Review of Annual Reports under the Follow-Up to the ILO Declaration on Fundamental Principles and Rights at Work* (Geneva: March 2000), pp. 1–3.

47. Ibid., p. 20.

48. ILO, "The Global Picture," ch. 2 in *Your Voice at Work.*

Chapter Seven

1. For the basic works in the theory of foreign direct investment, see John H. Dunning, ed., *The Theory of Transnational Corporations* (London: Routledge for the United Nations Library on Transnational Corporations, 1993), vol. 1.

2. Paul M. Romer, "Two Strategies for Economic Development: Using Ideas and Producing Ideas," in *Proceedings of the World Bank Annual Conference on Development Economics* (1992).

3. This volume does not address the positive or negative environmental impact of foreign direct investment.

4. Earlier, more detailed versions of the evidence and arguments in this chapter can be found in *Parental Supervision: The New Paradigm for Foreign Direct Investment and Development* (Washington: Institute for International Economics, 2001); and *Foreign Direct Investment and Development: The New Policy Agenda for Developing Countries and Economies in Transition* (Washington: Institute for International Economics, 1998).

5. The phrase *unambiguous control,* and the evidence to support the existence of the phenomenon, originated in John M. Stopford and Louis T. Wells Jr., *Managing the Multinational Enterprise* (Basic Books, 1972).

6. Raymond Vernon, *In the Hurricane's Eye: The Troubled Prospects of Multinational Enterprises* (Harvard University Press, 1998), ch. 3.

7. Paul Beamish, *Multinational Joint Ventures in Developing Countries* (London: Routledge, 1988); Bruce Kogut, "Joint Ventures: Theoretical and Empirical Perspectives," *Strategic Management Journal,* vol. 9, no. 4 (July-August 1988), pp. 319–32.

8. United Nations Centre on Transnational Corporations, *The Impact of Trade-Related Investment Measures on Trade and Development* (1991). For a theoretical explanation of why small plants are likely to proliferate even in large, protected markets, see H. Eastman and S. Stykolt, "A Model for the Study of Protected Oligopolies," *Economic Journal,* vol. 70 (1970), pp. 336–47.

9. Based on a 1995 evaluation of a General Motors assembly plant in Hungary that produces 14,000 vehicles a year and employs 213 workers. Karen Klein, *General Motors in Hungary: The Corporate Strategy behind Szentgotthard* (Washington: Pew Economic Freedom Fellows Program, Georgetown University, 1995).

10. Barbara C. Samuels, *Managing Risk in Developing Countries: National Demands and Multinational Response* (Princeton University Press, 1990).

11. See Huan Ngo and David Conklin, "Note on the Automobile Assembly Process," in *Mekong Corporation and the Viet Nam Motor Vehicle Industry* (London, Ontario: Richard Ivey School of Business, University of Western Ontario, 1996), 96-H002, app. 3.

12. Klein, *General Motors in Hungary,* p. 21.

13. Craig S. Smith and Rebecca Blumenstein, "Uncertain Terrain: In China, GM Bets Billions on a Market Strewn with Casualties," *Wall Street Journal,* February 11, 1998.

14. Ngo and Conklin, *Mekong Corporation.*

15. William Cline, *Informatics and Development: Trade and Industrial Policy in Argentina, Brazil, and Mexico* (Washington: Economics International, 1987); Claudio Frischtak, "Brazil," in *National Policies for Developing High Tech Industries: International Comparisons,* ed. Frances W. Rushing and Carole Ganz Brown (Boulder, Colo.: Westview Press, 1986).

16. Harvard Business School, *Mexico and the Microcomputers,* Case 9-390-093 (1990).

17. Ibid.

18. Wilson Peres Nunez, *Foreign Direct Investment and Industrial Development in Mexico* (Organization for Economic Cooperation and Development [OECD], 1990), ch. 5.

19. Edwin Mansfield and Anthony Romeo, "Technology Transfer to Overseas Subsidiaries by U.S.-Based Firms," *Quarterly Journal of Economics,* vol. 95, no. 4 (December 1980), pp. 737–50.

20. J.-Y. Lee and Edwin Mansfield, "Intellectual Property Protection and U.S. Foreign Direct Investment," *Review of Economics and Statistics,* vol. 78 (May 1996), pp. 181–86; Keith E. Maskus, *Intellectual Property Rights in the Global Economy* (Washington: Institute for International Economics, 2000).

21. Vijaya Ramachandran, "Technology Transfer, Firm Ownership, and Investment in Human Capital," *Review of Economics and Statistics,* vol. 75 (November 1993), pp. 664–70.

22. All inputs and outputs were valued at world market prices. Dennis J. Encarnation and Louis T. Wells Jr., "Evaluating Foreign Investment," in *Investing in Development: New Roles for Private Capital?* ed. Theodore H. Moran (Washington: Overseas Development Council, 1986).

23. The 183 projects were not explicitly coded for domestic-content and joint-venture requirements, but Wells confirmed, in a personal communication with the author, the association between these requirements and a lower or negative social return. Intensive use of energy subsidized by the host government also led to negative social returns.

24. Richard E. Caves, "Spillovers from Multinationals in Developing Countries: The Mechanisms at Work" (draft, 1999).

25. Barbara C. Samuels, *Managing Risk in Developing Countries: National Demands and Multinational Response* (Princeton University Press, 1990); Helen Shapiro, "Automobiles: From Import Substitution to Export Promotion in Brazil and Mexico," in *Beyond Free Trade: Firms, Governments and Global Competition*, ed. David Yoffie (Cambridge University Press, 1993); Shapiro, *Engines of Growth* (Cambridge University Press, 1994).

26. Fiat had preceded GM in using Brazil as an export platform for engines and other auto parts.

27. Peres Nunez, *Industrial Development in Mexico*, p. 124.

28. Ibid. For a description of the tension between union opposition to industrial restructuring and union cooperation in improving productivity in Argentina, Brazil, and India, see World Bank, *World Development Report 1995: Workers in an Integrating World* (Oxford University Press for the World Bank), pp. 81–84.

29. Rogelio Ramirez de la O, "The Impact of NAFTA on the Auto Industry in Mexico," in *The North American Auto Industry under NAFTA*, ed. Sidney Weintraub and Christopher Sands (Washington: Center for Strategic and International Studies, 1998), p. 83.

30. James P. Womack, Daniel T. Jones, and Daniel Roos, *The Machine That Changed the World* (Harper Perennial, 1991), ch. 10.

31. "G.M.'s operations in Brazil have copied Japanese manufacturing practices and have become the company's most profitable, efficient and flexible," observed the *New York Times*. Keith Bradsher, "G.M.'s Efficient Brazil Plant Raises Fears Closer to Home," June 17, 1999, p. 1.

32. Richard F. Doner, *Driving a Bargain: Automobile Industrialization and Japanese Firms in Southeast Asia* (University of California Press, 1991).

33. Klein, *General Motors in Hungary*.

34. Ibid., p. 6.

35. Kristian Ehinger, deputy general counsel, Volkswagen AG, "FDI Policy and Individual Country Experiences: The Volkswagen Experience" (paper presented at the OECD conference "The Role of International Investment in Development," Paris, September 20, 1999).

36. Seth Mydens, "G.M. to Tap Asian Market, and Two Nations Bid for Plant," *New York Times*, May 28, 1996, p. D-10.

37. Peres Nunez, *Industrial Development in Mexico*, ch. 6, pp. 109–36.

38. Institute of Developing Economies, *The Automotive Industry in Thailand: From Protective Promotion to Liberalization* (Tokyo: October 1995).

39. Ibid., pp. 19–21, table 4.

40. Rajah Rasiah, "Flexible Production Systems and Local Machine-Tool Subcontracting: Electronics Components Transnationals in Malaysia," *Cambridge Journal of Economics*, vol. 18, no. 3 (June 1994), pp. 279–98.

41. Linda Y. C. Lim and Pang Eng Fong, *Foreign Direct Investment and Industrialization in Malaysia, Singapore, Taiwan, and Thailand* (Paris: OECD, 1991), p. 115.

42. Michael Borrus, "Left for Dead: Asian Production Networks and the Revival of U.S. Electronics," in *Japanese Investment in Asia: International Production Strategies in a Rapidly Changing World,* ed. Eileen M. Doherty (San Francisco: Asia Foundation and Berkeley Roundtable on International Economics, 1994).

43. Rene Belderbos, Giovanni Capanelli, and Kyoji Fukao, "The Local Content of Japanese Electronics Manufacturing Operations in Asia," in *The Role of Foreign Direct Investment in East Asian Economic Development,* ed. Takatoshi Ito and Anne O. Krueger (University of Chicago Press for the National Bureau of Economic Research, 2000), p. 16.

44. Harvard Business School, *Mexico and the Microcomputers.*

45. Peres Nunez, *Industrial Development in Mexico,* ch. 5, pp. 83–109.

46. Roland Nordgren, president of Ericsson Mexico, interviewed by the author April 2, 2001. Ericsson's software engineering group in Saltillo, Mexico, has worldwide responsibilities for specialized applications for the banking sector.

47. Brian J. Aitken, Gordon H. Hanson, and Ann E. Harrison, "Spillovers, Foreign Investment, and Export Behavior," *Journal of International Economics,* vol. 43, no. 1-2 (August 1997), pp. 103–32.

48. Linda Y. C. Lim and Pang Eng Fong, "Vertical Linkages and Multinational Enterprises in Developing Countries," *World Development,* vol. 10, no. 7 (July 1982), pp. 585–95.

49. Ibid.

50. David G. McKendrick, Richard F. Doner, and Stephan Haggard, *From Silicon Valley to Singapore: Location and Competitive Advantage in the Hard Disk Drive Industry* (Stanford University Press, 2000), p. 170.

51. Rasiah, "Flexible Production Systems," pp. 279–98.

52. Giovanni Capanelli, "Buyer-Supplier Relations and Technology Transfer: Japanese Consumer Electronics," *International Review of Economics and Business,* vol. 44, no. 3 (September 1997), pp. 633–62.

53. The disk drive case comes from McKendrick, Doner, and Haggard, *Silicon Valley to Singapore.*

54. Ibid.

55. Michael Hobday, *Innovation in East Asia: The Challenge to Japan* (London: Aldershot, 1995); Hobday, "East versus Southeast Asian Innovation Systems: Comparing OEM- and TNC-Led Growth in Electronics," in *Technology, Learning, and Innovation,* ed. Linsu Kim and Richard Nelson (Cambridge University Press, 2000).

56. Hobday, *Innovation in East Asia,* p. 67.

57. A central feature of the Korean strategy of import substitution was to impose trade restrictions on consumer products, which penalized the country's own population, but not to inhibit the importation of machinery and capital equipment—which allowed the *chaebol* to equip themselves to compete in international markets. Korean protection of intermediate products, such as chemicals

and petrochemicals, and of computer and electronics goods and services, however, did penalize indigenous producers.

58. Hobday, *Innovation in East Asia*, p. 99.

59. See the selections by Frederique Sachwald, Luis Miotti, Marc Lautier, Kong-Rae Lee, Alice Amsden, Rene Belderbos, Bruce Kogut, and Lynn Mytelka in *Going Multinational: The Experience of Korea with Direct Investment*, ed. Frederique Sachwald (forthcoming).

60. Robert E. Lipsey, "Affiliates of U.S. and Japanese Multinationals in East Asian Production and Trade," in Ito and Krueger, *Foreign Direct Investment*.

61. J. Bradford De Long and Lawrence H. Summers, "Equipment Investment and Economic Growth," *Quarterly Journal of Economics* (May 1991), pp. 445–502; David T. Coe and Elhanan Helpman, "International R and D Spillovers," *European Economic Review,* vol. 39 (1995), pp. 859–87; David T. Coe, Elhanan Helpman, and Alexander W. Hoffmaister, "North-South R and D Spillovers," *Economic Journal,* vol. 107, no. 5 (May 1997), pp. 134–49.

62. Paul Romer, "New Goods, Old Theory, and the Welfare Costs of Trade Restrictions," *Journal of Development Economics,* vol. 43, no. 3 (1994), p. 34.

63. Ann Harrison, "Determinants and Effects of Direct Foreign Investment in Côte d'Ivoire, Morocco, and Venezuela," in *Industrial Evolution in Developing Countries: Micro Patterns of Turnover, Productivity, and Market Structure,* ed. Mark J. Roberts and James R. Tybout (Oxford University Press for the World Bank, 1996); Mona Haddad and Ann E. Harrison, "Are There Positive Spillovers from Direct Foreign Investment? Evidence from Panel Data for Morocco," *Journal of Development Economics,* vol. 42, no. 1 (October 1993), pp. 51–74; Brian J. Aitken and Ann E. Harrison, "Do Domestic Firms Benefit from Direct Foreign Investment? Evidence from Venezuela," *American Economic Review,* vol. 89, no. 3 (June 1999), pp. 605–18; Dani Rodrik, *The New Global Economy and Developing Countries: Making Openness Work* (Washington: The Johns Hopkins University Press for the Overseas Development Council, 1999).

64. James R. Markusen, "Trade in Producer Services and in Other Specialized, Intermediate Inputs," *American Economic Review,* vol. 85, no. 1 (March 1989), pp. 85–95; Markusen, "Derationalizing Tariffs with Specialized Intermediate Inputs and Differentiated Final Goods," *Journal of International Economics,* vol. 12, no. 3–4 (May 1990), pp. 225–42.

65. Florencio Lopez-de-Silanes, James R. Markusen, and Thomas F. Rutherford, "Complementarity and Increasing Returns in Intermediate Inputs," *Journal of Development Economics,* vol. 45, no. 1 (October 1994), pp. 101–19.

66. Sven W. Arndt and Alex Huemer, "North American Trade after NAFTA: Part 2," Claremont Policy Briefs 01-02 (Claremont Institute for Economic Policy Studies, July 2001).

67. Moreover, as indicated earlier, there is evidence that the presence of outward-oriented foreign investment in Mexico generated externalities for the host

economy by stimulating exports from nearby, but unrelated, Mexican producers. See Aitken, Hanson, and Harrison, "Spillovers, Foreign Investment."

Chapter Eight

1. Emergency Committee for American Trade, *Mainstay II: A New Account of the Critical Role of U.S. Multinational Companies in the U.S. Economy* (Washington: 1993); *Mainstay III: A Report on the Domestic Contributions of American Companies with Global Operations* (Washington: 1999).

2. Emergency Committee for American Trade (ECAT), *Mainstay II,* p. 99. Subsequent analysis by ECAT has adopted the more rigorous analytical approach recommended here.

3. C. Fred Bergsten, Thomas Horst, and Theodore H. Moran, *American Multinationals and American Interests* (Brookings, 1978), ch. 3.

4. Robert E. Lipsey and Herle Yahr Weiss, "Foreign Production and Exports in Manufacturing Industries," Review of Economics and Statistics, vol. 63, no. 4 (November 1981), pp. 488–94; "Foreign Production and Exports in Individual Firms," *Review of Economics and Statistics,* vol. 66, no. 2 (May 1984), pp. 304–08.

5. Magnus Blomstrom, Robert E. Lipsey, and K. Kulchycky, "U.S. and Swedish Direct Investment and Exports," in *Trade Policy Issues and Empirical Analysis,* ed. Robert E. Baldwin (University of Chicago Press, 1988), pp. 259–302. R. Svensson has argued that the expansion of exports from Swedish affiliates to third markets has displaced home-country exports, but Robert Lipsey concludes that the methodology leading to this conclusion is suspect. R. Svensson, "Effects of Overseas Production on Home-Country Exports: Evidence Based on Swedish Multinationals," *Weltwirtschaftliches Archiv,* vol. 132 (1996), pp. 304–29; Robert Lipsey, "Outward Direct Investment and the U.S. Economy," Reprint 2020 (Cambridge, Mass.: National Bureau of Economic Research, December 1995), p. 20.

6. Robert E. Lipsey, Eric D. Ramsetter, and Magnus Blomstrom, "Outward FDI and Parent Exports and Employment: Japan, the United States, and Sweden," Working Paper 7623 (Cambridge, Mass.: National Bureau of Economic Research, March 2000).

7. For reasons that are unclear, the results were not statistically conclusive for U.S. firms in Latin America, or for Japanese firms in East Asia when Indonesia was included. Edward M. Graham, "Foreign Direct Investment Outflows and Manufacturing Trade: A Comparison of Japan and the United States," in Dennis J. Encarnation, ed., *Japanese Multinationals in Asia: Regional Operations in Comparative Perspective* (Oxford University Press, 1999), pp. 87–99.

8. Howard Lewis III and J. David Richardson, *Why Global Integration Matters Most!* (Washington: Institute for International Economics, October 2001), p. 20.

9. Doms and Jensen, "Comparing Wages, Skills, and Productivity."

10. Lewis and Richardson, *Global Integration*, p. 20.

11. Eastman Kodak Company, *Kodak Wins with Trade* (Washington: 2000).

12. Mary E. Lovely and Stuart S. Rosenthal, "Does Spatial Concentration of Exporters Generate Productivity Spillovers?" (draft, Syracuse University); cited in Lewis and Richardson, *Global Integration*.

13. Lori G. Kletzer, *What Are the Costs of Job Loss from Import-Competing Industries?* (Washington: Institute for International Economics, 2001).

14. Lori G. Kletzer and Robert E. Litan, "A Prescription to Relieve Worker Anxiety," International Economics Policy Brief 01-2 (Washington: Institute for International Economics, February 2001).

Index